WHAT WE REALLY DO

Salle Church, Norfolk, recording Brumel's 12-voice *Missa Et ecce terrae motus*, in 1988.
Left to right, back row: Adrian Peacock, Stephen Charlesworth, Jonathan Markham, Sally Dunkley, Olive Simpson, Ruth Holton, Tessa Bonner, Rachael Platt, Donald Greig, Francis Steele.
Front Row: Ashley Stafford, Rufus Müller, Michael Lees, Simon Davies, Robert Harre-Jones, Caroline Trevor, Deborah Roberts, Jeremy White, Adrian Hill, Angus Smith, Nicolas Robertson, Mark Padmore, Charles Daniels, Nigel Short. *(Photo: Clive Barda)*

PETER PHILLIPS

WHAT
WE
REALLY
DO

THE TALLIS SCHOLARS

THE MUSICAL TIMES

First published 2003
by The Musical Times Publications Limited
22 Gibson Square, London N1 ORD

copyright © Peter Phillips 2003

Printed in Great Britain by
Biddles Ltd, Guildford

ISBN 0-9545777-0-1

FOR EDMUND FREDERIC SAYER PHILLIPS (b. 1997)

AND IN MEMORY OF NIGEL SAYER PHILLIPS (1926–1999)

JOHN MANSFIELD THOMSON (1926–1999)

JMT   PP

CONTENTS

Illustrations follow pages 60, 95, 190

INTRODUCTION

Beauty (in renaissance architecture) can only be achieved through 'a harmony of all the parts, fitted together with such proportion and connection that nothing could be added, diminished or altered but for the worse'.

(Leonbattista Alberti, in *De Re Aedificatoria*, c. 1460)

This book was put together both to celebrate the 30th anniversary of the proto-Tallis Scholars, who sang Obrecht, Ockeghem, Lassus and Victoria in St Mary Magdalen, Oxford, on 3rd November 1973, and, at the same time, to take stock of how the perception and performance of renaissance polyphony has fared since then. The group had no name at that first event, but it is fair to say that the Tallis Scholars were born that night, because the concert consisted entirely of renaissance sacred music, sung a cappella, two voices to a part, directed (or possibly mis-directed) by me. We were as green as grass.

As a celebration this book runs the obvious danger of turning into a se-ries of self-congratulatory remarks. Of course it didn't have to be written at all, which would have had the extra merit of allowing this anniversary to pass by unnoticed. Nothing puts a group more securely in the naff league than one which is forever trumpeting its anniversaries, a process which will start at 15, alight happily on 20 and 21 and proceed to 25. We did 25 in style in the National Gallery in London, with Sting and Sir David Attenborough as our guests, and we have had no intention of trying to follow that event for 30. But I knew that sooner or later I was going to write down an account of what it has been like to do this job, what it has consisted of; in fact I'd been doing it for some time, long before I came up with the idea of this anniver-sary collection. The Journal has been there since 1987, the *Spectator* articles since 1983, and the essay which forms chapter five was written some years ago on a rather depressing tour; so simple anthologising became an option. Instead, even though I hope there are many years still to go, I couldn't help summing things up as they stand in greater detail. This book will be out of date almost immediately, but I am hoping that a snapshot of now, and what led up to now, will have real interest.

Mindful of the dangers of seepage in the boasting department as the book progresses, I will dispose of a whole landscape of trouble by quoting once and for all our vital statistics. As of 3 November 2003, the Tallis Scholars have sung 1297 concerts of (almost) entirely renaissance polyphony, made over 40 discs, featured in several television documentaries and are about to release two DVDs. We have toured North America 36 times, Japan nine times, Australia five times, Taiwan three times, Israel twice, Colombia once, China once and sung (in 2003) in the Bolshoi, Moscow. We have given 131 concerts in London, 51 in Oxford, 38 in New York City, 32 in Boston, 30 in Utrecht and 29 in Tokyo. In 1994 we sang for Japanese and Italian television in the Sistine Chapel to mark the unveiling of the newly-cleaned Last Judgement. The phenomenon of the Tallis Scholars' sound-in-polyphony has driven a number of followers worldwide to try to recreate it, whether avowedly or not, including ensembles in: Novosibirsk, Siberia; Florence, Italy (where the tradition of singing polyphony had seemed to be dead); Barcelona and Granada, Spain (ditto); Lisbon and Evora, Portugal (ditto again); Tokyo and elsewhere in Japan; Sydney and Wellington; and a number of groups in the US and in the UK. It has also led to the creation of several courses dedicated to the study of the renaissance polyphonic repertoire and what it seems to require of its performers, of which the Oakham course (now part of the Tallis Scholars Summer Schools) and its dependent initiatives are the most closely associated with the Tallis Scholars themselves. And, inshallah, we are only half way through our career.

I can still hardly believe that so many people from different cultures have been drawn to music which was considered both elitist and incomprehensible in the years when it was being written, and which scarcely began to peep out of the 'eclectic and marginal' bin of modern concert-making until very recent times indeed. But I recognise the privilege these enthusiasts have given us: in effect *carte blanche* to explore the inexhaustible supply of renaissance sacred masterpieces, without having to dress them up as being anything other than they are. In 1973 whole concerts of polyphony were rare. Now they are commonplace, not only in early music festivals, but in straight up-and-down international artists' series in symphony halls around the western world.

This volume is a collection of essays which are intended to explain what it is like to dedicate one's working life to this unusual repertoire. I wrote the history of the group in chapter one not just to list the chronology of how we got going, but to explain what was involved in the task of convincing the world at large not only that a group of youngsters it had never heard of should be taken seriously, but that the repertoire the youngsters were peddling should be also. And although this was obviously going to be necessary if we were to make a life-long career of performing this music, I only came to realise it very slowly – there was no epiphanic moment for me. If this chapter wanders and tells anecdotes, it is because we wandered in the real life version too. Crucial to this process of advancing our general profile was the foundation and history of Gimell Records, which I describe in chapter two. I have no doubt that what musical skills I possess have been just as intensively called upon in editing the Gimell tapes as in any other work I have done. I have always found editing particularly fulfilling, in that I am left alone with the music and the voices making it, free to consider them at my own speed. Live directing is a hectic business, requiring one to be a diplomat as much anything else, and always to think quickly.

Nonetheless I have had a go at describing what I do as a director of polyphony in chapter three. One reason for writing this chapter now, and not after retirement when my experience should be greater, is that I was able to test out my maxims as I went along, often rushing to my dressing-room to note down some new angle on a problem connected to what I had just been doing. Related to this, chapter four introduces some of the initiatives which have sprung up around the work of the Tallis Scholars, in particular the course which first saw the light of day at Oakham School, and which is now set to expand to the US in 2004.

Chapter five is an account of what it is like to be constantly on tour. I wrote this quickly, during a week or so when we were singing in Italy in November 1999, and not feeling particularly pleased with the lifestyle despite being in Italy. What I have to say is not, of course, restricted to the life of an itinerant musician, but applies to anyone who travels constantly for work. Travelling rapidly loses its glamour, and yet one keeps doing it. Is it just because one hasn't thought of any other way of making a living? In my case the answer is no, but the route by which I get to the no is a twisted one.

The last three chapters are all kinds of appendices. This seemed as good a time as any to try to pin down all those special phrases we use on tour, put under the heading of our argot. We had good fun on the longer journeys remembering all that appears here. Chapter seven features an urge I couldn't resist to publish a 'let's reveal all' interview; and chapter eight is a copy of just one entry in the journal, of a tour to Latvia and Estonia shortly after the collapse of communism, to show what kind of information I think worth remembering immediately after an event. Finally, in the epilogue, I tried to put into words the aesthetic basis on which I enjoy polyphonic music.

The story of the Tallis Scholars in the last 30 years does not only consist of me having had a good and lucky idea and sticking to it through thick and thin. That idea has been put into effect by a small army of talented people who were there, presumably on the verge of doing something else, when I happened by. I refer of course in the first instance to the singers, and especially to the longest-serving members of the current group; for although no one who sang in that first concert sings full time for me now, Francis Steele and Robert Harre-Jones first appeared in 1976 and Deborah Roberts in 1977. Sally Dunkley, Don Greig, Tessa Bonner, Caroline Trevor and Ruth Holton first appeared in the early 1980s. Their collective sound, shaped over 20 years and more, is what set us up; and in the last ten years this sound has been refined by the addition of Jan Coxwell, Patrick Craig and a gallimaufry of tenors led most recently by Andrew Carwood, Nicholas Todd, Julian Podger and Christopher Watson. Behind the scenes the group has benefited enormously from the skills of Steve Smith, Julian Walker, Peter Bromley, Shauni McGregor and Lucy Rice; and the support and encourgement of James Brown, Dione Digby and Robert Brenton Betts. Add to these names those of the people who have worked alongside us – Juliet Allan, David Woodcock, Jan Joost van Elburg, George Steel, our librarians Dirk Freymuth and George Black, Phillip Chancellor, one-time verger at St Sepulchre's Church, EC1, the late Rev. John Paul and Martin Woods at St Andrew's-by-the-Wardrobe, EC4, where we keep our library and rehearse; and our foreign agents, of whom Jon Aaron has been the most outstanding – and the full picture begins to emerge.

The biggest debt I owe is to the people who have stuck to this project in difficult times, by which I mean when the future looked bleak and I myself seemed to be a less than satisfactory person to commit any part of one's future to. Francis Steele (1225 concerts) and Deborah Roberts (1087) are pre-eminent in this category. Standing on the extreme ends of the line, singing between them more than four octaves in overall range, they visibly as well as aurally represent the pillars on which this edifice has been built.

Julian Walker has been just as long-serving, having sung in the first concert as well as during 2003 – a unique achievement – and, in his professional capacity as an accountant, minded the finances of the group from the beginning. Thanks to his watchfulness we have never been in debt, which has been a bonus of incalculable value. I can vouch for the confidence and stability which healthy finances can give an organisation which is both pioneering and unlikely to attract government funding.

Ever since that first concert my intention has been to try to find a way of performing polyphony which would prove durable, a kind of classic style which would not fall into the trap of pursuing fashionable theories but, rather, survive them. It took as its starting point the realisation that polyphony had too often in the past been made complicated in an unsympathetic way. Polyphony certainly has its complications, most of them based in mathematics; but at one level it is a simple enough idiom for one to be able to say to potential performers 'just do it'. You need choral discipline, but not layers of overreaction generated by later thinking. In part this book is about the merits of simplicity; of the ordinary, obvious approach.

Our approach has resulted in a kind of performance which has sometimes confused people. On the one hand, all the discipline and clarity I believe polyphony needs in performance has been called cold, unsexy (even) and off-putting; on the other, this has been seen as a means to an end and scarcely mentioned. The confusion has been especially apparent among those who expect an older-fashioned sound and have been obliged to square their preconceptions with their emotional responses. This phenomenon has not necessarily been a thing of the past, as these words from the *Independent* (27 December 2002) show: 'The austere purity of the Tallis Scholars seemed to take on an anti-sensual, unworldly intensity that was quite overwhelming.' I find this remarkable, since it would never have occurred to me that austere purity could be overwhelming and I certainly have never been aiming for such an oxymoron. Austere purity has never entered my head as being something aesthetically desirable; I have hoped only that the power of our interpretations, conveyed by our collective sound, should be overwhelming.

I would call this sound 'modern': clear enough to benefit from digital recording (which didn't exist when I started), strong enough to fill three-thousand-seat concert halls without amplification or distortion, subtle enough to do justice to the religious texts involved, the sonic equivalent of what Virginia Woolf once wrote so tellingly about Marcel Proust's prose style: 'The thing about Proust is his combination of the utmost sensibility with the utmost tenacity. He searches out these butterfly shades to the last degree. He is as tough as catgut and as evanescent as a butterfly's bloom.' I can't imagine a better description of what I'm after than that.

But however potent and persuasive this style of singing may be, it is clearly not healthy that there should only be one style for such a widely-based repertoire, for two hundred years of music written throughout Europe. The styles of the future need to respect the nature of polyphony more than the styles of the past have done, certainly, but out of that respect should come variety. If renaissance polyphony really has established itself as a mainstream classical repertoire the ways of performing it should soon multiply. The Tallis Scholars and one or two other vocal ensembles from England and the continent of Europe have been privileged to have had the run of a vast repertoire of the greatest music without many questions being asked; but not even the greatest symphony orchestras are afforded that privilege any more. The accepted view of what they play has become too demanding, informed by new ideas, so that popular taste will no longer allow them to start a concert with a Brandenburg Concerto and end it with a Bruckner symphony. If this also happens in renaissance music there will soon be Spanish groups specialising in Spanish repertoire while drawing large crowds to hear them sing other polyphony as well, with their own sound, Italian groups will be doing the same for Italian music, and so on. The days of English imperialism in this world, which I have felt to be the case for a long time despite the wonderful achievements of some European groups, will have blended into something more international. I wonder how our style will seem by then. Classical?

ACKNOWLEDGEMENTS

I am grateful to Jane Armstrong, Sally Dunkley, Caroline Trevor and Steve Smith for reading and correcting the manuscript of this book; to Peter Campbell for his design work; and to Lucy Pilcher for compiling the list of singers. I am also indebted to the younger members of my family who have had to tolerate the constant comings and goings I describe here, an endlessly repeated process which should have been divisive, but through their understanding seems so far not to have been. Nothing could have been more supportive.

In St John's College Chapel, Oxford, 1973

I

A HISTORY OF THE TALLIS SCHOLARS

Interviewer: I've met a number of you English conductors who have come out of Oxford and Cambridge: Roger Norrington, John Eliot Gardiner, you and Harry Christophers, Andrew Carwood and Edward Wickham from the younger generation. You're all quite alike in not apparently having had much formal training in what you do. Was there any particular magic formula in what you experienced at Oxford?

PP: Nobody stopped me.

This was the simple truth. If we wanted to put on concerts, we just did it. Nobody cared if we did, nobody cared if we didn't. Nobody objected or put up barriers, but then nobody helped or encouraged. Maybe the Music Society of one's college would offer a small sum of money to get a project off the ground, but it was indeed small and it was certain that somebody else would get it next term. Concert-giving had nothing to do with the degree course one was engaged in: it did not count towards one's final result. There was and is no tuition in conducting at any of the British universities; and none of the conservatoires offers a course in choral conducting only. To all those people who have asked me how they can study and qualify in what I do professionally the answer is: you can't unless you either go to another country where such courses may for all I know be available; or you just get on with it and learn as you go along. All the conductors listed by my interviewer initially went to Oxford or Cambridge to do something else and left those places formally qualified in something else. But if one did decide to pass one's student days avoiding one's degree course in order to put on concerts, one gave oneself the chance to learn not only how to conduct but how to be an entrepreneur as well.

In theory, individual initiative is never discouraged by enlightened teaching. I think my interviewer, who is a professor at the Royal Conservatory in Stockholm, was interested because he knows very well the system by which places of advanced learning plan their degree courses, making the assumption that every moment of every term must be filled with some degree-related activity; and he wondered by what eccentricity these two famous universities could go about their business so differently. I do not intend here to write a paean to our ancient universities, whose hit-and-miss approach to tutoring means that a student can do just about nothing for three years, but this *laissez-faire* attitude does have an advantage for musicians. Just because they are not conservatoires, yet are packed with talented singers and instrumentalists filling up the chapel choirs and reading music, Oxford and Cambridge were and are the ideal breeding-grounds for young conductors who want to have a go. Almost every night of full term there is an undergraduate concert of some kind, while towards the end of those terms serious pressure builds up on the available dates, with the most favoured singers and players stretched very thin indeed, sometimes literally running between one venue and the next, between one chaotic solo and another.

In the conservatoire way of doing things, one studies a set of procedures laid down by tradition, qualifies in those procedures and goes out into a professional world which expects them. This is how it is, for example, with opera singers, for whom the Oxbridge experience, if they have it, can be nothing more than a bit of fun before signing up for real life. Traditionally the only musicians who could leave the Oxbridge system and go straight into a job were organists. Much of the old cathedral organist bias, incredibly, is still in place in the make-up of these music courses and their final examinations; but, like the British constitution, what seems on the face of it to be old-fashioned and useless has, behind the scenes, been adapted without anyone officially noticing. What these universities and their courses now provide is an unexceptional but sound grounding in music theory, almost unlimited experience for organists and choral scholars in church services, hovering between the amateur and professional worlds, and equally unlimited but totally amateur opportunity for entrepreneurs.

To be an entrepreneur is, by definition, to break moulds. An entrepreneur in music is likely to need an amateur context to experiment in, since the professional one is set in its ways. The relationship between what the entrepreneur is doing, what the public wants and whether the entrepreneur can eventually attract good professionals to his way of thinking is the unknown which every such person must confront. The history of painting is full of the breaths of fresh air which new geniuses have imposed on petrified tradition. Somehow in music it is more difficult. We cannot just put up a canvas and say 'look'. We must find like-minded people, argue about whether or how much to pay them, hire a venue and attract a paying public. And, hidebound though art colleges can often be, there is a way of thinking among art students which is revolutionary. If there are going to be political fisticuffs you can be fairly confident the art, film, writing and acting confraternities will be near the barricades. I have never had that feeling with music students. They are more cautious and more sensible. Making a living out of music is perilous, and in the last decades very few new ways of doing it have been found.

With none of this in mind ten undergraduates came together on the night of 3 November 1973 to sing a concert of renaissance polyphonic music in the church of St Mary Magdalen in Oxford. It was an event like a thousand others: too many rehearsals which not all the participants came to, a tiny audience, over-ambitious programming, and an almost complete inexperience, at least on my part, in directing and presenting the music that was finally sung. Obviously we had no idea that this was the start of something durable: this and many of the subsequent Oxford undergraduate concerts seemed as though they would be, and probably deserved to be, the final hiccup before oblivion. Our amateurishness was absolute. Either on this occasion or on one not long afterwards three of the singers arrived 15 minutes late for the start of the concert because they had been dining elaborately in Queen's College and had had to run up the High Street to get to the venue even when they did. I remember them arriving at the back of the church all out of breath and clutching their stomachs, the completely silent audience looking askance. All I could do was smile with relief, in a gesture of friendliness I have had to use many times since, when something stronger from me would only have upset the singing that was to follow. In the first concert we modified the programme as we went along. For some reason I had chosen Ockeghem's *Missa L'homme armé* to go alongside Victoria's *Missa O magnum mysterium* as the principal works, and backed them up with motets by Obrecht and Lassus. The Lassus and Victoria would have been familiar in style to the choral scholars, but the rest of it was guaranteed to cause problems, even to young men who were already highly experienced sight-readers. In the endless rehearsal on the afternoon of the day – probably the only time I had everyone together – we wandered through large tracts of the Ockeghem without any idea of where the music was going, intent on en-suring that it didn't actually break down. Ultimately this minimum require-ment meant restricting our efforts to the Kyrie and Gloria, despite the fact that the whole setting had been advertised. I think my team were miffed that they'd finally come across a vocal piece which they couldn't sing perfectly the first time through.

The singers were Julia White, Esther White, Jonathan Sharp, Ashley Stafford, Philip Cave, Alistair White, Julian Walker, Jeremy White and Stewart Haslett. This list impresses me in that I had set my cap at, and se-cured the services of people who were my seniors, both in age and experi-ence. Philip and Stewart were lay-clerks at Christ Church and therefore no longer undergraduates. Julian, Jeremy and Ashley were choral scholars at Christ Church and therefore, one would have thought, had more than their fill of choral singing every day without signing up for the vagaries of a con-cert led by the organ scholar of a minor college. Julia White (née Boalch) was the most sought-after soprano in Oxford at that time – I remember the day she finally decided that enough was enough and started to charge £5 for her services. I'm sure I didn't pay any of them for their appearances on this occasion, nor would I do so for years to come: none of the early concerts was underwritten in any way. But something of the later professional model can be glimpsed. Although as organ scholar at St John's I had my own chapel choir, with perfectly competent and enthusiastic singers in it, I didn't choose a single one of them. I knew there was better to be had and was determined to get it. Somehow I talked these luminaries into coming along, probably 'for a laugh'. The other constant was the make-up and style of the pro-gramme. Although in our 30 years we have shown, in many diverse places for the first time, that whole concerts of renaissance polyphony can be both an enjoyable evening out and a viable business proposition, this cannot be claimed for us in Oxford. The chapel choirs, from time to time, and the Clerkes of Oxenford, at least, had preceded us. But it was a rare enough thing, and the formula that we were to make our own was set from the very first piece we sang. To put it another way: what seemed at the time like a whole concert of easy notes and predictable rhythms being fluently more-or-less sight-read by some impressive youthful voices would turn eventually into mature interpretations of some of the most intellectually challenging music ever written.

That group of singers was given no name. The Tallis Scholars as such did not come into being until 1976. All the early concerts were entitled either 'Continental Renaissance Music' or 'English Renaissance Music', and the names of the singers were listed on the posters. My friend Jonathan Sharp and I designed all the posters ourselves and had them printed; I would then spend a very tiresome afternoon pacing about the city putting them up. I still remember the rough outline of that walk, the notice-boards to be visited, the other posters to be moved about in order to give prominence to my own. I was to do it many times: that and putting out the chairs in Merton College Chapel, where we were eventually allowed to give our concerts, were the purest chores of the amateur set-up. We sang only in Oxford until that first so-called Tallis Scholars concert in 1976, which took place in my old school chapel at Winchester.

I am often asked what happened to those nine singers; a question which interests me just as much is what happened to the 20 or so people in the audience that night. The one about the singers is easy; but I have never come across anyone who has been prepared to admit that they witnessed the inception of the group, who had paid their 35 pence (not many months earlier it would have been called seven shillings) for a ticket. I suppose I've never quite known when to ask. Nor is it likely that those present ever came to realise how important they might be to me. As to the singers: Philip Cave sang in one or two more of those early concerts and then disappeared from my life for 17 years. In 1992 he gave up being a teacher to join the professional singing circuit in London, and speedily established himself in the group. By the time he resigned in 2000 to become an organist and choirmaster in the US he held the record for the longest-serving tenor – 406 appearances. (To put the record straight right now I should point out that tenors, at this level as at every other, are the easiest singers to lose and the hardest to find. Phil's record is a splendid one, fully a hundred more than the next tenor challenger; but on every other voice part there are those who have doubled this number.)

Julian Walker, whom I met on my first day at grown-up school in January 1967 and is thus by far my oldest friend, has always been a close contender for the role of most suitable singer for polyphonic music that I've ever come across: his voice always easy, melodious, instinctively phrased and perfectly tuned. I remember him at school singing with me the first tenor part in Harris's *Bring us, O Lord God*, and then slotting in the second bass bottom D flat in the final chord, because he was the only person who could. He freely admits that he has preserved the easiness of his voice by deciding very early on not to become a professional, as a result of which he is also one of the most reliable singers I know. Of all those first nine present in November 1973 he is the only one who still quite regularly sings with us; though he has contributed just as much to the health of the group as an accountant. I don't remember why there were nine singers taking part in this concert, instead of eight or ten, which would have yielded two to a part.

Esther White was married to Alistair; Julia White was married to Jeremy. Jeremy White sang for some years longer for me, appearing on a number of the earlier discs and starring on our Russian Orthodox record in John Tavener's *Great Canon of Saint Andrew of Crete* as the bass soloist. He eventually gave up choral music to concentrate on opera, currently having a soloist's contract at Covent Garden. Apart from all the many tenors I could list, he and the countertenor Michael Chance are the singers from the other voice-parts that the regular group has lost to an out-and-out solo career. Ashley Stafford sang for 20 years more in the Tallis Scholars – he and Robert Harre-Jones were more or less the standard alto line for some time – before turning to teaching and osteopathy; Jonathan Sharp did a lot of design work for us before disappearing without trace. Stewart Haslett never sang for me again, dying in the 1980s of liver failure.

The second concert we gave, on 1 December 1973, has not been so widely remembered as this first one, though in a way it should have been since the programme included Tallis's *Spem in alium*. Not only was this the first time the group had undertaken this colossus, but performances of it were so rare in those days that it was probably the first time any of the singers had sung it. On this occasion I had invited choirs from the various institutions I had attended, which resulted in two choirs from Winchester (College and Cathedral), two from the Royal School of Church Music and the other four from around Oxford, principally drawn from my chapel choir at St John's and from Christ Church. The only available edition of the music was the unmistakable Oxford University Press publication, originally edited by Michael Tippett and later revised by Philip Brett, available to this day but now normally replaced by something less unwieldy. Of course no choir could afford to buy a set of these copies, so they would be hired. It became known that Plymouth Public Library had a set available for this purpose, and we were duly supplied by them, with postage covered by some internal library delivery. Those copies had quite possibly been used in every performance in the country for many years. In time for our next rendition, in 1978, I had bitten the bullet and written the whole thing out, transposing up a minor third and rescoring, in the process inventing the system by which one could make a reduction of the score onto A4 paper. It took me a month of constant work.

People singing from the complete OUP edition must necessarily stand at some distance from each other, acquire acute pains in their arms, especially if they happen to be in choirs seven or eight, and stand every chance of getting lost. The conductor, incidentally, will have the same problem of keeping his place, especially if the soprano in choir one (whose part he can follow most easily) is unreliable; and is faced in every venue with the business of finding a music stand tall enough to stop the copy flopping over at the top and ripping whenever he turns a page. When I failed to find a stand big enough for this copy even in the Royal Albert Hall, I realised that it must be exceptionally tall even by orchestral standards.

The copies, the unfamiliarity of the music itself and the fact that the various groupings hadn't been able to rehearse together before the afternoon of the concert, led to a performance which, like so many others since, can barely have hung together. My only memory of it now is of a sea of shiny copies and eighty legs. It is easy to underestimate the difficulty of *Spem*, and no doubt we did so on that day. It is a particular error of judgement to assume that because there are so many voice-parts it becomes something akin to a piece written for a choral society (Striggio's 40-part *Ecce beatam lucem* is nearer this mark, being more chordal). In actuality *Spem* is fully polyphonic, which means that every part in it has its own individuality and importance. But unlike smaller polyphonic conceptions, in order to avoid consecutive movement between the parts, Tallis had to cut up his lines, making them rhythmically highly involved. The uncertain singer can hide behind quite a lot of this kind of writing – no one is going to hear it clearly – but hidden in those thickets of notes lurk one or two leads which can make or break a performance. I have looked into the faces of choral society singers struggling with, say, tenor choir four or alto choir eight, as the one crucial note in their part approaches, the one that is massively ringed in the copy, and seen sheer panic. I know from long experience whether any given singer is going to sing that note, and what will follow if he or she doesn't.

It is a great test of nerve, singing *Spem*, and the same can be said for conducting it. One is constantly being threatened with burial under a very weighty edifice, and yet, astonishingly, I have never heard it actually stop. In some of the amateur performances I have been involved with I have heard it so cacophonous that one would assume it was about to stop – the sound of massed tenors and basses wandering about in the texture coming at me like a vacuum cleaner with attitude – but the very size of it is a bonus in moments like these. The singers waiting to come in cannot hear anything they need to know, but they are far enough away from the others not to have their thinking destabilised. With clear leads from me and a good basic sense of tonality it is quite possible for them to come in on the right note in the right place, despite everything. It takes courage; and I must pay tribute to the many women I have heard singing the top two parts in the eight choirs, who time and again have saved the day. Those are the parts everyone can hear, including the other singers.

In 1973, performances of *Spem* by anyone at all were occasions of real note. News of them was passed around the musicians' grapevine so that everyone could feel vicariously involved: every performance and every recording was guarded as part of a collective folklore. Robert Brenton Betts, who later helped to found Gimell Records, first heard of the Tallis Scholars when he read an advertisement for our 1978 performance of it, and flew over specially from Athens to attend. I assumed from this that he was endlessly wealthy, in the way British youths think all Californians must be, but, despite his help with Gimell, this was not really the case. He just wanted to hear *Spem*. On the recording side, everyone knew the 1965 King's, Cambridge recording under David Willcocks, which had influenced and informed a generation, though as a matter of historical interest the two names that deserve most to be remembered in this context are those of Boris Ord who directed what was probably the first modern performance of it in the 1930s, and Michael Tippett, who not only made the first published edition of it but also made the first recording, in 1949 on 78s. After the King's recording came those of the Clerkes of Oxenford (1974), the English-language version, entitled *Sing and glorify*, of Andrew Parrott (made for radio in 1981), Pro Cantione Antiqua under Mark Brown (1982) and ours in 1985. On the concert side I can list from memory that we sang it in 1973, 1978, 1984 and 1985 as part of the same project, 1989 and 1992. After that it began to become more commonplace, and recently has been something of a party piece. Between January 2001 and August 2002 the Tallis Scholars sang it 18 times, three times live on BBC Radio Three, including in the Proms, four times in France and ten times in the US, with us furnishing the first ten voices alongside 30 American amateurs. It is worth recalling that Tallis himself probably never heard it.

A performance of *Spem* is more or less guaranteed to yield a full house, though at considerable extra cost to the promoter – four times the usual number of Tallis Scholars for a piece which lasts about nine minutes. Allegri's *Miserere*, however, costs the same as usual, lasts about thirteen minutes and is even more of a draw. As a result we have sung it more than any other single piece – 227 times by the 3 November 2003 – despite not realising its potential until 1979, when we first sang it. Almost all those performances have featured Deborah Roberts as the soprano soloist who soars repeatedly up to the famous high C, something she seems to be able to do with perfect ease and tuning in all circumstances. I have even heard her sing it when she was too ill to speak. It is a dazzling aural experience; and no one cares that the music itself is a freakish mixture of folklore and twentieth-century doctoring, neither renaissance nor polyphonic. We agree to do it as a special dispensation, to encourage new audiences, grateful that on the back of its 13 minutes we can fill the rest of the programme with music we are keen to put forward. Those groups who are obliged to perform Handel's 'Messiah' for their visiting card can of course do nothing else all evening, being tied into a concert of two and a half hours in length.

The Allegri has brought us some unusual opportunities. Despite having great difficulty pronouncing just about all the consonants in the two words in question, the Japanese asked for it as an option on each of our first five tours, happy that it should appear in some otherwise scrupulously constructed national programme: 'English Music (and Allegri's *Miserere*)' or 'Josquin and his Flemish contemporaries (and Allegri's *Miserere*)'. But it did the trick, and now we tour Japan without having to sing it at all, renaissance music and our association with it established. The history of our touring in Australia has followed the same pattern.

At the other end of the spectrum, we sang it in the Sistine Chapel, by special invitation of Italian and Japanese television, to celebrate the unveiling of Michelangelo's newly-cleaned *Last Judgement* in April 1994. For me this probably was the high point of my career so far (something I am asked periodically to identify). It was, after all, the Allegri's natural habitat, the solo group singing from the choir gallery where the original solo group had stood, and where so many of the greatest renaissance composers had once stood, the sound just as they all would have known it. The moment we were let into the chapel for the first session I dashed, laughing like a schoolboy with my friend Bo Holten (whom I had smuggled in as a singer) up that staircase to the famous loft, to marvel at the frescoes on the ceiling, now so much nearer, and to sit in the place where we imagined Josquin had sat, awaiting his turn to sing. For once the unconscionable amount of time that cameras take to get themselves organised was pure pleasure. They could have taken all week so far as I was concerned, a more or less empty Sistine Chapel being such a rare delight. For the time they did take I was required to stand in my place in front of the *Last Judgement* with nothing in between me and it except the singers, and look.

One of the bonuses of the Allegri is the opportunity to divide the two choirs into separate groups and dispose them about whichever building we may be in. I suppose the original idea was to recreate just those (supposed) circumstances of its performance in the Sistine Chapel, alternating between the loft and the floor. In a gothic cathedral the concealing and/or raising of the so-called 'solo group', which makes their sound more distant and indistinct, does add an extra frisson to a performance; and just recently, under the guidance of Andrew Carwood, we have also put the singer responsible for the chant verses in a third location. I realise only too well that this goes completely against the way we approach the rest of the music in our programmes, which is to leave it as simple, as undecorated as possible; but I accept that the Allegri has a special role to play, provided that it remains a one-off and does not lead to demands for us to sing baroque music, and provide spectacle, more generally. Down that path lies the end of the distinctive existence of the Tallis Scholars. It is worth observing, incidentally, that *Spem in alium* is not at all suited to the divided choirs format. Only a small part of it is in the *cori spezzati* idiom: the rest is properly polyphonic, which becomes a nonsense if its strands are dotted all over a building. Promoters of a light cast of mind, some of them French, are forever trying to turn *Spem* into something from a quite different era; and they then wonder why the result sounds like second-rate Gabrieli.

Attempts to recreate the Sistine Chapel effect in some of the concert halls we sing in have led to near-farce. If ever there was a piece which presupposes a churchy ambience, the Allegri is it. In order to fake some sort of atmosphere in prosaic places we have resorted to various forms of subterfuge, like putting the solo group behind partially closed doors, in corridors, in the royal box, in the organ loft, in the projection room of the Cinema Jacques Tati. In some of the Japanese halls there has been no other choice than to place the solo group somewhere else on the stage. On a scale of ten from utilitarian to paradise (eight being a gothic cathedral like Norwich, ten being the Sistine Chapel), modern concert halls would perhaps register as two, one being the Seymour Centre in Sydney, which was akin to a gymnasium. In fact there we did manage to remove the group behind a door at the back, but the surroundings killed the sound concrete dead. As the singers say, the sound didn't just die the millisecond it was produced, it was sucked back into the throat. The Opera House in Sydney would register about six on the scale, and count as a thrilling venue to perform such a piece, if the obvious place to put the solo group was not the organ loft, which is so raised up that I found it hard to focus on the singers standing there without feeling I would fall over backwards. For any singers who suffer from vertigo it is very difficult to concentrate: some have told me how they cling onto some part of the superstructure and dare not look down.

By its nature, the placing of the solo group off-stage may prove hazardous. The most entertaining episode was in the Hong Kong Festival towards the end of the British colonial era. The concert took place in Victoria Hall, an old concert hall with enclosed boxes. The idea was that the solo group would sing from one of these boxes, which as it happened was next to the royal box. We tend to sing the Allegri as the first piece in the second half, so that if necessary the group can be led to whichever eyrie has been set aside for it before the rest of us go on-stage. The piece was duly performed and, in the ensuing applause, the main group on the stage took a bow and waited for the others to come down. This they did by walking through the auditorium from the back to the front, expecting to regain the stage by some steps which had been put there in the rehearsal specially for them, but which in the meantime had been removed, leaving a climb of four feet. They re-traced their steps and vanished, soon to get lost in the corridors back-stage in a perfect rerun of one of the best spoofs in *This is Spinal Tap*. Minutes went by, the applause ceased, and the rest of us stayed on-stage trying to look as though this was all quite normal. Suddenly, with a clarity we had not entirely noticed during the singing, the acoustics of the building rang out with the words 'Oh shit', as the leading singer opened yet another door and came face to face with the Governor and his wife.

The first concert to carry the name 'Tallis Scholars' took place in February 1976. Finding a good name for the group took a lot of agonised thought. I disliked Latin tags – phrases involving words like 'Cantores', 'Voces', 'Nova' – and felt uneasy with medieval spellings in English, despite the example set by my heroes, the Clerkes of Oxenford. A composer's name seemed like a good idea, to make it clear what kind of music we were specialising in, but in those days there were already groups dedicated to Byrd, Taverner and Sheppard. There was also a group dedicated to Tallis, called the Thomas Tallis Society Choir and Orchestra, for whom the main connection with Tallis is that they are based in Greenwich where the master lived and died. Since they are a much larger group than ours, specialising in choral society repertoire from later centuries, I hoped they would not object to the dupli-cation, and the fact that we both still exist is proof that no harm was done. Not that I asked them. Nor did I ask The Scholars, an ensemble of four soloists which also still exists, and on whose toes I more directly trod when I decided that since the first members of my group held choral scholarships, this fact might be reflected in our name: such was the difficulty of finding a title that did not immediately send out the wrong signals. 'Tallis Scholars' was not bad, though I would not choose it today. I find the 'scholars' ele-ment too forbidding, even though in the cases of Sally Dunkley, Francis Steele, Andrew Carwood, Deborah Roberts and others it is perfectly accu-rate. But none of us conforms to the popular image of a scholar toiling away in ill-lit libraries seven days a week; and from time to time it has cost me a lot of effort to correct that wrong impression.

I would stand by Tallis, though. I didn't fully realise it at the time, but Tallis was the perfect choice in the sense that there is never any embarrass-ment programming a piece by him, and his Englishness and technical resilience suit us rather well. His relatively small output in so many differing styles maintains an unusually high overall level of compositional achievement, and it is an added bonus that it is possible to know everything he wrote. This is not the case with Palestrina and Lassus, for example, and if it ever does become so via a complete recording of their music, things will have to have moved on a long way from where they are now.

Having settled on the name 'Tallis Scholars', I decided in March and April 1978 to put on Tallis's complete Latin works in London. This was my big push to establish a reputation for the group outside provincial Oxford. It must have taken a lot of planning, though I hardly remember that now, since a good half of Tallis's music was not available in editions we could use, quite apart from the logistics of publishing a booklet to accompany the series. It transpired that Tallis's Latin output, plus a handful of English pieces and one or two organ voluntaries, could be fitted into four concerts. Obviously the last would culminate in a performance of *Spem*, which took place in St John's Smith Square. The first of the series was also held there, the second in the Little Oratory, Brompton, and the third in Marylebone Parish Church. I have a cassette recording of that last concert, made by a friend with a hand-held tape-recorder. I wonder if modern amateur performances of *Spem* sound quite so timid, and yet are quite so accurate. It is ironic that the one merit our rendition had – clarity – just goes to underline how far we were from making a real performance of the piece. That timid accuracy was a hallmark of our singing throughout the amateur years. The Clerkes, who also relied on amateur singers, could also sound small and white on occasion but their director, David Wulstan, rarely failed to produce a performance, which was the difference between the two groups for some time.

To a certain extent I achieved my ambition with the Tallis series. We received notices in several of the main London newspapers, which were generally favourable, and a respectable number of people came to hear the concerts, especially the two in Smith Square. In addition I was building up a useful library of music, much of it unique in that we had made the editions or transcriptions ourselves. But although our name was now more widely known, the next stage of our advancement was infinitely more difficult to secure. The problems awaiting us were that the group was still almost entirely amateur – I paid for the Tallis series out of door receipts – and was therefore at the mercy of the singers' real jobs and commitments; the unions were about to come down heavily on unpaid ensembles which they considered to be taking work away from registered professionals; and the BBC rejected us instantly, more or less permanently and without hope of redress.

The cliché about prophets being without honour in their own land provided me with cold comfort for the next ten years, and still has some application. Without the demand for our work outside Britain I doubt the group would have survived, for there was forceful opposition to what we were trying to do at home, which no one could ever be found to come forward and explain. Perhaps we really did have nothing to offer in 1978; certainly I annoyed people by being over-confident, and had offended Wulstan's contacts by setting up my group in competition with his. But if the BBC exists to do anything it is to encourage young British artists, and our repeated, almost hysterical, rejections at Radio Three by a clique of highly-strung young men who were answerable to nobody outside their own hierarchy became in time a scandal. We were officially banned, without any explanation being offered, until 1987, when a campaign of lobbying on our behalf led by Bruno Turner finally succeeded in convincing the powers of the day to take our name off the blacklist. In fact the Radio Three people had little choice by then, since we were within a few days of winning the *Gramophone* magazine's Record of the Year Award, which even they realised would show them in a bad light. There have been some distinguished names on that blacklist, incidentally, including those of the composers Robert Simpson and George Lloyd, who might be a lot better known if they hadn't been on it; but I think all of us would say the experience has left a bad scar. The BBC, which the British pay for through licence fees, claims to represent us all and yet, like the worst quango, has no obligation to justify itself. Petty vendettas and prejudices can run almost indefinitely in organisations that the public at large are keen to think irreproachable, which is why such organisations can be so absolutely terrifying.

The attitude of the BBC to our work was the most difficult to stomach, but there were other lesser obstacles. In 1982 I was visited by a representative of Equity, the union to which professional singers of every kind belong, who explained that I would not be allowed to employ professionals and amateurs together. I pleaded, as John Eliot Gardiner and others had also done, that my group depended on certain essential members who in those days were just as likely to be amateur as professional, since the professional circuit provided relatively few voices which were able to sing polyphony in the way I wanted it sung. This was academic to the representative, who assumed I was indulging in special pleading. In the end a tacit compromise was reached by which I could ask anyone to sing provided I paid them all the same. In fact I discovered we were not famous enough to be made an example of; not compared with the Clerkes anyway, who had been threatened in 1979 with the prospect of pickets outside one of their recordings, whose purpose was to vilify the Equity members taking part for supporting a group which was prepared to employ amateurs in a professional capacity. Unionism was at a peak then, Margaret Thatcher goading the miners into the ultimate showdown a few years later. Once that historic confrontation was over it was not long before Equity came to be described as 'the mouse that roared'; but for a time I really believed that I would have to continue my work either with amateurs only, or with Equity members only on full rates. The former was not attractive because that was how the Clerkes were constituted, and I knew well that they had been restricted in what they could achieve by never having made the leap into the professional world. I had myself sung for them. I also knew that some of my best young singers were about to enter the profession, thereby creating a stratum of professional singers who could sing polyphony as I wanted. These people, who included Francis Steele, really made the choice for me. We began to ask for fees which paid everyone the basic Equity minimum rate, my preferred amateurs as well.

After ten years of singing as an amateur group we thus entered the fray in 1983. It was a very difficult moment. With the BBC hostile, no reputation outside the UK, no outside funding and with the sudden obligation to pay our way, we had very few resources to fall back on. The worst of it was that we were held by our peers to be just another mixed singing group which specialised in music people really only wanted to hear performed by cathedral choirs (i.e. with boys and men in robes, preferably those of King's College, Cambridge). Having had 27 concerts in 1978 we had just six in 1983, and our recordings effectively had no outlet. Gimell, founded in 1981 because the established labels were interested neither in us nor the music we represented (see p. 74) had got nowhere. I took a part-time job as a teacher at the Royal College of Music.

Trying to start something in one's own country is like trying to establish oneself as an individual in one's own family. Everyone knows you and will support you in an indulgent way, but will assume that what you have to say would carry more credibility if it were said by someone they don't know. You have to prove them wrong, upset preconceptions which are comfortable to them, prove that the whole of you is more than the sum of all the parts they have given you and are familiar with. British music-lovers in the early 1980s, compared with their counterparts in other countries, knew quite a lot about the kind of amateur or semi-professional singing I was espousing: many of them had been involved with choral music, possibly in a cathedral choir. Some of them also knew quite a lot about renaissance polyphony, having heard it in perfectly good performances either on record or in religious services, sung by the leading cathedral and collegiate choirs of the day. We were asked then, and sometimes are still asked, what we are bringing to this music apart from extra costs. It was written for a cathedral choir with boys, wasn't it? Then the local cathedral choir can sing it perfectly well, and at a fraction of the cost. As a latter-day example of what I mean, we still have not been invited to sing in the City of London Festival specifically because they have long-established links with one or two London liturgical choirs; and we sang for the first time in the Three Choirs Festival, which is put on in rotation by the cathedral choirs of Hereford, Worcester and Gloucester, in 2002.

The answer I've always given is that we are specialists hoping to bring a deeper understanding of how the music we have chosen works, as well as a wider knowledge of the repertoire it has to offer, than non-specialist choirs can easily do. This is where the indulgent supporter used to lose interest, and the not so indulgent former choir member, who knew it all, lost patience. Who were we to set ourselves up? Were we claiming to know more than the (usually thriving) local choral scene? I came to understand later that the problem for anyone wanting to repeat what we had done in other countries was that renaissance music was a novelty to which the public had to be converted. In Britain the opposite was the problem: there were too many preconceptions of the rights and wrongs of how to sing it. I have never faced such routine hostility as when I have taken public discussions with choral singers in Britain of a certain age who 'sang for years' with so-and-so, rigid certainty usually going hand in hand with old-fashioned practices. Of course those preconceptions also carried a seed of hope, since at least the holders of them were potentially interested, putting the onus on us to convert them to our way of thinking. We had a start in Britain such as nowhere else in the world would have been able to provide, both in knowledge of the music and in finding singers to sing it; but the corollary was suspicion and condescension.

1983 was make or break time: that time which some of the semi-professional choirs I now direct outside Britain are having to face up to. We survived on a mixture of qualified support from the few people in Britain who were interested to see what we might achieve, and the first serious intervention by an organisation from abroad. Without a near-miraculous invitation from Musica Viva to tour Australia in 1985, which was made over two years before the event and which obliged us to keep going, I believe the group would have foundered. In retrospect it seems right that our first prolonged foreign visit should have been to Australia: a country which was free of the snap judgements about British singing groups we were used to at home, and yet was sufficiently like home to enjoy us without having to undergo a major cultural overhaul; but at the time the logic of the situation escaped us. Given that we had hardly sung on mainland Europe by 1983, had made no discs proved to have travelled outside the Home Counties and had no idea what fee or conditions to ask for, this really was a leap of faith on the part of a large international organisation and we were duly very impressed. When Francis Steele and I went to meet Kim Williams in a London hotel early in 1983 all I knew was that we had no track-record in touring and could only fumble when asked what our conditions would be. I waited to see whether our hesitations would sound alarm-bells in Kim's head at that meeting, since the idea had been all his and it must have been obvious we had almost no clue what we were talking about. But he maintained a calm exterior, and got a good deal. By the end of the tour two years later, I had spent all my fee and a good bit more on bare subsistence during a stay of nearly a month in an expensive country. This could easily have been avoided by asking for a realistic per diem rate, but to do that was beyond us. We were too desperate not to lose the gig. I never did find out what we had done to attract the attention of someone who lived in Sydney, deciding it was tactless to ask.

In the event, that Australia tour really sorted us out, plagued as we were by troubles brought on by doing something testing for the first time. People fell out with each other, some of the singers never sang in the group again and two-thirds of the team were ill, some for days on end. We had regularly to change programmes on the night, as the roll-call of the incapacitated became available, which forced the fully fit into all manner of vocal contortions, sometimes in front of crowds numbering close to three thousand people. Caroline Trevor, booked as a second soprano or 'mean', actually sang soprano, alto and tenor in one concert in Melbourne, which was broadcast live on the ABC. She can afford to remember moments like that with affection now, but at the time it seemed that we were on the verge of concluding a career before it had really begun. Nor was the tour an unqualified success for Musica Viva, who didn't ask us back for another seven years, though I think what put them off was not the running crisis behind the scenes (the tapes I have of that tour show we sang perfectly well despite everything) but our physical appearance on-stage. Another of our little naïvities was that we had not really worked out what to wear in public, and it did matter, much as we wanted it not to. Unfortunately the night we appeared at the Sydney Opera House one of the sopranos decided to wear a skirt (and I mean skirt) which had always been too short for formal wear quite apart from its other disqualifications, and had become shorter during the course of the tour due to wear and tear. The critic of the Sydney Morning Herald mentioned this outfit in his review and I imagine our reputation took quite a while to recover from it. On a subsequent occasion I have had reason to notice that the Australians are as quick to comment on what people wear as the Italians, and equally have the vocabulary to express their findings. (In 1995 the same man put an end to some years of the sopranos wearing shot-silk dresses by referring to them as 'bridesmaids' frocks'.) He did talk about the fact that the Opera House had never heard the like of Byrd's Five-part Mass before, but that is not what has been remembered.

The illnesses were to be expected. Touring at that length, so far from home, is a strain even on holiday. Having to perform just about every night as well adds pressures which it takes years of experience to recognise and find one's way round. On that first tour all the difficulties I am so often asked about – having to sing after being in dry, air-conditioned aeroplanes and hotel rooms; having to breathe germ-laden recycled air; having to sing with jet-lag; once ill having no opportunity to recover properly – piled in on us. The remarkable thing is that it has never happened again, at least nothing like on that scale. Occasionally a voice has had to be rested for a night or two, but from that day to this I have not had to change a programme (though see below page 36). For some years after this Australia tour we would carry round copies of standby four-part pieces we could sing if we had to, like Palestrina's *Missa Brevis*, but we never sang them and the practice has long since been discontinued. What happened was that the singers became professional even in the matter of not becoming ill. They learnt how to rest on concert days, how to diminish the effects of jet-lag, how to sing through nascent colds and infections in such a way as not to make their throats worse while still contributing, if at all possible, to the concert that night. And should a singer really go voiceless the programme will be saved by the fact that in theory we have two voices on each part (or, if that doesn't work, sopranos who are willing and able to sing alto, altos to sing tenor, tenors to sing alto, baritones to sing tenor, tenors to sing baritone and Fran is never ill).

My current colleagues reckon that the lack of illness in the touring group these days is little short of extraordinary. The older ones recall the days when no self-respecting group would fly and sing on the same day, even if the journey was to a country as close as Belgium. The John Alldis Choir once demanded and got A WEEK to recover on arriving in Australia at the beginning of a tour: I suppose our 1960s and 1970s predecessors still remembered the days when intercontinental tours had to be undertaken by boat, and took months. Nowadays we always travel and sing on the same day, if it is physically possible; and will sing the day after our arrival in the US. In Australia we get one blank day. By the old standards we should be very ill people, and perhaps long-term we are without knowing it; but in the short term the singers attribute their reliable good health to one thing only: that I encourage them to sing properly. They tell me that if I were to adopt the faux reverential approach, which so many conductors of early sacred music do, and try always to make them sing softer and yet softer, they would be at least vocally ill much more regularly. During the course of 2003 I have heard more about the problems caused to singers who are not allowed to sing out in polyphonic music than in all the years before, which makes me think the issue may be coming to some sort of head. Of course it is easier to get a blend from a group of singers if no one is sticking out, but the paleness of the impact of such an ensemble sound is so disappointing in a live event (as opposed to on a recording, when you can just turn up the volume knob) that I have instinctively never gone for it. Once the initial hurdles of the touring life had been vaulted in 1985, it became apparent that quite unwittingly my aesthetic preferences were going to make it easier for the singers to survive and even enjoy these long tours: a strong, energetic method of voice production is healthier for the throat than a held-back one. That it is also psychologically healthier doesn't surprise me in the least.

[I leave the last two paragraphs exactly as I wrote them some months ago, but now, at the last moment before publication, add this one. On 4 June 2003 we were finally obliged, not by illness but by the unreliability of aircraft, to change a programme completely. Of course it was a miracle that this had not happened before, but this was of little vital interest to the six singers who finally stood up with me before a thousand people in Milan Cathedral to explain that it is not possible to sing Gesualdo's Responsories for Tenebrae with a group of this size, at least not if there is only one tenor present. The other tenor and three others, travelling separately, had spent the day in Gatwick waiting for a healthy aeroplane. They arrived just as we left the building at the end of a concert which had required both the highest degree of professionalism from those who were there, and, yes, copies of Byrd's Four-part Mass and Palestrina's *Missa Brevis*. As I say so carelessly above, we didn't have these with us; but we were just in time to find old versions of each in Ricordi's music store up the road from the cathedral before it closed for the day. On no rehearsal we sang these Masses one after the other, while Andrew Carwood interspersed their movements with chant propers for Ascension Day and Pentecost. He was also sight-reading, from unfamiliar notes, in a volume which someone had found in a library seconds before we went on; though this volume was not to be found, it was noted, in the cathedral choir library itself, since they own no chant copies of any description, let alone copies of polyphonic Mass settings. Given their apparent lack of interest in traditional sacred music, at least in its more printed forms, we found it ironic that the concert we were giving was part of a series marking the six-hundredth anniversary of the foundation of the cathedral choir. I suppose my bag is now going to be burdened with one or both of these Mass copies for the foreseeable future, until we become blasé about them again. But we still have not had to cancel a concert.]

By 1985 we had begun to sing in the nearer European countries, in events like the Holland and Flanders festivals (in Flanders in 1982 we sang 39 separate items in four concerts, many of them new to us); and in England we had equally begun to sing in major venues. By far the most loyal of the English promoters were situated in the west country: the Bath Festival under William Glock, and Dione Digby's Summer Music Society of Dorset. If Kim Williams may be said to have taken a punt in 1983, Glock certainly may be said to have done so in 1977, when he first asked us to sing in his Bath Festival. He then went on to invite us back every year for the following seven years. Such belief in an untried ensemble was worth more than even he could have known, though he did it in part because he loved the repertoire and had few other groups to turn to. Dione Digby went even further in a sense, not only, eventually, giving us concerts in her series but allowing us to rehearse for whole weekends at a time in her house. To date we have sung 14 times in the Bath Festival, the fourteenth in 2003; for Dione's Society we have sung a total of ten times, twice performing Tallis's *Spem in alium* (at full fee), the second time in 2002.

But it was very slow going, and no doubt would have remained so if we hadn't won the *Gramophone* Record of the Year award in 1987. Those not familiar with the *Gramophone* Awards should know that they are structured by initially dividing the discs into many categories: Early Music, Baroque Instrumental, Opera, Orchestral, Contemporary, and many more. Each category parades a winner which has been decided upon by the experts who review in each of those categories for the magazine. These winners then go on to be judged between themselves, by the whole reviewing staff of the magazine. Any Record of the Year must therefore win its own category first, before it can go on to the next stage. Our record of Josquin's two Masses *Pange lingua* and *La sol fa re mi* not only won the Early Music category (which we have done twice subsequently) but went on to be preferred to all the other winners. This was the first time, and remains the only time, that a disc from the Early Music category has won the overall prize; and the attendant publicity helped the general public to begin to imagine that our repertoire might be something mainstream rather than something marginal, for church services or whatever the preconception was. The fact that 'minnow' Gimell had beaten the likes of EMI, Polygram, RCA and the rest of the majors with all their financial clout did the story no harm either. Very briefly I was a minor celebrity, appearing on radio news programmes and featured in newspaper articles. Suddenly Gimell was a going concern as a business and, not so suddenly, the Tallis Scholars began to be considered for international artists' series in concert halls. We first toured the US as a professional ensemble in 1988 and Japan in 1989.

The history of our touring in the US actually began in 1981 when Robert Brenton Betts, who had given us a small sum of money to start Gimell, gave us some more to tour the US as an amateur ensemble. This series of concerts did not teach us very much about the realities of a task we would later come to know so well, since Bob was with us to make sure his preparations went according to plan, and we reluctantly agreed to stay in private houses (see 'Hostilities' in chapter six). It was amateur enjoyment at its most complete – singers falling asleep in the sun after large meals and missing events, the events themselves alternating between formal concerts before substantial audiences and singing for church services. Just before we were due to leave on this tour the first so-called Gimell record (CDGIM 001, Palestrina's *Missa Benedicta es*) became available, though the final stages of its preparation had to be rushed to meet our departure date – anathema to Steve Smith and a mistake never repeated, not even when distributors have been crying out for product as they used once to do. Nonetheless we were able to take some boxes of heavy black vinyl 12-inch records with us on the tour, and sold them at the concerts, while I later tried to find a private distributor for them in New York. The only problem was that in the haste or the heat or both the vinyl was not reliably flat. One shop – Olsson's Books and Records in Georgetown, D.C., which had a Tallis Scholars bin more or less uninterruptedly from that day to just recently when they finally closed – said they could probably sell these discs provided their customers didn't look at them sideways. I blushed with embarrassment to see the stylus climbing and falling like a ship in a storm on those records. This was how Gimell started in the US.

In December 1985 we were invited to give ten concerts in the Folger Shakespeare Library in Washington, D.C. with the resident Folger Consort. In some ways this was just the sort of concert-giving I did not want to be involved with, verging on the wearing of 'authentic' costumes, using instruments to create a merrie Elizabethan atmosphere, second-rate music everywhere. In fact we were allowed to sing whatever we wanted in our own slots, and I duly dealt a possibly unsuspecting public some pretty solid eight-part counterpoint in the shape of Crecquillon's *Andreas Christi famulus*. We still didn't get much idea of what touring the US would be like, since we never moved from a house round the back of Capitol Hill, but I did have time to go to New York and meet Jon Aaron, for breakfast.

At first Jon took little notice of me, as he piled into the expansive meal he had chosen, there being other supplicants at the table. But I was carrying a review from the *Washington Post*, which happened to say that we were doing a good job, or words to that effect, and Jon had little option but to read it. The noise of collective masticating made sure there was no pregnant silence while a brave new world was born; but in the split second between scanning the newspaper and resupplying his mouth Jon said: 'We could fly the flag and see what happens.' It was an understanding which led to 32 tours under his management, an arrangement which only ended in 2002 when we decided to move to Frank Salomon.

In the event the flag was hoisted in 1986/7, and our first professional tour took place in April 1988. The main problem was not repertoire, of course, nor even venues, which on the early US tours were mainly churches, but money. Unlike in Australia in 1985, the list of costs was our responsibility, since Jon only acted as agent not impresario and, as was entirely normal, took his percentage of the highest fees he could command. But on a first tour of anywhere one is starting from scratch. Those fees were small: the concert in New York which brought me together with Douglas Dunn and Gordon Beals paid $1000, which had to make its contribution to everything, from hotels and international flights to fees and living expenses, for 11 people. The other 13 concerts didn't do significantly better, and I calculated afterwards that even though we scarcely came home with anything left of what was supposed to be our fee, the trip had lost six thousand pounds overall. I emphatically did not have this money to lose; it had to be 'found'. It was found eventually, by sleight of hand, but the worry of it was something I lived with for a long time. Nor did the next US tour, a year later, do much better, though slowly the deficits reduced. If I had acted with a kind of amnesia towards the future in setting up the group in the first place, and backing it to the exclusion of everything else, the irresponsibility I showed in allowing this first US tour to go ahead bordered on the criminal. I had no idea how it was going to be paid for and almost no idea in advance how much it would lose.

Yet we had to start somewhere, since I don't think anybody even today would pop up out of nowhere and invite us to tour the US twice a year, as we have actually done for 15 years, with every penny in place. It's true that that is what happened in Japan and Australia, which are the comparable countries for us to visit in terms of distance and numbers of engagements that will make any tour cost-effective; but ticket prices in the US are nothing like as high as they are in Japan – people expect to pay $40 on average to attend a concert there; and there is no organisation in Japan or the US like Musica Viva in Sydney, which completely dominates the concert-presenting scene, standardly pulling in the largest crowds we receive anywhere in the world – nearly three thousand people in Sydney and Melbourne, even in 1985 – with its own network of agents country-wide and substantial government subsidy. Nor do our own national organisations like the British Council offer any help in a country as wealthy as the US. Their attitude is that if people in rich countries want you they will pay for you, and it is not the business of the British taxpayer to help you establish a reputation in the first place. Everything I describe here makes the US the most difficult market to approach, and yet, as the number of tours we have given there shows, the most welcoming once the groundwork is in place. And it is no coincidence that it has proved to be by far our most consistent market for record-selling.

Welcoming and rewarding in one sense, but the finances have always remained uncertain. Whoever takes the risk – which in our case was, in order, me personally, Jon Aaron and latterly the Tallis Scholars Trust – will not get a great return on that risk. The overheads are too high and the chance of really coming good with renaissance polyphony is remote. We have tried live television appearances at prime viewing time, as on *Good Morning America* one mid-December with more or less straight carols in spoofed-up cosy fireside surroundings, and got absolutely nowhere, of course. We have tried signings in record stores, especially after winning an award from one of the glossier magazines, and made no impact. When we were with Polygram we tried to interest their film department in our music for sound-tracks – a well-worn path to instant stardom – and failed. We have done studio programmes from coast to coast, master classes at countless universities, and have been featured in glamorous publications like the *New*

Yorker. The result has been the slow but steady building of a presence which has acquired a formidable profile, but led to no pots of gold, no fairy-god-person looking down on us and saying, 'You've worked hard; here is a little bonus for all those hours of toil'. No doubt in the back of our minds there is still the hope that this *deus ex machina* moment of congratulation will come, but, as I say elsewhere, in the discussion of Gimell's selling-power, the reality of the situation is that our repertoire can sustain decades of attention in the public eye only if it is allowed to realise its potential at its own slow speed. We have performed to untold numbers of listeners, both in concert and on disc, who have collectively paid out the kind of fortune that directors of companies only respect if it comes quickly. We have reaped that fortune, but spread out over many years. Not glamorous, but a wonderful career, undistracted by memories of having made it really big when we were young, like the typical pop star, and for ever after trying to find that fame again, long after all the money has gone.

The upside of the story is that these many days, amounting to months, even years spent on the road in the US have provided some of the most positive experiences of our working lives. Unlike Japan or Australia, which have been much more occasional pleasures, North America has been a constant destination for us. In 2003 I went there on seven separate trips for work, and never came back saying that over-familiarity had been an issue. Perhaps I am an extreme case (see chapter five) but surely one only hates going somewhere if the circumstances of the trip are hell, when one can manage little other than to feel homesick (or just sick?), and ours to the US have never been that. The music is too good, the average standard of performance too high, the warmth of the reception from our audiences too evident for anyone who is committed to this way of life to say they could never do it again.

That first tour, like every first speculative venture in a new market, was designed to make contacts which would lead on to something better. No precise plans were laid, of course, but in fact we were lucky. Louise Basbas gave us the chance we needed in New York City by inviting us to sing in her Music Before 1800 series; as a result I met Douglas Dunn and Gordon Beals, who would later sponsor many of our New York appearances. And on the same tour Jon Aaron's network of friends in Boston introduced me to Kathy Fay of the Early Music Festival there. Douglas (until he withdrew from the fray in 2001) and Kathy together came to provide the backbone of almost

every tour we have given to their country, in the two cities most likely to provide a convenient jumping-off point for regular visits. Kathy needed no talking into action, since she was at the helm of an organisation that had already
staged several biennial early music festivals, renowned as the showiest of
showcases for leaders of the early music revival of the 1970s and 1980s,
which in turn had spawned a concert series which ran throughout the year.
This organisation flourishes now, almost entirely thanks to Kathy's deter-
mination and her loyalty to groups such as ours. We have tended not to sing
in the festival – though we did so in 1991 and 2003 – but we have given 29
concerts for Kathy as part of our regular touring at other times of the year,
traditionally just before Easter and just before Christmas.

New York provided no such ready-made vehicle for us, or indeed for any
ensemble or orchestra specialising in something the public held to be marginal, a prejudice which more or less continues to this day. Douglas and I sat
in the Oyster Bar under Grand Central Station, the day after our New York
debut in a small church untrendily too far up Manhattan to attract the regular concert-goer, bemoaning this state of affairs. If Boston had an organisation dedicated to this repertoire – and there were rumours of the same
thing happening in San Francisco, Los Angeles, Vancouver and even San
Antonio – why shouldn't New York? (The answer, incidentally, is that people who spend their time thinking about money tend to be unimaginative
when it comes to thinking about anything else, especially artistic things.
Mozart's operas – the safe and the tried – have more potential sponsorship
than can possibly be good for them. The Shakespeare industry in the US is
well out of control.) I said, in a random and only half-mindful way, 'Why
don't you start your own festival? I'm sure it would catch on.' In fact for some
time he and his partner Gordon didn't follow this up, at least not to the letter, though from the our next tour in 1989 they did agree to put us on pri-
vately. So began an extraordinary run of concerts in Manhattan, first in
'Smoky' Mary on 42nd Street, until it was closed for restoration, and then,
after one or two experiments, in St Ignatius Loyola on Park Avenue. That
wonderful building (and its organist Kent Tritle) hosted some of our most
memorable concerts anywhere in the world, including our 'thousandth',
with augmented forces and grand repertoire to match, in 1998; the John
Tavener extravaganza in 2000, when Paul McCartney appeared alongside us
(and I appeared alongside him in the final bow and had a first-hand taste of

what it is like to face a crowd that has gone feral); and finally, after the demise of Douglas's enterprise, the charity concert we gave for the victims of the Twin Towers disaster.

Douglas's Gotham Early Music Foundation, established in the autumn of 1996 and financed by Gordon Beals, should have been the perfect answer to the lack of profile for early music in New York. Douglas has impeccable taste in music, only ever inviting ensembles at the top of their respective areas of expertise. To read the roll-call of artists who worked for him in the four and a half years that the Foundation existed is to see that New York was offered a feast which has scarcely ever been convened elsewhere, even in Europe: it was like one of those small but perfectly complete collections of paintings – the Frick in New York or the Gulbenkian in Lisbon come to mind – whose reputations are carried on having one exceptional example of everything. Yet the audiences for Gotham were slow to build up. Cheaper versions of the same basic idea might have been more feasible, but Douglas was never interested in compromise. He also thought that the *New York Times*, after an initial interest, did little to support him (and indeed they are now talking about reducing the amount of classical coverage across the board, saying that their public needs more pop). Gotham closed its doors in 2001 and it looked as though our regular visits to the incomparable Big Apple – and that corner of 76th and Broadway near which, in the Milburn Hotel, we have always stayed and called home – were over. In fact, having fulfilled one or two special commissions, like singing in the Mostly Mozart Festival in August 2001, and underneath the Christmas tree in the Metropolitan Museum of Art in December 2002, we were adopted by George Steel at the Miller Theater of Columbia University. Our new singing home appears to be Riverside Church (or St Paul's Chapel at Columbia), and the regular visits have recommenced.

New York and Boston were not the only places in the world where we were invited to perform under the umbrella of 'early music' and the concept of authentic performance. The most outstanding of these was Utrecht, where the Festival Oude Muziek had an astonishing success in the 1980s and 1990s, and continues to this day with just the same spirit of folk-happening, but with classical music. We gave 27 concerts there between 1981 and 1996, and it was there that we first had a taste of how popular polyphony could be.

For the first time there were microphones everywhere, audiences stretching as far as the eye could see in beautiful churches, people sitting literally at our feet; there were concerts that started at 11 o'clock at night and carried on well past midnight, round-table discussions in smoke-filled bars in the small hours, earnest strangers quizzing one about performing editions in the middle of the street. The early music revival is probably not quite like this any more. One of the problems the organisers in Utrecht have to face now is that the young people they want to attract to their concerts are resistant because their parents have been supporters for 20 years and more, and these concerts actually run the danger of being seen as conventional. This is ironic. In many parts of the world early music still has the reputation of providing something daringly alternative, even revolutionary in artistic terms, providing a convenient tool with which to beat the classical music establishment; but the Dutch were years ahead in this game.

It would seem that the words 'early music' are a turn-off with some people in both Utrecht and New York these days, but for opposite reasons: in one there is too much of it, in the other it is insufficiently understood and respected. For the rest of us, caught in between, those words always made one think twice, even in the pioneering days; and those other words – 'authentic performance' – which went with the first words were never more than an embarrassment. I wonder how honest I was about this. Our repertoire was not being revived. It had been sung in an unbroken tradition in our cathedrals from the 'early' period to our own, and not only in the UK. Palestrina has similarly been sung in Rome, and Lassus in Munich. True, we were singing it with women rather than boys, and a lot of people have made a lot of fuss about that, but as one of our greatest cathedral organists and composers of church music, S.S. Wesley, said in 1849, 'Boys' voices at the best are a poor substitute for the vastly superior quality and power of those of women; but as the introduction of the latter at Cathedrals is inadmissible, it is necessary to cultivate boys' voices with due diligence.' Well, we weren't running a cathedral choir, but a professional concert-giving ensemble. We weren't reviving, and we weren't being authentic; but we were demonstrably singing music from an 'early' period, and we were doing it in a way we wanted to be heard as new. In fact we were caught in a rather unusual loophole in the whole early music business, whose *raison d'être* is the discovery of instruments from past centuries and what they can teach us about the sounds people heard before the invention of recording. By keeping to voices we were not an integral part of the scene.

I did not feel a fraud in joining the early music bandwagon because we were also trying to do something mould-breaking. The revolutionary mood of the early music 'movement' or 'revival' applied to us just as much, though our push had different emphases from those who were presenting instrumental repertoire. We wanted our music to be accepted in concert halls, as being just as much part of the long tradition of western classical music as any later repertoires. As much for the music as for ourselves we wanted to take it out of the church and the context of worship, where it is an endlessly interruptible adjunct to another purpose, and put it in lights by itself. For the pioneering early music groups this was never the problem: the music they played had always been accepted – even Vivaldi had come of age before the drive to authenticity had begun in earnest – though the proliferation of bands specialising in baroque instrumental repertoires probably fuelled the current enormously expanded state of general knowledge about music from the seventeenth and eighteenth centuries. Their challenge was to take the accepted way of playing this music out of the hands of non-specialist, modern-instrument orchestras, and show how the music is better served if it is not given the whitewashing modern treatment. As everyone knows, this struggle has been a great success and the revolution has largely succeeded, the headiness has gone out of it and all that is left is the mundane requirement to play the notes rather more confidently than was once the case. Our struggle is very far from being over, partly because on a smaller scale it is actually more ambitious. Instead of trying to convince the public to listen to music they already know they like in a way which may briefly make them feel uncomfortable, we are selling them an entire repertoire, also performed with a sound which will be new to them, but which in every detail is as modern as it can be. Instead of trying to recapture old sounds in the service of the music, we have no option, because there is no evidence of how people sang in the past, but to make up a sound which we think is appropriate. We are therefore asking our audiences to make a leap of faith twice over.

It has not escaped me that all along we have sung to larger audiences if we were being presented in international artists' series, alongside string quartets and other recitalists of every kind, than in festivals which had a special theme or went in for some kind of special pleading. From 1985 onwards the really big crowds have come to hear us in theatres and concert halls which have no other purpose in life than to offer a space to promoters who are prepared to take a risk on something which has to be mainstream enough to pull in audiences in the low thousands. Many promoters we have worked for have not been inclined to think beyond the church element they hear in our singing, and have scaled down their ambitions for us while ensuring an ambience which they think will give the concert an appropriate halo, and which their public will turn out to experience. Since the 11 members of the Tallis Scholars do not cost the same as a symphony orchestra, this approach has often worked perfectly well and everyone has been satisfied. But large though cathedrals may seem, they are not nearly as accommodating when it comes to providing seats with a good view and a good sound (not to mention the provision of adequate back-stage facilities) as a medium-sized concert hall. Nor as a general rule do they have such a loyal following. My own ambition to bring polyphony out of the margins has never looked more hopeful than when we have sung to nearly three thousand people from the stage of the Sydney Opera House, or the Melbourne Concert Hall or the Orpheum Theatre in Vancouver or the Auditorium 'Titien' in Nantes or the Osaka Symphony Hall or (to rather more) in the Royal Albert Hall in London. And in case it be thought that the sound in those places, unmiked, must be inferior to that achievable in the reverberant acoustics of a cathedral, in my experience state-of-the-art buildings like Symphony Hall, Birmingham, and the Bridgewater Hall in Manchester (and the Symphony Hall in Taipei – more of a fluke because older) are unrivalled in producing the perfect environment for polyphony: ensuring a sound that is rounded, blended and above all clear.

Mention of the Osaka hall reminds me that our far eastern touring, more than anywhere else, has been built on the supposition that we belong to the mainstream of western classical music-making. The whole notion of early music must strike our Asian audiences as being irrelevant – the subsection of a relatively small branch of an alien culture. As we know, in mainland China, the Philippines, Taiwan, Singapore and South Korea, as much as in Japan, the interest is in western artists who are seen to be famous at home. What matters are the western magazine reports, the awards, the good reviews, which they take at face value and want to experience for themselves. We would never have visited any of these places if our discs had not been reviewed well in Europe. The *Gramophone* and other record magazines (but mostly the *Gramophone* because that is the one they think we rate the most highly) have provided all the publicity we needed. Whenever we visit Japan we are obliged to sing music from our latest disc, otherwise there is a danger that we will not be seen as being up to date. I don't know whether it is possible for a western artist to build up a sufficient reputation to carry him or her beyond this pressing need for topicality, but after nine tours we certainly haven't managed it. The moment Gimell and the flow of discs seemed uncertain, so too did our touring in Japan. To be fair, our 2003 tour was also reduced in scope by the slow decline of the Japanese economy.

Many interviewers in the western world have asked me why I think so many people from such radically different cultures from ours have come to hear us. The only answer is that their need for culture, in a much more general sense than just early music or Catholicism or 'choir-music' as they call it, is great. They are curious without feeling threatened. Whole choirs standardly attend our concerts; one in Seoul for example, numbering 40 people, came armed with individual copies of the music. I remember the numbers because I was asked to sign every copy, though 40 is insignificant compared with the numbers attending some of the organised signings we've had to do after concerts in Japan and Taiwan. Obviously western music is filling an emotional need, yet I don't get the impression the next step for these peoples is to try to become a westerner. We are admired, but kept at arms' length.

Our one tour to China, in 1999, provided the most extreme examples of how unpredictable appearing in the far east can be. In Japan we have an agent; in China the incomparable Sibylle Mager of Hazard Chase had to do everything. There were officials on the ground who were technically responsible for us, but the line of command and responsibility above them was so long that they had no authority other than to order us about, while not knowing the answer to anything important. They were trapped between employers who had no respect for them, and some rather expectant professional musicians. Our two appearances in Beijing were less than glamorous, indeed the British Embassy staff reported that advertisement for us had been stifled by officialdom, possibly because of the religious content of the texts we were singing. These appearances culminated in an official banquet the next day (at 11.00 a.m.), attended by a thousand Chinese amateur singers, some government ministers and 9 of the 11 Tallis Scholars (since we had been given no warning of this event two of our number had revolted and gone sightseeing). To my horror there was a speech praising (and boasting of) the fact of our presence, at the end of which I was given a Chinese screen which fell apart in my hands as I stood there, the pieces ending up on the floor at my feet. This debacle was followed by an abrupt announcement that we would sing something. 'No, we won't', I said. Our minder, who all the time had been insisting that my colleagues get to their feet and perform, was not amused, presumably fearing for her job.

Guangjou (old Canton) must stand in relation to Beijing as Venice once did to Rome: when the conservative hierarchy in the capital tell you how things should be, you thumb your nose at them. The air of freedom in Guangjou is all the more noticeable for theoretically being offside. Unlike Beijing, Guangjou has a state-of-the-art modern symphony hall, which in 1999 was holding its opening season. Our travel there from Beijing had been so delayed (by about seven hours) that we had actually taken off after the starting time for the concert; and the flight took 90 minutes. This was a very low moment for Sibylle, who had spent months trying to make this happen, for we automatically assumed that the concert was lost. But we were reckoning on our own terms of reference. When we arrived, late and tired, the organiser clapped her hands, said 'hurry up', and bundled us into a bus. In an oxymoronic mood of rebellion at yet more rudeness, with a desire to live this experience to the full (and oiled by some very, very sweet-talking from me), the singers finally agreed to go on-stage with a slightly shortened programme. We were greeted by an uproar such as even the Koreans might have felt some respect for. To our astonishment all 2,500 ticket-holders had waited nearly two hours for something I doubt one of them had ever heard before. We blinked, failed to form a convenient line on a stage we had not been able to rehearse on, shuffled uneasily around and started up to a barrage of noise and incomprehension. It was a critical moment of cultural interaction. The listeners were eventually seduced, not least by the Allegri, which was given a heart-stopping rendition by Deborah Roberts despite everything. As she knows only too well, when the chips are down, midnight beckons and programmes are being shortened, Allegri is your only man. The rest of this Chinese tour took us to Hong Kong and Taipei, where we had sung before and knew the ropes (or the ropes knew us). Needless to say, this deeply flawed experience is the one many of us mention early on when we are asked where our work takes us, though our recent (February 2003) appearance in the Bolshoi has been rivalling it.

Special circumstances in the far east apart, the early music colours were worth serving under for a while; and in one or two places they still have some force – most notably in the Utrecht and Boston festivals, where audiences have been consistently supportive and loyal to the cause. In Britain the early music banner served a purpose for some years, before the focus turned back to the mainstream and what orchestras and singers had learnt from the new ways of thinking about music. The number of festivals dedicated specifically to the principle of authentic performance fell away. In Germany the idea never properly caught on, despite the presence of some leading ensembles: the Alte Tage of Regensburg was and is famously the worst-paid music festival one can be invited to perform in, a stark contrast to what goes on in Germany when it comes to the acknowledged mainstream. In France, Italy and Spain the interest has always been in the baroque, with a generally relaxed attitude to the theories behind the performances. In fact just recently in some southern European countries, long after the heat had gone out of the early music movement in the north, there has been a quite sudden flourishing of stylish singing in both baroque and renaissance music. What for so long had seemed as unlikely as it was desirable, has to some degree come about in the last five years. It was as if their leading practitioners had been biding their time, waiting to pick out the elements of the northerners' work which most suited them, and which they could adapt with their own flair.

Even in the early 1980s, when the early music revival was at its most marketable, I was careful not to identify the Tallis Scholars with it too completely, partly for the reasons already given concerning my sense of ambivalence towards our role and partly because I always had an eye on those symphony halls. At the same time I was also at pains to point out that we did not seek to perform in churches as a matter of course, as so many promoters have assumed, again through a sense of ambivalence towards our role in secularising what was originally intended for churches in a different context, and again with an eye on those symphony halls. There is still a way to go in convincing concert-goers that polyphony could be part of their standard fare, though there have recently been some very brave attempts to advance this cause. In October 2000 we sang Ockeghem's *Missa Au travail suis* in the

Philharmonie in Berlin as the first part of a concert whose second part consisted of a performance of Mahler's Ninth Symphony, played by the Berlin Symphony Orchestra under Kent Nagano. The hall was filled to capacity for this experiment, more for the Mahler than for us of course; and we received quite violently divergent criticisms. One newspaper said the hall was not the place for a Mass to be sung; another said this kind of thing should happen more often. No one said that the eight singers were too soft for such a vast auditorium – and the place was full for a reprise of exactly the same programme on the following night.

But in general, Germany and the German-speaking countries have been the most resistant in western Europe to our music. It is a fact of life that the core of western classical music-making has been led for centuries now by composers, conductors and performers from Mitteleuropa, and those musicians have never done anything more than pay lip-service – if that – to polyphony. For them, and for millions who have taken their word for it, classical music became interesting when the first identifiable symphony orchestras were formed and written for. It does not help one iota that the German world did not produce any composers of the front rank until well after the turn of the seventeenth century; not a single polyphonist who was a native German speaker has become a familiar name: I offer you Gregor Aichinger, Hans Leo Hassler and the three composers called Praetorius. Germany, like France, and even Italy until the 1550s was under the sway of the Flemish masters. And here we come to a fact which explains so much about the excellence of renaissance sacred music, while also explaining why it can be so difficult to present to modern audiences: 90 per cent of the best of it was written by composers who were born in the country which is now called Belgium, lands that were initially part of the Burgundian empire, for long known as Flanders. It helped that Flanders was a restricted geographical area, where generation after generation of brilliant musicians could develop and mature a set of compositional techniques. No doubt the members of each of those generations knew each other well, before they set off on their travels all over the renaissance world, and knew the achievements of their predecessors equally well. There has never been such a powerful musical force in European music, not even when the Germans got going in the late seventeenth and eighteenth centuries.

Yet one has to admit that the facts of this case have not helped us in our struggle. Belgium is too small a country to be able to support and promote such a colossal musical heritage single-handedly. Indeed in this very year the anniversary of the death of Philippe de Monte in 1603 was planned as a major theme in the Flanders festival, but the anniversary celebration was more or less cancelled in its entirety for lack of money. De Monte was an ideal candidate for showcasing, since he was both prolific and varied in his output, very highly rated both in his lifetime and since by the *cognoscenti*, but unknown to the wider public. The Tallis Scholars were to have summed up a week of concert- and symposium-giving with a gala concert in Ghent Cathedral, but instead sang a potboiler programme featuring Allegri's *Miserere*. And the other side of this coin is that the Germans do not seem to feel much affinity with the Flemish composers who dominated their musical life for so many decades, in particular Henricus Isaac and Orlandus Lassus; nor have the French particularly identified with this school despite having always referred to it as Franco-Flemish, done their best to claim for themselves those with French names, like Josquin des Prés, and physically taken possession of some of the towns and counties in what was once Flanders, such as Tournai and Lille. The French, like the Germans, tend to support their own people, and it comes as no surprise to find that their interest in French baroque music far outweighs their interest in the Flemish renaissance. This is not to say that these peoples are not open to the possibility of listening to something new – both have a strong instinctive feeling for mathematically complicated music – but there is an extra hurdle to clear in suggesting polyphony to their main festivals, and there is an obvious temptation for the organisers to stick to what they know their public knows.

The pull of the familiar should not be underestimated. In Italy and Spain we are standardly asked to sing music by their nationals, by men whose names look approachable on the page (Flemish names like Adriaan Willaert, Hayne van Ghizeghem and Gheerkin de Hondt seem to put people off before a note is sung). Fortunately in a sense the Flemish cultural empire began to wane before the end of the renaissance period, which allowed one or two local composers to shine, if not in Germany and the rest of 'France' then certainly in Italy and Spain. Almost the only significant beneficiary of this waning in Italy was Giovanni Pierluigi da Palestrina, but he has proved to be enough. We can do whole concerts of Palestrina in Italy (with the Allegri, which is not strictly speaking a renaissance piece) and everyone is satisfied.

For years we have sung for the Societa Santa Cecilia in Rome, and have sung a Palestrina Mass every time. It helps that this society, which nowadays boasts a symphony orchestra and chorus and a brand-new concert hall, was supposed to have been founded by Palestrina, amongst others, and has been putting on concerts ever since Palestrina's time. The scene in Spain is even better from our point of view. Although Flanders was colonised by the Spanish in the sixteenth century and many of their leading musicians went to work in Spain, local talent was never crushed by them. Indeed there are significant native Spanish composers going well back into the fifteenth century, and Spain continued to produce geniuses throughout the sixteenth. The vast majority of our concerts in Spain have involved native compositions, or those of first-generation Spaniards living in Mexico, with Victoria's incomparable six-voice Requiem to the fore. Indeed, Spain should long have been the perfect touring venue for us, with good support for culture from the banks and a well-disposed public, but the potential has not yet been realised because of the dog-eat-dog practices of concert agents in that country.

And then there is the English repertoire, which has the unique distinction (outside Poland) of having escaped the influence of the Flemish, at least until well into the sixteenth century. As a rule English concert promoters are not so stuck on asking us for a native programme as happens elsewhere. Tallis and Byrd are known composers to English audiences, through cathedral performances and a long tradition of recording their music, in a way that does not apply with renaissance music anywhere else. And a certain general familiarity with the style of polyphony means that British audiences are more ready than most to consider turning out for a name they've never heard of. This is also true in the US, but more for the reason that they are prepared to take on trust that whatever we say we want to sing will be worth the ticket-money, the difference between Byrd and Lassus in many cases being quite literally academic. English renaissance composers are probably more popular in the UK than any others, but the sheer length of time that this has been so has led to a desire to explore further afield, as the BBC's programming illustrates when they remember polyphony at all. The only drawback with the English composers is that they tended to be less prolific than their counterparts abroad, with the possible exception of Byrd. For example, we sang all of Tallis's Latin music in four concerts in 1978; Robert Parsons's contribution has been published in one fairly slim volume. On the one hand, there is more variety in Tallis's music than in Palestrina's immeasurably larger output; on the other, one has no option after a few years but to repeat what one knows of Tallis.

It is a commonplace that after 25 years an ensemble with a particular message to promote, and no government subsidy to sustain it, is usually beginning to fade away. The original members of the group, as well as the message, begin to tire, and the reputation of the ensemble starts to be overtaken by new attractions on the block. Those groups which survive longer do so by a constant process of reinvention. The leading early music ensembles to have passed the 30-year barrier have managed it by coming up with new ideas and new repertoires, while still performing them better than anyone else. I very much admire groups like the Hilliard Ensemble, the Amsterdam Baroque Orchestra and the Academy of Ancient Music, and conductors like John Eliot Gardiner, Roger Norrington, Nikolaus Harnoncourt and Philippe Herreweghe for the liveliness of their minds and the sheer doggedness of their professionalism. Most of these people started their careers in one corner of the early music map, and slowly worked their way round to others, extending the territory as they went. It was partly as a result of this process that the term 'early music' began to be applied even to compositions written in the twentieth century. But the Tallis Scholars have not done this. We have not branched out and we can scarcely be said to have reinvented ourselves, unless promoting the music of Gombert and Crecquillon, after Clemens and Sheppard, may be called a reinvention.

One of the ingredients in our survival has been the depth of our chosen repertoire. I notice that one danger for longer-lasting groups is that they can run out of good music from within their chosen speciality. If this happens they must either adopt a new profile, which their public may not like, or start digging up unknown 'masterpieces' for fear of coming to rely on the same small round of acknowledged masterpieces. Baroque specialists are particularly prone to this since the baroque achievement is not as deep as that of other periods, as is constantly being illustrated. Even a Beethoven cycle causes less excitement than it once did among the public; and if Mahler can still be said to do this, it will not be for much longer. We have the privilege of being able to pick at leisure from a repertoire which seems to know no limits. Different publics may have their different preferences, and familiarity with renaissance music may not be as widespread yet as that of the orchestral repertories, but once inside the territory one can be like the proverbial boy in a sweet shop, eyes wide with incredulity at what surrounds one. I still go to the library and open a volume of the complete works of someone I've recently heard people talking about and choose at random, without hearing a note before the first rehearsal. That is the kind of trust which 30 years with these composers has inspired. And so incomplete has anyone's knowledge been of the polyphonic repertoire that one is just as likely to stumble across a Mass by Palestrina that is as good as his most famous settings and never been performed, as to find one which is merely good. It is an irony of our situation that the library shelves have been supporting these complete editions for anything up to a hundred years now, in many cases without a single note of them ever having been heard. I and conductors like me can't believe our luck.

Nonetheless if we had been restricted in our touring, as many groups are, to Europe, I think we would have had a hard time of it. Perhaps we would have survived, but with such a significant reduction in activity that our rate of development as a performing ensemble would have slowed, to the point where we might have done little more than mark time. Our knowledge both of the repertoire and of how to present it in all its different facets has come from constant and regular practice, just as an instrumentalist explores and practises for hours a day at home. We can't do this as a group at home, and it is too expensive for us to rehearse just for the experience of it, so we have to have concerts. Europe has regularly proved unreliable in giving us these. Japan, Australia and above all the US have been much more certain; and because tours to those places last weeks, they have inevitably formed us more intensely as a group than the one- or two-night trips within Europe. It helps the intercontinental tours that payment to the singers is much higher when we work night after night for two weeks, than when we work for one night and take three or even four days over the project, as can easily happen in Europe.

As I have already said, the home scene was idiosyncratic. At first we had as many concerts as we wanted, provided I did everything in the way of publicity and no one was paid. Once we turned professional we were in trouble everywhere, but nowhere more than with people who had not been used to paying us and who had the choice of employing umpteen other vocal ensembles, some of them offering some renaissance music. It was essential that these promoters should want the sound we made if we were going to get anywhere, and this didn't begin to be recognised for what it was until about 1983. Even then British promoters blew hot and cold for many years, with the honourable exception of one or two loyalists mentioned above, and it has only been in the last five years, under the auspices of Hazard Chase, that Britain has begun to provide really high-profile and consistent employment for us. If the casual observer were to think that a concert like the one we gave for Peter Davison in the Bridgewater Hall in January 2003, to an audience of 2200 people with a live broadcast to back it up, was the sort of thing we had come to expect, they might be right if they were to look outside this country, but not within it.

As Janet Baker once said, if you're any good you'll probably start your career at home with good notices, and, once you've survived the middle period and become part of the establishment, end it with good notices; the problem is that middle time, when you are just doing what you always did, and the critics have run out of positive-sounding adjectives or are a little bored with you and can still say so. You are no longer new when other people are. In our case there was a limit to the number of times writers could talk about the purity, the clarity, the blend, the tuning, how the women sound like boys, angels, glimpses of heaven and so on. People got self-conscious. And they began to assume that something must be missing. In England we were dismissed as part of a malaise – fluent but passionless note-reading – which everyone knew was endemic because it was practised in the cathedrals, and therefore tolerable but not likely to yield something first-rate.

Abroad this story was reversed. We were first heard by many critics who were used to listening to very different kinds of singing, and judged insultingly bland. One French newspaper, in the late 1980s, referred to a concert we gave as 'monotone et ennuyeux'. At about the same time an Italian said we performed like robots, implying that Palestrina could only come alive if we sang him with a full range of operatic expression. It is a wonder we ever broadened our base in these countries, since originally they were not particularly thrilled at the idea of an expensive English choir coming to sing anything at all to them, and some suspicion certainly remains. But slowly the idea of this unusual kind of concert, backed up by awards for our discs in the local press, caught on, and has flickered and faltered ever since.

In some European countries, mostly the larger ones – France, Germany, Spain, Italy, Austria and Switzerland for a while, Belgium – we came to rely on a string of local agents. In the smaller ones – Holland, Ireland, Finland, Sweden, Portugal, Israel, Greece, Slovenia, Poland, Hungary – where there is no regular work for us, we dealt directly with the promoters. This has long been the case in Britain as well, largely because until about ten years ago Britain had much less money to spend on culture in general than was clearly the case on the continent, and an agent's commission on top of all the other necessary costs would have lost us the concert. At the Bath Festival in the early 1980s, for example, we were only employed if we could account for every single penny spent on the sheet music for that event, or mile of petrol consumed in getting to Bath. With sterling much stronger now relative to the euro and its predecessors, this has changed.

Our dealings with those agents over the years would illustrate splendidly how the European Union couldn't possibly have functioned harmoniously before the turn of the century, and how it just might now. From the disdainfully aristocratic Frenchman who was our first experience of a foreign agent to the Portuguese woman with numbered bank accounts which the British Council refused to pay their money into, we fought hard to get our concerts. Only the Belgian agent – Luc van Loocke at Lilian Weinstadt – is the one we started with. The general pattern was that we did quite well in the larger countries as a result of the *Gramophone* Award of 1987, until about 1994, when the graph turned inexorably downwards (13 concerts in France in 1990, none in 1997). We had become an old story, and had failed to establish our music as mainstream. The degree of success and collapse varied. Germany was always a near-impossible struggle, for concerts and records alike, yielding little overall variation year on year. In France and Italy – in the years when Britain was so disappointing for us – it briefly looked as though we could do anything up to six mini-tours a year. France was the most promising of all, if we agreed to stay in third-rate hotels on motorways and travel everywhere by train or too-small minibus. Servicing the summer festivals was an especially memorable occupation. For July after July 11 of us would routinely expire in a 12-seater van as it veered from one gothic abbey to another, often in the remotest places. The Abbaye Notre Dame de l'Assomption de Châtres, vaguely near Saint-Brice in Charente, for example, has no windows, is crawling with bird and insect life and is in the middle of a field with no facilities of any kind. There was a certain frisson to be had from performing nocturnal music in these places, but the audiences were small, and the real problem was that it didn't have to be us. In those days it seemed to me that what the French really wanted was either a consort of monks (for late-night contemplation) or a baroque orchestra (for every other time of the day). Polyphony didn't quite fit any of the clichés.

We sang in countless small festivals in France in this way, totalling 96 concerts to date. Very few had us back, though two were sufficiently faithful to ensure that this charade of international touring had a backbone for a good seven years. One was Jean-Luc Soulé's festival in St Amand de Coly; and the other was masterminded by the Abbé Orhant in the cathedral at St Malo. With reference to the latter (and meaning no disrespect to the former, who has remained a close friend of mine) I don't think we have ever come across a man who has impressed every one of us so unreservedly. It wasn't just that he had us back six years running when it was clear his festival had very little money: indeed, we were the only fully professional group in it. It was his saintliness. Every word he spoke (most famously 'Bonjour') and every gesture he made, had an authority that most politicians would die for. Before every concert we gave in St Malo cathedral he would introduce us to the audience, each year the description became a little more embroidered, until by the last time he was saying, as he nodded gently to each of us: 'Vous êtes les ambassadeurs palestriniennes par tout le monde' – a pause to raise his right hand and point to the vault – 'JUSQU'AU JAPON'. Then, lowering his voice: 'J'éspère, chers amis, que parfois vous vous souviendrez de St Malo quand vous êtes loin d'ici, car St Malo pense toujours a vous.' And it was true in a way. We did, and he at least did, though his colleagues and congregation never shared his enthusiasm and our audiences were largely made up of tourists. He died suddenly in late 1993 during a routine check-up in hospital, a fact I only knew about because a letter I had written him was returned months later with the franking 'décédé', which is one way of finding these things out. He had no family to pass on the news, and the church itself very quickly forgot him, as I was to discover. But he had already invited us for the 1994 season, and we returned to sing the Victoria Requiem for him, which this time was preceded by a eulogy from me. It was not an easy concert to do. A number of us have gone back to St Malo for holidays in the years since, my family and I about ten times to date.

By 1994 we were on the slippery slope that can come after 20 years of doing the same thing. Since we were not much employed in Britain, Germany or Spain the first obvious signs of it were in France and Italy. The agents, who as a breed can easily lose interest if work for a group has to be fought for, began to make excuses. Once again we were kept going by the long tours, and by the continuing success – or relative success – of our records. The urgent question was whether we could get any further in our campaign to make polyphony a normal point of reference for averagely educated and interested music-lovers, not something one needed 'to know about' to enjoy. By this time the problem was not really our standing: we were well known enough to represent the music if people wanted it, and we were not being pushed out by other groups. I knew very well that if a festival was going to give our space to another ensemble it was almost certainly not going to be to one offering polyphony. The organisers would simply have decided that their audience was not going to turn out for this repertoire.

The campaign continues, and the verdict will not finally be known for some years. But between 1996 and the present our profile has slowly changed for the better. This has partly come about as a result of James Brown and Lucy Rice at Hazard Chase selling us to the kind of halls and concert series which will correct the impression that we only appeal to specialists; and partly by our using our increasing years of experience to advantage, both in the way we plan our programmes and in the way we deliver them. Which is another way of saying the public haven't got the impression that we're bored or past it. The concerts I've mentioned above in Manchester and Berlin were representative of the change; I could list others in the Birmingham Symphony Hall, the Philharmonic Hall in Liverpool (and yet others, like the protracted negotiations to appear with the Milwaukee Symphony Orchestra which collapsed at the last moment because the organisers panicked).

During 2002 we appointed new agents in France and Italy, whose initial task was to bring us back from the living dead. In the case of Daniel Gutenberg in Paris this was approached with some trepidation, but he found that after six months or so he no longer needed to say 'do you remember that group that had a reputation here ten years ago?' By going straight to the top for concerts from the beginning – the Musée d'Orsay, the Cité de la Musique, La Folle Journée de Nantes, all of which were broadcast – he was soon able to refer only to what we had done very recently, which meant the past never became an encumbrance. In Italy it is still early days in our resurrection, but we have found that promoters are simply pleased to hear that we are available again.

A group that survives for decades does so on the average standard of what it does. At the back of this story are ten musicians, dressed as if for a chi-chi dinner party of yesteryear, agreeing to stand there and sing. These ten are the latest configuration of hundreds of singers employed by me over the years, who collectively bear witness to the genius for singing which obtains in Britain. In truth these hundreds are hardly representative of what makes up modern British society, let alone of what other nationals can do, since we have scarcely ever employed any 'outsiders'. From the beginning we have looked to a very particular type of person to sing in the group, probably someone who has been through a cathedral or Oxbridge college choir if male, or even, these days, if female. Some read music at university, or studied voice at a conservatoire, many had musical parents. And although London plays host to many hundreds of professional singers from all over the country, offering more paid work than any other city in the world, this can be a difficult scene for an outsider – by which I probably mean a foreigner or a Brit with the wrong attitude or even accent – to break into. It is even unwise, at least when starting out, not to have a London telephone number. Despite running into the hundreds these singers belong to a quite intimate circle, living easily with themselves at close quarters, their days spent grouping and regrouping in airports, bars, buses and on stage: an instinctive union of professionals in trade if ever there was one.

It is a traditional British scene. It reminds me of a kind of Britishness that I used to read about in historical studies of the nineteenth century, the prototype being the radical artisan. These were the people who made the industrial revolution possible, who had a skill and a brain. They were the new people, who asked awkward questions about how they deserved to be treated, and always knew how to make things work. They were proud people who cost a specified sum: instinctively suspicious of fine language or abstractions, very often with a dry, ironic sense of humour, especially when the management were making their lives hell. They had a craft which, like their humanity, they knew no one could take away from them, and they were able and willing to put both unstintingly at the service of anyone who employed them fairly. I think of this model of the artisan sometimes when we find ourselves doing what we do in terrible circumstances – jet-lagged, hungry, cold, ill – yet going for it flat out, because we owe it to ourselves and our colleagues not to take it easy. No wonder the average has been so high.

Before the Tallis Scholars: in Magdalen College cloister, Oxford, February 1977. Left to right: Michael Cockerham, Peter Hayward, Francis Steele, Neil Lunt, Jeremy White, Julian Walker, Julia White, Louise Glanville, John Crowley, Alison Stamp, Mike Brown, ?, Julia Williams, Andrew Wright, Verity Curry, Robert Hayward, Helen Dixon, Gillian Russell, Christopher Moorsom, Petronella Dittmer, David Parker, Harry Christophers, Alistair White (taken by a local photographer who specialised in weddings).

Outside Bath Abbey, in 1983. Front row left to right: Francis Steele, Deborah Roberts, Tessa Bonner, Sally Dunkley, Alison Gough, Charles Daniels, Nicolas Robertson. Back row left to right: Michael Chance, Douglas Leigh, Graeme Curry, John Milne, Rufus Müller, PP, Jeremy White, Robert Harre-Jones.

Ouside the Danish Church, London, in 1984, in preparation for the Australia tour of the following year. Left to right: PP, Sally Dunkley, Alex Donaldson, Alison Gough, Robert Harre-Jones, Caroline Trevor, Nicolas Robertson, Jeremy White, Deborah Roberts, Francis Steele, Charles Daniels. *(Photo: Clive Barda)*

Inside the Danish Church, London, in 1989. Left to right: Deborah Roberts, Caroline Trevor, Rufus Müller, Robert Harre-Jones, Francis Steele, PP, Michael Lees, Donald Greig, Charles Daniels, Sally Dunkley, Tessa Bonner. *(Photo: Clive Barda)*

Outside St John's Smith Square, London, in 1991. Left to right: Paul Agnew, PP, Sally Dunkley, Donald Greig, Caroline Trevor, Tessa Bonner, Francis Steele, Ruth Holton, Deborah Roberts, Robert Harre-Jones, Robert Johnston. *(Photo: Hanya Chlala)*

In Ham House, London, in 1996. Left to right: PP, Philip Cave, Robert Johnston, Deborah Roberts, Robert Harre-Jones, Tessa Bonner, Ruth Holton, Francis Steele, Donald Greig, Sally Dunkley, Caroline Trevor. *(Photo: Clive Barda)*

In a studio in 1999. Left to right: Caroline Trevor, Sally Dunkley, Philip Cave, Francis Steele, Jan Coxwell, PP, Deborah Roberts, Donald Greig, Steven Harrold, Patrick Craig, Tessa Bonner. *(Photo: James Brabazon)*

2

A HISTORY OF GIMELL RECORDS

Any artist hoping to make a career out of classical music will want the double whammy of maintaining a high average standard in concert while releasing recordings which attract good notices. Of the two, giving good concerts is the more important since most music-lovers are still wedded to the idea of music as spontaneous expression, an ideal which is premised on live performance. This has meant that almost every successful concert artist has sooner or later ended up in the recording studio, if only once or twice, if only to produce a kind of memento; but prominent recording artists have not always had an easy time finding concerts. It is hard to put down deep roots with recordings alone.

If the relationship between concerts and recordings is inevitably symbiotic, the exact balance of the relationship is at the mercy of the marketplace, with records the more volatile element. Of course concert work can fluctuate, but in our experience it does so on a much narrower scale of ups and downs than record sales, which reflect tensions completely outside the control of the artist. If one gives a good concert, one may expect to be asked back: anything can happen to a good record, from being sunk by a rogue reviewer who has an axe to grind (usually an academic with a pet theory) to the whole industry being convulsed by some new crisis of identity. One rather vividly remembers the time when CDs were new, income was up, and record companies could afford to be as interested in repertoire as they were in artists. For some years The Complete Works of an Interesting Composer, recorded by unknown 'specialists', could make as big a splash as the latest recital album of a Very Famous Soloist. But the CD is tired now, as the LP was, and performers who relied on eye-catching recording 'projects' will be wishing they had spent their glory years treading the boards in as many places as possible, relentlessly giving very good concerts. On the back of giving outstanding concerts one may sell some records these days, which is exactly how it was when we started in the 1970s.

Anyone who allows himself to think that a record exactly represents what musicians do on-stage is my friend, if a gullible one. Of course, as with film-making, there is an element of voluntary delusion – one wants to believe it is as perfect as the representation suggests it is – but everyone knows that records are made with edits. In a recording studio one is giving one's all to a conductor, a microphone and an empty space. One does this several times over, as necessary, until everything is in place and there are no aircraft overhead. Eventually one's best clean efforts will be stuck together. The disc will inevitably come from a series of takes which presuppose that the performers have constantly stopped and started, which ironically is the one thing in a live performance which is not allowable. Wrong notes, bad tuning and outside noise are all tolerated in concert so long as they do not actually cause the music to stop. If it does, then everyone is embarrassed. Equally ironically, given the doublethink involved, unedited discs of whole concerts are not usually successful with the public. The hope is that the raw passion of the moment will have been captured in a way that is assumed not to be possible in the cold atmosphere of studio sessions, yet the leap from the heat of the moment in the concert hall to a set of speakers in one's front room is not so easily made. My view was always that the listener actually wants something different in the two places, for all that the stated ideal is that the recording should come as near as possible to a live event. When people come up to me after a concert and say, 'You sound just as perfect live as you do on your records', I do not believe them, though I am glad they think it. What I imagine they are saying is that the good, immediate, human things about the concert have substituted for the calculated perfection of the disc. But the concert will not have been as sonically perfect as the disc – the presence of an audience would make sure of that. I will be thinking, as I have so often thought while listening to radio broadcasts after an event which had seemed perfectly good at the time, that had they bought a disc of the concert and played it at home they would have been disappointed; just as it goes without saying that if the concert had consisted of the playing of a disc they would have been disappointed.

So I make no apology for making discs which are artificially controlled: as I say, it is foolhardy to offer anything less. Obviously one wants passionate interpretation, which may be difficult to achieve on the sixth take of a piece of music we all know very well (or can sight-read very easily); but if one believes, as I do, that the sheer sound in polyphony is its most powerfully expressive agent, then it is worth spending time and money trying to maintain that sound throughout the length of a composition. Indeed to me 'interpretation' has come to mean maintaining the sound. Little is achieved if a piece starts off well and then audibly tires, something which can happen as much in Tallis's *Gaude gloriosa*, which lasts 17 minutes in performance, as in the most modest motet. In-depth editing has been the inevitable result of achieving on disc what I have wanted to hear.

For a while I was defensive about the amount of editing Steve Smith, my partner at Gimell, and I used to do; until I remembered that, as with so much else in trying to establish polyphony in a marketplace which was controlled by the dictates of later music, polyphony might have its own requirements. It is not the same thing to record a big piece with ten singers as to record a big piece with a symphony orchestra, or with a piano, or even with an opera singer: the first two of these are fixed-pitch instruments, and the third will only sing a fraction of the number of notes which a polyphonist will sing in a session. The demands are different: recording polyphony with two voices to a part means in effect that everyone present has to take on the role of a soloist – since every tiny thing they do will be audible – while actually having to blend with a partner. This is difficult enough with an instrument, but to do it with one's voice alone requires a kind of physical stamina which players are not normally required to display. They will have other efforts to make on session, but my point is that when we started making discs the received view of how a session should go was determined by the needs of an orchestra recording a symphony. In their world it is sufficient to run a piece twice, always going flat out for a challenging interpretation, everybody except the conductor sitting down, everybody confident that the collective sound will be rock solid from the first attack to the last chord. In fact the cost of having so many musicians around for many more takes than two would have been prohibitive even in the glory days; so the norm was established of very few takes and therefore very little editing. The analogy that this made the result 'like' a concert performance hovered conveniently around in the background. Polyphony didn't fit this straightjacket as it didn't fit so many others, which could be difficult to explain to outsiders and led to a sense that what we were presenting on disc was somehow faked or manufactured. The gap between what we were releasing on disc and what we were able to do on-stage in those days was too wide. It took long years of giving concerts in which we customarily sang pieces as 'perfectly' as on disc to silence those who thought we couldn't do it without artificial aids, which initially we barely could. The experience of doing sessions obliged us to raise our standards as concert artists. But I don't see why that should be held against the discs themselves.

The general unease about faking was doubly tiresome to me. I have never claimed that what we put on record is equivalent to what we do onstage, but maintained that an edited recording has a legitimacy of its own. At the same time we have not looked for a way of manufacturing the actual singing. Every sound we have ever put out on a disc was made by the singers: we have not tried to process and reproduce their sound electronically. It is true that we have been able marginally to alter the pitch of notes and, in a repeated passage, make two versions out of one original – and we have always been able to edit out unwanted notes or phrases or noises, in recent years with an ever greater control over how natural the joins between the takes sound ('cross-fade editing') – but without the raw material we can do nothing. We cannot, for instance, take a perfect note from one phrase and put it in another: the vowel-sound will be wrong, or the overhang from the previous chord will differ, or the tempi won't match. Even worse, there is nothing we can do if I have misremembered the tempi on session and secured perfect notes at different speeds for the same passage, unless one makes the edits as short as a single note, and then there is still the danger that that note will not lie perfectly in place.

Compared with what goes on in mixing studios with pop and jazz session tapes we have deliberately restricted our options. Even by the standards of orchestral recordings we have gone for the natural sound, using only one pair of mikes, one poised above the other, on a single tripod. By doing this we have put our trust in the actual balance of the group and turned our backs on the array of microphones and banks of knobs and dials which standardly appear on sessions. As a result we have never been able to boost up one voice-part over another, or conversely tone one down. Much of the success of our recordings has therefore depended on the exact placement of the tripod – the 'sweet spot' in a building – positioned not only to catch the natural balance of the group but also to include just the desired amount of sound from the building. Considerable skill and confidence is needed to find this optimum position which, once identified, is scrupulously marked and remembered. Partly for this reason we have used very few venues, effectively only the chapel of Merton College, Oxford and Salle Church, Norfolk. As a result of this simplicity we look with some alarm at the paraphernalia which turns up for radio broadcasts, though I understand that the optimum point for the tripod, if that approach were to be adopted for concert record-ings, would be in the auditorium where the public would knock into it. We have also noticed with radio recordings how close the engineers put the mikes to us at first. They retreat immediately we start singing, and then slowly retreat a lot further as the group warms up, or the high singing starts. The extent of this retreat has become something of an in joke with us; but I wonder what expectations have led to the clichéd closeness in the first place. On session the tripod is a long way away. The impact of Steve's decision (made in 1977) to record us in this straightforward way cannot be overstat-ed.

The advantage of recording for oneself, obviously, is that no one can tell you what to do. From the very beginning Steve and I between us built up a method which we felt suited us and the music: one which entirely depend-ed on the group producing a good balance unaided. It is highly probable that if, when we first pooled our ideas in the 1970s, we had been employed by an established company, we would have been recorded according to the nor-mal practices of those days, with rows of mikes and concomitant mixing desks. That I met Steve as early as I did meant that in this respect at least polyphony was not subjected to what was found convenient for later reper-toires. In 1977, as undergraduates at Surrey University on the Tonmeister course, he and his friend Terry Davies (nowadays an award-winning or-chestral arranger and conductor for the National Theatre) had written to me to ask if they could record one of our concerts in Merton College Chapel as part of their final portfolio submission. During the course of that day Steve asked me if we wanted to make a record, which we did some weeks later. I think all the essential elements of what became our working practices were in place from that first day, though we didn't have the money to ask the singers to do more than a couple of takes of each piece on the earliest session, which otherwise I'm sure we would have done. However my desire to edit everything with care was certainly in the picture because I think initially Steve was surprised by it. Irritated at my repeated requests to have yet another go, he pointed out that if the singers couldn't produce the sounds I wanted he couldn't manufacture them. What I was hoping for was that we should listen to all the available options all over again, trying yet again to find the best possible matches, while relying on him to have the technique to edit them convincingly together. That is what we still do, with more takes and cleverer technology at our disposal.

One of the problems with this approach, as Steve registered on that first editing day, is that it is very hard work. It is the kind of meticulous work which one associates more with manuscript illumination than with making a commercial recording. Indeed the way we go about it does seem to assume an almost medieval style of existence, in which time is no object and dedication to perfection has no price. The degree of concentration required on session to repeat and repeat until every uncertain thing has been elimi-nated from the tapes has driven all of us, and especially the singers, close to distraction at times. I realise this does not conform with the standard romantic view of an artist building up to one magnificent interpretation, in one inspired burst of music-making, but our kind of music-making meant we had to be sure that the sound was in place. With a piano or an orchestra it is automatically in place; what we were doing with our repeated takes, especially in the early days, was honing a sound through which the music could speak. I have never found the music we have made any less expressive on the sixth take, indeed there is every chance I will find it more expressive if we have been working intensively on short sections to refine what we are doing. The skill in editing is to find the optimum moment for the develop-ment of the ensemble sound in any given passage; and it is in the nature of vocal polyphony that that is likely to come several takes later on average than in sessions of music with instruments. Latterly, with the sound more secure, its requirements better known and understood by young singers, the take quotient has come down, making it possible to consider releasing discs of (almost) live events. For these – *Live in Oxford* and *Live in Rome* – there were on average two takes (because we gave the concerts twice). I leave it to the listeners of our discs to decide whether anything has been gained in the way of inspiration of the moment, or lost through the lack of fine tuning, in the 'Live' format. If CDs were to be released of genuinely one-off radio record-ings I think there would be a widespread sense of disappointment.

To say that every Gimell record has been handmade is to state the obvious. From the design of the booklet and the logo, the choosing of the artwork and the writing of the notes, to the recording of the sound, the choosing of the takes and the editing of them together, the work has been done in-house, mostly by Steve and myself. Since this story covers over 40 discs, and a number of compilations, it can be imagined how much effort has gone into it. But it has always been an effort I have found rewarding, not least because the basic requirements – a dogged memory, tireless interest in the music, never accepting second best, becoming so familiar with the singers' voices that I can second-guess what they will do in any given situation – were of lively and constant interest to me. In fact, given how fulfilled I am after a day's editing, I suspect that nothing in this multifaceted job I do is quite so suited to me as this. It is the satisfaction a miniaturist must feel as something of supreme beauty slowly blossoms from laboriously shaped and formed raw material. It is a very different satisfaction from what the live concert can give, when the raw material is red hot and its forming minutely observed by an expectant public. Then one has no choice but to throw everything into the moment; and calm reflection, if it comes at all, comes afterwards. But in editing being calm is an essential part of the process, and I thrive on it. It is a tiresome (and mistaken) cliché that music-making must always be a succession of impulsive gestures, no matter how well trained and considered in advance they may be.

Another problem is that it is expensive. In recent years a new recording of ours has been certain never to break even: the costs of running the business have been covered by the continuing popularity of our back catalogue, an interest which tends to surge every time we bring out a new release. The continuing returns on some of the discs we made 20 years ago and more – especially the Allegri and *Spem* discs – put these items in a special category of achievement, not to say historical recording. But now, at last, the market has shrunk to the point where we cannot justify these costs any more. The time has come for other strategies, in particular making DVDs and relying more on almost-live new releases. The quality of the Byrd tapes we made for the BBC and Gimell in September 2002 suggested that the years spent being meticulous had prepared us collectively for a less elaborate approach to sessions without a serious drop in standards. The only proviso is that what we record in the future will have to follow much more closely on from what we have been doing in concert than it did in the past. The 'project' approach meant we had time to rehearse substantial new works just for the purpose of recording them. Whether this will cramp our style remains to be seen. With 15 years to go before reaching the official retiring age I rather hope not.

Gimell Records was founded at the worst possible moment, as a last resort. Not only were the Tallis Scholars as a group not wanted by any existing record company, which was not entirely surprising in 1981, but the repertoire we represented wasn't wanted either. When we finally did make a disc for a 'major' company – the Allegri in March 1980 for EMI – and made a considerable success of it in terms of numbers sold in the crucial first year, it was in vain that we tried to interest them in a proper series of renaissance sacred music recordings. The only concession they made was to take a punt on an album of madrigals – the popular view that everyone loves a quick madrigal was to the fore – which flopped (and remains the only post-1978 recording of ours never to have been released on CD). At about the same time Bob Betts was offering us some money to record three Palestrina Masses he happened to like, which we had no reason to refuse, though we had little sense of 'founding' anything when we went into the sessions which eventually yielded Gimell 001.

1981 was not a good time for small record labels. It might be thought it is bad now, and there are similarities in that the black vinyl LP then, like the CD now, had become stale in the public mind and there were too many of them for serious money to be made from any one release. But the scene was more traditionally-minded then. Every touring artist wanted the cachet of seeing his or her photograph in every shop window with the DG or EMI logo attached to it; to be considered established required little less. A lot of moulds remained to be broken or recast in those days, and going with a completely unknown tiny label was the hard way of learning about how things worked. The mould has been recast now in that the falling revenue from classical CD sales is hitting the majors as much as the minors, with the result that the people most likely to survive are those with the smallest overheads coupled to the most appealing repertoire ideas. And belonging to an old name is no longer the automatic passport to bookability it used to be, except perhaps in the hard-core traditional classical repertoires we were out to dilute in the first place.

For those with the collector's instinct we had made four discs before the Allegri in 1980. The very first – called *English Sacred Music of the Sixteenth*

Century – was the one that Steve Smith proposed on the first day I met him, outside Merton College Chapel in March 1977. The idea that he should record that concert of ours had come from a first-year postgraduate at Oxford, John Milsom, previously an undergraduate at Surrey, who was later to play a considerable role in the future of Gimell, both as editor of some of the music we have recorded and as critic at the *Gramophone* magazine (remember the one about Gesualdo – 'Is this great music or merely weird?'). In fact the conjunction of John, Steve, me and Merton College Chapel that day was uncannily fateful. Steve asked me if I would like to make a record, which would be of the starter-kit variety – 1000 copies, to be marketed by ourselves and recorded on Surrey University equipment. We made the disc in less than a day, on 2 April 1977, with singers coming and going at random – evensong time around 3.30 p.m. removed several of them for a while – and if that was not quite typical of the sessions of our maturity, the editing which followed this day gave Steve and me quite a strong foretaste of what was to come. Eventually the tape was delivered. I designed the sleeve to the extent of typing out the back of it myself without knowing how to get the typewriter to justify the right-hand margin, so I used longer or shorter words as necessary to give the right general effect, and then had great difficulty finding anyone to print it, since this broke union rules. The one great regret over the CD format, incidentally, is that its sleeve is not twelve inches across, as the vinyl ones were: with such a big space the possibilities of design were greatly enhanced, especially if one wanted to use whole paintings. The technique now is to find a telling detail.

Soon my flat was piled high with copies of this record, which I sold by footing it around the independent record shops of London and Oxford – there were more of them then – and talking the assistants into taking some, almost invariably being given cash on the spot. I also sent some by post to these shops, having scoured accumulations of rubbish in the street for suitable packaging. I was later told that not all of these discs arrived in a suitable state to be sold; nonetheless, somehow all thousand were sold, and I assume that the money earned from them went to pay for the concerts of those years. The recording was even sold (for £90) to an American company, called Everest, which released it under the grandiose title, *The Combined Choirs of Oxford and Cambridge*. This was the first time of many that we thought we were well launched.

In fact what came next was an invitation from Peter Fellgett of the Cybernetics Department of Reading University to help him develop a microphone, for which he had received some kind of grant. We made two discs for him, probably in 1978, one of music by Thomas Tomkins which included verse music with organ, and another of compositions by Guerrero. These were the only sessions we have ever done without Steve Smith at the controls and they did not go well. Neither disc was ever released, though I did hear some of the Tomkins on tape; while the Guerrero was never completed because halfway through the allotted time it was discovered that everything that had been recorded up to that point had been accidentally erased. Nonetheless that microphone, if not our recordings in the service of it, did have a long-term future as the SoundField microphone, used by Nimbus and others to make their Ambisonic recordings.

The Guerrero sessions were the first time I worked with Bruno Turner, using editions made by his new independent publishing house, Mapa Mundi. Bruno and I appreciated the fact that we were both in the business of breaking moulds, and in our vision of the future we would need each other. Mapa Mundi was followed years later by Jon Dixon's Joed editions, and now, with computer software available to everyone, well-presented copies are there for the asking. It was not ever thus, and one willingly forgets how often we had to sing from copies which inevitably tripped us up. These might standardly sport original note-lengths, a written pitch which might be as much as a fourth away from the sounding one (we adopted a rule of no more than a minor third), the page thick with editorial suggestions for dynamics and phrasing. We even on occasion sang from C clefs, though this requirement had more or less passed into history by the time we started. Worst of all was the state of the musicological editing in some of the complete editions which one was obliged to rely on in the pre-computer days. The music might look safe enough on the page, as one sat in the library poring over those heavy volumes, but to put it in front of one's singers in the constrained circumstances of a professional rehearsal without checking the notes, the ficta (those notes which may or may not have been instinctively inflected – raised or lowered – by the singers at the time) and the ranges was to court disaster. Before the academics responsible for those editions had the chance to hear what they were publishing – a debility which lasted many decades – every carelessness imaginable was commonplace. It was as if renaissance music was to them more like a proposition of Euclid than a living work of art.

Another first attempt to hit the big-time was launched with the help of Ronnie Bell at United Artists in 1977. Steve and I spent months talking to Ronnie, who gave us encouragement because he was obsessed with a romantic vision of monks making the pilgrimage to Canterbury. Anything which touched this nerve sent him into reveries, and we represented Tallis as the obvious exemplar of his obsession. It was with great difficulty that we kept him to the point, which for us was a series of discs of polyphony by our eponym, since his interest seemed to be in processions, monkish habits and ritualistic services he had no knowledge of, but finally, after many setbacks, we were commissioned to make what came to be called *Thomas Tallis Volume One*; and indeed the UA label reissued our very first effort for good measure (more stained glass and depictions of monks in the cover design). As has happened more resoundingly in recent years, the promise of a big name underwriting our work evaporated, as it seemed for no particular reason, overnight. We began to learn the lesson that this job was never going to be done effectively by people who had formed their ideas on other repertoires, and that it was going to be a very uphill struggle indeed. Our next venture – the Allegri with EMI – was only successful in the long term because Steve, during the course of the negotiations, had been obliged by EMI to pay for the sessions himself and then to licence the tape back to them, initially for a period of five years. Of course we had not gone into the project expecting to have to pay all the costs, but in fact this turned out to be a blessing in disguise. If EMI had paid they would have kept the rights. Five years may have seemed an eternity to us in those days – borrowing money was anyway very expensive in 1980 – but by 1985 tapes like our Allegri were in high demand in the new CD market. Steve refused to renew the licence. Given that the Allegri is still selling well, it is fair to say that Gimell would have been weakened beyond telling if it had not had the income which that disc has generated.

I remember the editing of *Thomas Tallis Volume One* with especial clarity. Over the years the equipment Steve and I have used has developed, as new technology has become available. Nowadays the whole process is done off computer screens and keyboards, the software for which must be unbelievably intricate given the number of detailed commands it can process. At the touch of a button we can hear any part of any take, which means we can make immediate comparisons between tiny subsections of different takes. But in 1977 there were no computers that we could use, only reel-to-reel tape-recorders and yards of tape on a spool. It could take a while to find the exact moment on the two takes one wished to compare, and to have six options of the same passage was to begin an almost open-ended process. The whole thing now seems incredibly primitive; the beginning of each new take was marked on the tape by a low-pitched sonic noise, which could be heard if it was pressed to the heads at speed, in either forward or reverse, by someone's finger as it passed through. Once we'd heard the 'booop' we would start to look for the bars in question. If the takes we needed had been far apart on the sessions, five minutes and more could elapse before they were identified; and swapping between them for quick comparisons was impossible. One simply had to remember which was preferred. Once the decision had been made the edit was fixed there and then by cutting the (only) source with a razor blade and joining it with a clever kind of sellotape to its other half on the top of the tape-machine. One did not normally have a second chance to do this; and during the editing of this disc we managed to oxidise the tape, which meant that the blade was dirty in some meaningful electronic way and had destroyed some of the recorded material on each side of an edit. There was no redress; and those who can find this rare record, and know the music well enough, will hear that the running time is about a second shorter than it should be. For years afterwards 'oxidising the tape' became an in phrase for losing control of a situation.

The Tomkins sessions were the first we undertook in Merton College Chapel, though we had given concerts there before that. The Allegri sessions of March 1980 were the first in my hearing to make the most of this unusual building, whose particular sound comes from its T shape. Because the nave was never built, and the surviving choir and transepts are on a grand scale, any note sung at the altar will travel the length of the choir before becoming trapped in the transepts, where it acquires an extra but more distant reverberation before coming back to where it started. If the nave existed this sound would pass through the transepts, go down the nave and dissipate, as in a cathedral. By putting the solo group of the Allegri not only in the transepts but round the corner of the main pillar at the crossing, actually out of sight of the single microphone placed by the main choir at the altar, we hoped to have the perfect distant choir effect, distant but made solid enough by the Merton acoustics to enable the detail to be heard. I doubt we have found a better venue for the special effects of this piece, unless it was the Sistine Chapel itself, where that same balance between distance and clarity was possible. The solo group on that occasion consisted of Alison Stamp, Jane Armstrong, Michael Chance and Julian Walker, of whom only Michael Chance went on to be a professional singer. Alison Stamp's top Cs set new standards at the time for effortless good tuning at very high altitudes.

The Allegri sessions were the first time I felt the terrifying pressure of time inexorably passing, while trying to interpret music whose founding principle was, as it were, timelessness. If ever one can be said to experience an oxymoronic state of mind, it must be while recording something like the Allegri with one eye on the clock. And because quite serious sums of money were at last involved, and scarcely-formed reputations were on the line, time was not the only pressure. Bigwigs from head office came to watch; singers who had never been on session before found they had to sing exposed passages perfectly every time, which for the inexperienced is a very tall order. One or two of them almost cracked under the strain, especially during the recording of Mundy's colossal *Vox patris caelestis*, which I had insisted on including alongside the more famous Allegri and Palestrina's *Missa Papae Marcelli* as an example of what we were really trying to do. Above all I began to learn about outside noise, in time acquiring a sixth sense about when a car was beginning its journey towards us from the far end of Merton Lane, which is cobbled. On bad nights I can still hear tyres on cobbles, the sound beginning from far away, making me try to guess when Steve would say the take must be abandoned, with all the intense frustration that that entailed. The upside is that I can also still hear *Vox patris caelestis*.

Because of the inexperience, we used more than two singers to a part on those first Merton records. For *Vox patris*, which only has six voice-parts in the full sections, we used nineteen people; and that slight nervousness about the fullness of the ensemble sound lasted for a while. The Taverner *Missa Gloria tibi Trinitas* was also scored up with a sense of safety in numbers, as was the Russian Orthodox Music we recorded in Charterhouse Chapel. Perhaps I had not yet fully realised that two to a part at least with trained voices is the ideal for polyphony – large enough to be called a choral sound, but small enough for all the participants on the line to be able to hear each other and phrase together. Even with three singers per part it is harder to do this well. But by the time we were recording Palestrina the blueprint for the next twenty years of sessions was soon established.

Bob Betts's capacious library contains a set of the Kalmus miniature reprints, all in green, of the old Casimiri edition of the works of Palestrina. Although his fancy had originally been taken by volume XL which contains the Masses *Nigra sum*, *Sicut lilium* and *Nasce la gioia mia*, all inconveniently scored with two tenor parts, I managed to interest him in an altogether bigger setting by Palestrina, which in those days was known as the *Missa Sine nomine*. Scored SAATBB and soon found to be based on a superb motet by Josquin, it did us no harm to launch our new label with a masterpiece which hitherto hadn't been properly identified. Bob, who had flown over from Athens specially to hear our performance of *Spem* in Merton in 1978, now offered us a sum of money not only to do our first tour of America (see p. 38), but also to record the *Missa Benedicta es*, hoping we would eventually go on to record the three Masses he had always had in mind, which we did. Once the tape of *Benedicta es* was edited Steve and I made half-hearted attempts to sell it to existing companies, but quite quickly in 1981 we decided to establish Gimell. The enterprise floundered at first of course, but with Bob's permission we shelved the Palestrina project for a while, which at one stage was going to include all 107 of Palestrina's Masses, to record some of the more basic repertoire – Tallis's anthems, Byrd's Masses, Palestrina's *Missa Brevis*, and finally Tallis's *Spem in alium*. On the strength of those recordings, and with the Allegri returned to us, Gimell eventually took off, though this was not possible until the invention of the CD in 1984. In fact the first digital recording we ever made (for black vinyl) was the one of English madrigals, in Deene Park in April 1982. The technology was sufficiently in its infancy for the new equipment to have to be 'wound up' before each take, which involved waiting for it to catch its breath and prepare itself. More fidgeting and anxiety about time passing.

The costs of the *Spem* recording were in a different league from what we had managed hitherto, and were met by a wealthy stock market speculator named Christopher Selmes. Given to impulsive gestures, like buying vintage cars by the half dozen, he suddenly decided that his 40th birthday, which fell in December 1984, should be adorned with a performance of *Spem*. He was not the last person to have thought of this, but, apart possibly from Queen Elizabeth I, so far as I know he was the first. To scout out the ground he summoned me to an elaborate meal at a smart West End restaurant and asked me how much such a concert would cost. Since I had not had any warning of the question, and a recording was rapidly becoming part of the discussion to boot, I stared hard at my plate and guessed. 'Ten grand', I said. It was just enough.

Steve Smith's second stroke of genius was to back the new CD format from the very beginning, committing every penny the company had to it. At the beginning of the CD era there were only three manufacturing plants in the world – in Japan, Germany and at Nimbus in Wales – and anyone wanting a run of CDs was restricted to a tight quota, which at first was not much more than five hundred a month. Steve was so keen that his first order to the plant at Nimbus had the stock number 02 on it, which was in stark contrast to many of the established companies, who were inclined to ignore the whole CD thing. Nonetheless within a short period of time demand was well ahead of supply, and slowly the capacity and the number of the plants was increased. Our quota went up to a thousand a month, to two thousand, and finally we could reissue the whole catalogue as it then stood. By 1986 we had a business on our hands, though its future was still uncertain because of the unchallenged hegemony of the 'majors'. The world was not used to and did not respect minnows in those days; and I use the word 'minnows' deliberately because that was the term *The Times* of London applied to us when we won the *Gramophone* award in 1987. As a result of this income Gimell was able to set itself up properly around this time as a business, with a staff and a warehouse; before that it had more or less been run out of Steve's front room. Pre-eminent among the staff was Peter Bromley, a half-Italian teacher of languages who brought his own flair to the designing and translating of our booklets, which remain distinctive to this day, as well as a way with people which constantly delighted me when we were on tour in the Mediterranean countries. Without his fluent Italian and his gentle but determined cultivation of contacts within the notoriously slippery Vatican hierarchy I doubt that either of our 1994 Roman extravaganzas would have come off.

The profits to be made on CD sales in the early days seemed almost miraculous. The retail price of a vinyl LP had come down to about £2 a disc for a new release, with EMI's Classics for Pleasure – the label which released both the Allegri and *English Madrigals* – originally costing 49p, increasing to 99p by the early 1980s. The new, shining, iconic CD, if one could find one to buy, yielded anything up to eight times the price of a 'full-price' LP, for something which cost at the most three times as much to manufacture. With every new release turning in a healthy profit it was suddenly in our interests, commercial as well as artistic, to make new recordings; and a golden period was launched, which lasted for nearly ten years. Having few concerts in those years we threw ourselves into sessions. Six discs were made in 1986, seven in 1987, six in 1988; then the rate slackened, but in the ten years between 1981 and 1990 inclusive we had completed 33 discs, many of them award-winners around the European classical magazine circuit.

'Completed' should be underlined here, because around 1989 we suddenly seemed to have great trouble finishing anything. Perhaps this is the way such enterprises go, but it is clear to me in retrospect that we became more and more careful – about outside noise, about tiny imperfections of singing, and about taking risks with new and potentially difficult repertoire, which we were prepared to broach, but only if the safety-net of available recording time was increased. Inevitably costs rose; and the physical demands made on us all rose with them. No doubt we were concerned that our public was becoming ever more discerning, and that we had not only to maintain standards but raise them. By the time we came to record the Obrecht CD – one of the later ones – it seemed incredible to us that we had dared to put down two Josquin Masses, or the whole of the Cornysh record, in two days apiece in 1986. Not only were we now taking three, four or even six days to complete a disc, but we began to lose whole days to the weather. By transferring from Merton to Salle – a large gothic church in the middle of rolling acres of Norfolk countryside – we swapped aeroplane and cobble noise for aeroplane, farm vehicles and wind noise. Whereas we had finished every Merton record within the allotted time, we now found ourselves having repeatedly to go back to Salle to patch or re-record. In fact we had had good warning of the capacity for rolling countryside to generate unlooked-for noises on the very first day we worked there in 1986 on the *Christmas Carols and Motets* disc, when we had coincided with the harvesting of the fields around us. The tapes were covered in the sound of tractors and whole pieces were written off. But it was the obtrusive sound of the wind in the trees around the church which eventually cost us so dear. Ironically the

'Western Wind' Mass sessions went through without a hitch.

But it was partly because of noise that we had left Merton in the first place. With changes to the flow of traffic in Oxford High Street, Merton Lane had become audibly busier; and anyway Merton was no longer able to accommodate our new rate of recording, since it was only possible to use the building out of term-time. I first set eyes on Salle Church one day when I was staying with Michael Chance in Norfolk in the mid-1980s. I had asked him whether he thought there were suitable buildings around that relatively underpopulated county that we might be able to use for sessions. He had mentioned a few, and we started our search at Binham Priory. But a farm with an audibly functioning grain-drier next door to the church had dissuaded me, beautiful though the interior of the building was. Next we tried Salle, which seemed to have everything: it is the size of a small cathedral, yet serves, and has only ever served, a community of a few houses. The road outside is as minor as country roads can be, and the RAF and US airforce bases at Mildenhall, Cotteshall and Lakenheath (Norfolk and Suffolk are blessed with many of these) were as docile that day as the wind. Its interior is the rival of any of the many fifteenth-century churches in the area, which is saying something, since many of them were built or enlarged with the profits made from the highly lucrative wool trade of that period, which explains how such an elaborate building could have been erected more or less in the middle of nowhere. But best of all were the acoustics, which we tested by standing at the extreme ends of the nave and conversing without raising our voices. Every word was clear. I had started my search with the intention of finding acoustics which would carry the detail of polyphony without any distortion from obvious reverberance, yet which had an encouraging natural sound. When I reported my findings to Steve Smith I said I thought all that was necessary was to find the right place to put the microphone, to catch the sound of the singers from one direction while preserving the all-round contribution of the building. In the course of time that was exactly what he did, and we went on to make 25 discs there. Eventually we so convinced the world of the merits of this place that the BBC started to use it regularly for studio sessions – too regularly for the local farmers; and other groups even started to give concerts there. I fear that for one reason or another Salle is again as silent as it was before I had that conversation with Michael.

Our move to Salle in 1986 more or less brought an end to the sequence of records we made in Merton. We went back there during the night to make the Sarum Chant record in 1987, but didn't do so again until December 1996, when we gave the concerts which became the *Live in Oxford* release. Meanwhile, we had experimented with St John's Church in Hackney, London, for music which seemed to require bigger acoustics – recording Victoria's Requiem, his Responsories and Byrd's Great Service in there – but gave it up because the background rumble was too constant. It was a minor irony that our principal tormentor in this place was the Number 38 bus, which, a little further along its trajectory, has served me faithfully for many years. The only other records we have made outside Salle or Merton were the early Russian Orthodox disc (in the chapel of Charterhouse school) and the *Live in Rome* extravaganza in Santa Maria Maggiore in Rome. The performance we were asked to give in the Sistine Chapel some two months after the Santa Maria Maggiore concerts was recorded by Italian and Japanese television, but not made commercially available.

Our move to Salle also introduced us to life in the country, or at least to life in the countryside around Reepham, where our hotel was to be found. The setting was as good as anywhere, as Pevsner makes clear in his *Buildings of England*.

The Market place is pleasant to look at, especially the row of houses along the North side. This starts with an excellent house of c.1700, Dial House (or Brewery House), and continues with minor Georgian houses. Dial House is of seven bays and two storeys and has a broad porch with fluted Corinthian columns, a carved frieze, and a segmental pediment also with carving. Staircase with slim twisted balusters.

It was the fate of that staircase which gave the clue to what had happened during the latter part of the last century, since the outside had been preserved and is still attractive. The staircase is there, more or less untouched in its lower flight, but it is surrounded by cheap false walls and flimsy boarding, which divide something that was once spacious into smaller, meaner compartments, no doubt in the search for greater 'convenience'. The bedrooms had suffered even more from this fate: the grand rooms at the front of the building bearing the marks of repeated rearrangement, unconvincingly masked and remasked by decorations in timelessly bad taste. By the time we last went there, in 1999, the place was onto its umpteenth owner or minder, though there were signs that the imperatives of a 1950s life-style had given way to something more contemporary.

For one thing the food had improved. In the mid-1980s the food served in the dining-room had always been the reliable proof that England's regional cuisines had been drowned in cheap fat and clichéd 'international' ways of thinking. With schoolboy humour which seemed appropriate to the place we would inscribe our initials on the crab shells, waiting for them to reappear on some subsequent occasion. In fact only once, so far as I know, did the dual processes of freezing and then deep-frying actually allow any bacteria through for long enough to make anyone ill: Mark Padmore was once served a sardine that was glowing a malignant green when he cut it open, having made the mistake of eating some of it before he did so. Nearer the more normal daily experience was the business of being served by unimpressionable young ladies who thought the modest food on offer very grand. The deployment of French on the menu for example was lost on them, as they bore the plates from the kitchen with a ringing 'Beef?', 'Fish?', and so on. Robert Harre-Jones once was bold enough to cross-question one of them, in a tone so mild I still feel nervous for him, with the words 'suprême de volaille?' 'Chicken', came the inevitable riposte as the plate crashed down in front of him.

In many ways breakfast was as much a test of character as dinner; but then hotel breakfasts surrounded by one's colleagues always are. Of course we had to be confined to a group table, though the real problem was that the meal was over by 9.00 a.m. This really was a nuisance, especially if there was to be a session before lunch and we had stayed up late the previous evening enjoying the local beer (which was the one completely authentic aspect of what was on offer). At 8.58 a procession of musicians would make its way into the relevant room, all demanding the full cooked breakfast of a staff who had long ago concluded that their task for the morning was over. The woman who originally presided over this meal was one of the most fearsome people I have encountered. It was unwise to make one's order too complicated, though on one occasion Nick Robertson tried to specify exactly which of the usual seven or so different foodstuffs that make up an English cooked breakfast he would like on his plate. When the plate arrived it included at least one item he hadn't asked for. 'Well, you don't have to eat it', said the woman, as she banged it down. A few visits into this process it was apparent she had conceived violently ambivalent feelings towards Charles Daniels, who made it his habit to appear at 9.08 and yet ask for the works. At 9.03 she would stand hands on hips and demand, 'Where's Charles?' We all knew the answer, of course, and in time, and to our collective relief, she came to mother him. Eventually she was replaced by a man who had worked as an engraver for one of the leading London music publishing houses, a now defunct art. This was potentially of interest to both sides, since he had actually set some of the music we were singing; but the collapse of his profession in the face of modern technology and the almost total loss of his eyesight in its service had embittered him, and he showed little inclination to find out how useful his work had been.

But we were not unhappy there, even if the quality of the beds and bedding made it hard to sleep. The Norfolk countryside is exceptionally pretty, dotted with gothic churches: three or four towers are in sight from any vantage point, and many more if one takes the trouble to climb to the top of Salle tower itself and survey the scene. And the usual more secular country delights surrounded these sacred buildings – pubs, country houses, restaurants – the plenitude of cash in the centuries preceding the last guaranteeing that they were well built. One of my particular pleasures was to visit Blickling Hall with its fine gardens and seventeenth-century interior, and then to have dinner in the pub in the village. It may be asked how I had time to do this, given that we were supposed to be making records, but one of the refinements of our method as time went by was to book two or three days of sessions before a weekend, have the weekend off to refresh ourselves, and then get back to it on the Monday morning for another two or three days. This was indeed the luxury edition of session-planning, of the days when CDs sold well.

Salle Church itself was the prize, though. I have never once gone into that building and felt the worse for it, not even when the wind was guaranteeing the forfeiture of thousands of pounds; nor when there was only one session to go and too much music to record in it. In our line of business we have been privileged to stand in many beautiful places, but, as with polyphony, it helps to go back repeatedly and feel again what it means to you. Salle is my Tallis Lamentations: I never got bored. And it wasn't only the proportions of the architecture, the inspiring use of light inside the building, the sense of joy which all these things together could instil; but also the view across the fields when we'd finished working. There was one particular evening, at 8.30 p.m. on a June evening after a day of recording Morales, when we had worked ourselves to the bone as usual and were starving hungry. We opened the small chancel door to make our escape and saw the sun hanging huge and milk-pale yellow over the hedges. Everyone stopped to look at that, fatigue forgotten, mesmerised. Recording studios may keep the wind out, but in the end one doesn't mind a bit of wind, still less bird-song on session. They give the word 'authenticity' a new lease of life.

It is probable that none of these later and more elaborate projects, including the two in Rome in 1994, would have taken place if our recording of Josquin's Masses *Pange lingua* and *La sol fa re mi* hadn't won the top *Gramophone* award in 1987. It is true that most of the back catalogue was turning over reasonably well before the prize was awarded; but, as I said in chapter one, the cachet which that prize brought us and our repertoire was irreplaceable. Beforehand we were an adjunct to the classical music scene, afterwards we were an awkward presence in the mainstream - and Gimell had made enough money to plan for the future.

The benefits came slowly but surely, both to Gimell and to the Tallis Scholars individually. The most immediate were to Gimell. On the morning of the ceremony I was to be heard on Radio Four's early news programme, *Today*, airing the merits of Josquin's music and this disc to a million people or so, while every newspaper of any standing had been published with some sort of report. To them the newsworthy aspect of the story was not so much Josquin, Tallis Scholars or early music, but that a tiny record company had taken on the vastly better-funded giants of the industry, and beaten them. Nowadays this happens more regularly because the giants have taken such a pasting at the hands of the consumer in recent years and been cut down to size, which has left more of a free-for-all in what is left of the marketplace; but then it was quite a spectacle. The style of the award ceremony itself was more informal then than now, the notables standing around balancing a glass and rubbing shoulders. I got myself photographed with Elisabeth Schwarzkopf, who was the Guest of Honour, after both of us had made speeches which I'm sure the organisers didn't really want: over-long, over-pleased with ourselves and using the forum for beating some sort of drum, she on Walter Legge and me on the joys of just about everything in sight. I notice this trait on the part of the winners has continued into the present day. The most touching moment for me was when

Roger Norrington stood forward from the crowd and very deliberately made sure he was the first to shake my hand. After that we remained flavoursome to the *Gramophone* magazine for some years – winning the early music award again in 1991 and 1994 – and I was invited to give away all the early music awards in one other year. Eventually the eternal search for novelty, from which we had benefited so greatly, saw us off.

To the Tallis Scholars, apart from more recordings, came more concerts, a trend which peaked in 1992. Whereas prior to 1987 our international profile had brought us invitations from early music festivals, like the one in Utrecht, now we were asked by organisations in the German-speaking world – in Lucerne, Vienna, Berlin, Bonn, Bremen, Hamburg, Carinthia – which from time immemorial had relied on the Berlin Philharmonic with Karajan and very little else. Lucerne was the most hospitable, in the sense of inviting us several times, though they had only ever had one annual 'Alte Musik' event, just as they then only had one 'Zeitgenossische Musik' concert, as a kind of nod to changes in taste which the planners gave little impression of sympathising with. I'm not sure I ever met an Artistic Director of the Lucerne festival, despite directing a live broadcast one year; and it was in Lucerne that I walked the streets noticing the kind of publicity a rich record company could turn on for their featured artists and, despite the award, feeling small. No doubt this sentiment fed into my dealings with Polygram, some years later. But this flirting with renaissance early music never went more than skin-deep in most of the Germanic towns which had so cautiously opened their doors to us after 1987. Baroque, whether Bach or wittering, in its more authentic manifestations was already sweeping the board, finally creating a real alternative to the Berlin Philharmonic in the public mind.

All this activity culminated in the few days we spent in Rome in February 1994, celebrating the four hundredth anniversary of the death of Palestrina. For just a moment we were able to behave like a well-funded television station or major record label, spending what it cost to make a high quality artefact of what we believed in. For the night of the anniversary itself, 2 February, and the next night, we hired Santa Maria Maggiore, had the traffic stopped in the vicinity, imported cameras and engineers (from Cardiff), tons of lighting equipment (from Manchester), electricity generators (because we didn't trust the local supply), invited the entire curia and countless other notables from many countries to attend, and gave a concert of music by the great man (and Allegri's *Miserere*, of course) which was filmed from every angle and recorded on the most modern equipment, while the building itself furnished the producers with the most perfect fifth-century mosaics in the world to illustrate the eventual film. It was a ball of a very individual kind, released later that year as *Live in Rome*, on CD, videotape and even laser disc, and not quickly forgotten by anyone who was there. Needless to say, despite what these recordings may suggest, there were some interesting alarms off-stage. The most dramatic of these, which Steve didn't tell me about at the time, was a bomb scare with the place full of cardinals and ambassadors. This necessitated the kind of police search which in more northerly countries would have delayed the start of proceedings by hours, but on this occasion made very little impression. Another difficulty was caused by a senior figure who was sitting in the front row constantly clicking the arms of his spectacles together, a sound which the microphone in front of him picked up very clearly. Peter Bromley's most emollient Italian was pressed into service, and the problem silenced.

How one would have loved to make a habit of projects like that! To go to every city in the western world that had ever spawned a great polyphonist and make a film about him. We only once came close to doing this elsewhere, in Bruges for ITV's *South Bank Show*. This 'personal odyssey' of mine was filmed in 1990, this time with the backing of a fully-financed television company, and told the story of how the different musical traditions related to each other in the renaissance period. It was the privilege of a lifetime to present a show like that; and it required very special funding. *Live in Rome* itself eventually broke even; but it presupposed an enormous sum in the bank before any return could be had – a sum we didn't have again – and nerves of steel. We had also made one serious miscalculation. We had supposed that every television station of repute, once they saw the high specification of the filming, and the quality of the music-making, would want to screen the result. Only one did – a Japanese satellite channel – but the deal with the singers meant that we hardly made anything from it; and so there was effectively no revenue from a source we had counted on, only from the sale of the discs and tapes. This was dispiriting, and introduced us to the myopic way television stations tend to think and commission. This and the effort of planning such an enterprise with a tiny staff and little first-hand knowledge of what to do had exhausted us as a company; and, worse, it had distracted us from noticing what was going on in the record business more generally.

1994, partly aided by Palestrina, was the last year Gimell could be said to have been riding a crest, and even then the signs of decay were there to be seen. The CD boom was over. Suddenly there was more material than the public wanted; retail prices began to fall until – incredibly in the terms of previous years – magazines were giving CDs away. The independent distributors, on whom we relied, were already having a bad time, and soon some of them would disappear altogether. The major labels, with huge investments in terms of back catalogues, experienced staff, and reach into different markets, began to look unbeatable. They thought so too, and made a series of mistakes based on over-confidence. Eventually they began to lose money at a rate which even they had to notice, opening the way for the dramatic takeovers of the late 1990s in which leading classical music labels found themselves at the mercy of people who dealt in whiskey – or was it water?

We had had an invitation from Philips Classics as early as 1990 to join forces with them. They felt they needed an early music department which could rival those of their colleagues within Polygram: Archiv at DG and L'Oiseau Lyre at Decca. Despite the facile asseverations made recently on a BBC Radio Three phone-in programme by the current head of Decca, Costa Pilavachi, that we should have joined Polygram then and there, we did precisely the right thing to stay out. Why share good profits with a multinational? It was only when there were no profits to speak of that we needed them – and we still sold them our shares, when the time came, at a rate that suggested we were doing really well. By 1995, however, we were obliged to reconsider their offer. Having sounded out a number of other companies, including EMI, we realised that the real interest was still at Philips. So the negotiations began: they were to last well over a year, during which time we had to confront another end-of-year set of accounts that showed quite clearly we were falling off whatever pedestal we had been on in terms of sales. Steve and I had an anxious moment when these figures became available, assuming that the Philips executives would read the signs and renegotiate the purchase price. Of course no one at that time could foresee the commercial devastation that was to follow, above all to the big companies, but I still find it incredible that nothing was changed. Perhaps there really was an old-fashioned sense of honour, especially with Hans Kinzl, who was about to retire after many years in charge, whereby a serious record label committed itself properly to an artist and did not argue the toss. We were certainly treated with great respect in the early stages of this relationship, both Kinzl and Pilavachi simply keen that we should go on making the magic we had made over so many discs, undisturbed, while their powerful selling machine would realise a potential to which the independent distributors had not been able to do justice.

The final arrangement between Gimell and Philips has sometimes been misrepresented. Gimell remained an independent company within Polygram, with five directors on the Board: three appointed by Philips, to reflect their 51% share-holding, alongside Steve and me. This meant that we had to give our consent on every decision; that we had not sold out, but spoke at the board meetings as fellow shareholders. As every businessman knows, the small print in contracts which marry two concerns together is probably not going to be referred to until things go wrong; but when they did and it was, our part-ownership was crucial, even though originally the retaining of 49% of the shares had seemed a technicality.

The honeymoon period lasted perhaps 18 months, beginning with the release of the Ockeghem disc to celebrate the five hundredth anniversary of his death in 1997, amidst great trumpetings. Steve, Peter Bromley and I were paraded around innumerable meetings with the local reps, all of whom seemed to be motivated and intelligent people, pleased to be working with good-quality product. In fact meeting us should have got us a bad reputation, since without fail the moment we had said goodbye they either lost their jobs or were moved on; and anyway we might have done better if we had talked to the actual shop owners, who had a very different and more realistic agenda. They knew that records of Ockeghem's Masses were not going to deliver the kind of sales head office was projecting and demanding, and it was not long before this became abundantly clear, at which point the whole initiative ran speedily into the sand. The business went straight into the red, aggravated by the undertaking of new sessions, which obliged Polygram to put in more and more money in the frequently expressed hope that all would come good in time. Steve and I were not complaining about this

– except to observe that there were no dividend payments – since we knew very well that this money was gold-dust in the context. And it kept coming until 1999.

We went through all the motions that in earlier times would have been expected of an international artist joining an international record label. The two *Live in Oxford* concerts in December 1996 were held partly in order to introduce as many Polygram employees to our music as could be got down to Oxford. Wherever we went on tour the local office would oblige all its staff to come and hear us, after which there would always be a reception and speeches. I particularly remember the one in Tokyo because I mischievously used the word 'symbiotic' in my few well-chosen words, and waited with interest to see what the translator would do with it. She faltered and giggled, as did I in sympathy. Costa Pilavachi himself did the honours in Holland, where Philips was based then. The people in Germany were especially impressive, and powerless as it turned out to improve our track-record in that substantial market. Polygram USA, who assumed they owned the whole business from top to bottom and spoke slightingly of their European masters quite openly, had very little time for us from the beginning, which at least was honest. I gave up attending their meetings. They reminded me too vividly that in transferring to Polygram we had been obliged to say goodbye to old friends in the independent sector, who in some countries had done us a better job than Polygram could ever do because they understood the product, were small enough to keep an eye on it, and cared for it and us. Pre-eminent amongst these was René Goiffon at Harmonia Mundi USA, who had become a close personal friend. The same could be said of Mr Miazawa in Tokyo, who had taken our defection badly, and there were a number more. They needn't have worried. Within five years we were back with them.

So long as Polygram and Philips Electronics, the majority shareholder in the overall business, were of one mind, conversations with our fellow shareholders were rational and helpful. The difficulties really started when Philips Electronics sold out to Seagram, Philips Classics merged with Decca, and a cycle of big business take-overs began. Suddenly the skids were under everyone, no one seemed to be in control of their future and the rate of dismissals increased to the point where it became a waste of time trying to ask anyone to do anything for the business because there was little chance of ever speaking to them again. Even our board members came and went.

The sense of paralysis throughout Polygram was total, but perhaps especially difficult to bear for us, who only a year or two earlier had had complete freedom to run the show as we thought best. Now we had to wait for edicts to filter through from a figurehead on the other side of the Atlantic, for whom classical music as a whole probably seemed like a commercial irrelevance, let alone our tiny corner of it. I wrote a tongue-in-cheek piece in my *Spectator* column at this time pointing out that of all the businesses this fat cat had acquired as a result of his take-overs, the one he should be most proud of was ours, there being little competition in real terms between a bottle of whiskey and a Josquin Mass. Unsurprisingly the flow of cash to our business was finally stopped, and Gimell was technically bankrupt.

There then followed the most destructive period of all, when lawyers fought and the distribution of our records effectively ceased: the system had completely broken down. The reputation we had built up over so many years for being something reliable was trashed, and our name disappeared from the shops. This was serious not only for Gimell, but for the Tallis Scholars more generally. Concert promoters like to have a sense of their artists being at the cutting edge of their professions, and although by this time it was no longer essential to have the support of a major label, it was necessary to have some sort of recording programme in hand. In Europe it proved possible to ride out this storm, because it didn't last too long, but in remoter places, especially in Japan and Australia, a new release rapidly became an imperative. The concert-going public require novelty, and the up-to-date reviews which new releases spawn. It may be true that most new recordings these days make very little money for the company who releases them, but to the artists they have a hidden value in terms of standing. It is therefore ideal if the record company and the artist can work together towards a common goal.

We didn't need to be told this. Although it had been years since Gimell had had a budget for advertising concerts, the principle behind doing so had always been respected by Steve. From the start the Polygram executives had taken a different view, at first understanding, latterly totally dismissive, which could never lead to a properly symbiotic relationship, whatever the word for it in Japanese might be. Such niceties were lost to view in the meltdown which Polygram was confronting. Yet even now they made an attempt to keep us. An edict was delivered to the effect that if Steve and I would part with the remainder of our shares we could make one record a year for a number of years for a pittance. This meant handing over to a now completely faceless and provenly incompetent organisation all our assets, especially a back-catalogue which we knew had some life left in it, and the tapes of the discs we hadn't yet released, of which at that stage there were five. I suppose the executives thought we would think we had no option but to accept their proposal; perhaps they even thought they were being generous in the circumstances. We actually thought that to hand over the assets would be suicide.

The upshot was that we refused the offer, Gimell went into receivership, and Polygram lost not only the substantial sum of money they had paid for their 51% of the shares less than four years earlier, but all the money they had pumped into Gimell since. For our part we had taken a serious risk. We were betting that no one wanted the assets of Gimell as much as we did, and that any potential rivals would soon lose interest in the bidding for them, if indeed they ever noticed that bidding was going to be required of them. Of course we realised that it was not only Polygram we might be up against: the thought of trying to outbid EMI, for example, did not appeal. And without any corporate financing behind us, there was every chance we would simply have to drop out of the race, having lost the lot. Through late 1999 and early 2000 the process ran its course, the size of the bids increasing until they reached our breaking point. We were never told whom we were up against (almost certainly not EMI); but suddenly the fighting stopped. Standing on a street corner in Washington, D.C. one day in March 2000, a public telephone receiver jammed into my ear, I learned from Steve that the nightmare was over and the work of 20 years was ours again to do whatever we liked with. We had no hopes of returning to the glory days of pre-1994, of course, but we did have a certain confidence in the longevity of the product we had to sell.

There is a great strength and a great satisfaction in being a specialist. I used to marvel at the chairman of our board at Polygram who would come into meetings and say, like a liturgical refrain, 'Is it being marketed aggressively?' whenever the reported sales figures didn't match up to his wild estimates. It seemed to me self-evident that a Clemens Mass or an Iberian Requiem was never going to be susceptible to 'aggressive' anything. What this music needs is years, if not decades, of gentle promotion – through concert performances, published copies, newspaper articles, talk and general interest. And in time discs of it may realise the kind of profits the executives expect in a matter of weeks, if one is patient. Looking back on the Polygram days, I think we had all fallen victim to the assumption which I outline in the epilogue (p. 235) that out there somewhere is a huge market which is crying out for what one does, if only the product can be presented in a challenging new way which appeals to it. The issue here is size. There are always people who are going to be interested in good quality music-making, in repertoires they may not yet have come across. And to attract them one should stick to one's guns, be severe if severity is part of the picture, and not cheapen anything. To be fair to Polygram, there wasn't time to explore the downmarket option in its finer points: the deluge came too quickly. The cover of the compilation *Lamenta* was as far as it went. But we allowed ourselves to imagine those tens of thousands, when I could have reminded myself that the lesson of our 30 years has been to specialise, to perfect and to expect modest returns.

Gimell Mark II has just completed its second year of trading, re-released the entire back-catalogue of just on 40 discs, and released the Morales and the two Gombert Magnificat discs. Of course we do not have easy answers to the problems which are afflicting the CD industry at the moment, any more than anybody else does, but it has been heartening to see that even in the current climate, records we made 20 years ago, which have sold well throughout the intervening years, have continued to show themselves to be astonishingly resilient. The whole industry is into a new era, one aspect of which is represented by the two DVDs we are about to release – one of the *Live in Rome* film with extra material, the other a television programme on Byrd which we co-produced with BBC4. The amount of music I want to record seems to grow daily, and since the singing of the Tallis Scholars has never been so consistently good there is every incentive for us to get back into the studio. It is worth remembering that, paradoxically given the negative press about the state of the CD market, the survival of Gimell (now called a 'boutique' as opposed to a 'vanity' label in the *Gramophone* magazine) is actually more certain now than it was in the past. Small labels are normal these days; it was in the 1980s that we were so unusual and had to fight so hard to exist.

Above: Cold weather work, recording Gesualdo's *Responsories* in 1987
Right: Recording Lassus's *Missa Osculetur me* in 1987

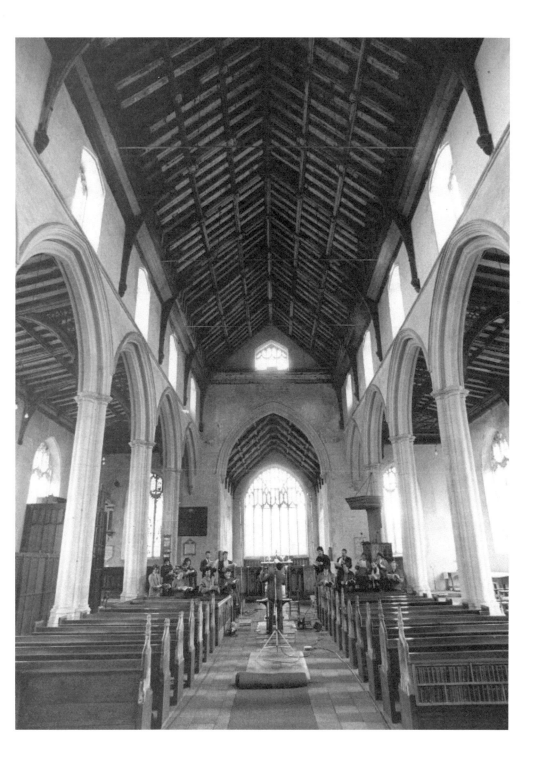

Recording the plainchant *Missa in gallicantu* in Merton College Chapel, Oxford in 1987

Steve Smith in the control room
(a.k.a. the Parish Hall) at Salle in
1999

The *Gramophone* Award winners in 1987, including Klaus Tennstedt, Bryden Thompson, Roger Norrington, Brigitte Fassbaender, Rosalind Plowright and Elisabeth Schwarzkopf

The way we used to edit: in the Keeper's Cottage, Minterne Magna, Dorset, with a Revox reel-to-reel, an amplifier and a razor blade.

Some examples of the Gimell house style.
In the case of the Tallis Christmas Mass the angel's wings have been computer-extended.

3

PERFORMING POLYPHONY

Joseph Brodsky, the Russian-American poet, once wrote of Ezra Pound:

The Cantos, too, left me cold; the main error was an old one: questing after beauty. For someone with such a long record of residence in Italy, it was odd that he hadn't realised that beauty can't be targeted, that it is always a by-product of other, often very ordinary pursuits.

This could stand for many old-fashioned interpretations of polyphony: take a piece of music that looks simple, something apparently elementary in its technique and naive in its expression by comparison with what one knows, and impose beauty on it. Louds, softs, rubatos, crescendos, diminuendos, the works. Then the ordinariness – that simplicity which can yield beautiful results – will surely be crushed.

The discussion which follows is more concerned with how to avoid a boring performance of polyphony than a bad one. It might be thought that the two were the same, but that is not true. A bad rendition, which shows no respect for the very nature of the music, by destroying the clarity of the lines, obliges the sensitive observer to leave the room immediately. The experience is completely hideous. A boring performance by contrast is likely to be one which indeed shows rather too studied respect, where the singing is 'white' rather than colourful, where the performers are putting on a 'renaissance' tone of voice which means only half-singing in order to secure a more successful blend.

There is little I can say to those in the former category, now fewer in number than they were 30 years ago. Perhaps I have said all I can by building up a following for the 'clarity' approach, and broadcasting it as far and wide as possible. It is the boring practitioners who are so prevalent, encased in self-confidence, subtly turning audiences everywhere against the music, and taking their vision of polyphony just so far but never further, making it pretty. It is easy enough to be misled by the sheer beauty of renaissance music into thinking that that is all there is to it. What more is needed?

Religion is the place where we shunt off all our good thoughts and fragrant wishes; surely this custom-made old music was designed to complement this? Such a point of view forgets that for almost all the composers we have chosen, sacred music was the only music that they composed, compared with the contemporary situation when sacred composition is a rarity, usually forming only a small part of a composer's work. Renaissance composers had no other outlet for their emotions, good, tempestuous and bad, than their church music. They may not have been as highly trained as we are in self-analysis, with all its attendant anxiety-inducing complexes, but there surely was more to them than prettiness.

In what follows I have tried to address the practical problems of achieving clarity in polyphonic singing. That is both more elementary and easier than defining how not to be boring, which is more open to individual interpretation. I can only offer my interpretation, beginning with what I see as some of the more entrenched and unhelpful attitudes to choral singing in the amateur world.

There can be few things in music-making more opposite than the amateur and professional approaches to rehearsing polyphony. The amateur view, at its most extreme, sees polyphony as an adjunct to later 'choir music', sung perhaps by people who cannot read music and conducted by maestri who don't know what to say if they cannot lead by melodramatic and probably egocentric example. This view has clearly developed from nineteenth-century choral practices, when community singing from musical scores was new, and it tends to find the reserved nature of polyphony – the lack of accessible melodies and exciting chromatic harmony – unhelpful. The sheer number of unmemorable notes in the simplest polyphonic motet presupposes countless hours of rehearsal for choir members who need to begin with solfège, a process which can run the risk of overwhelming a gentle piece and killing it stone dead. The professional approach is that the notes are so easy one hardly needs to rehearse them at all, which runs the opposite risk of never really getting to know the music in its finer points, a kind of death by underwhelming. I contribute to courses where I take over a choir which has just been conducted by someone who has, to take an extreme example, made the singers put their heads between their legs and shout out the first three chords of a Mass movement, in an attempt to hold their interest; and yet when it comes to my turn I find I can do no other than represent the professional approach, despite the astonished and total silence at my first downbeat. Eschewing sectional rehearsals, or piano play-throughs, half an hour later we may collectively have blasted our way onto the second page, a dispiriting, unimaginative and endlessly repetitious process which I pursue because for me rehearsal is a means to an end – the concert performance; and I believe my method is ultimately the quickest way to achieve that end. In amateur singing, rehearsals are exciting, physically communal events of elastic length, with a meaning of their own; for professionals they don't exist without a concert that day or the next and even then are viewed as a necessary evil.

The irony is that despite such vastly different routes to the eventual performance of a piece of polyphony, when the concert begins we are all in exactly the same situation. The time for histrionics, perfumed or threatening exhortations is past. The only question is whether the notes will be right, and whether the singers have acquired any feeling for them.

Most of this is academic to the vast majority of the non-specialist concert-going public, who are not aware of the kind of professional expertise I have just described and who still harbour inappropriate ideas of how 'choirs' should be treated. These mistaken expectations put the exponents of polyphony in a terrible bind. Either one has to confront the idea of the large choir, in which no one takes significant responsibility for their part, or of the cathedral choir, for whom rehearsal time is very restricted, and in which the boys inevitably dominate the ensemble sound. Of course the cathedral model is closer to what the Tallis Scholars do, but unfortunately it is the other one which comes to many people's minds when they see us, for the moment a group of singers is seen to be mixed, and conducted, they tend to be treated as if they need to be led by the hand in all circumstances, no matter what they sing. The choral society approach does not suit polyphony, nor does polyphony suit singers who are used to doing no more than singing along. Any four-part motet by Palestrina will show this, but the classic case is Tallis's *Spem in alium*, whose size may mislead people. It is indeed a piece for a large group, but it is not suitable for a choir whose members never sing by themselves. Essentially it needs eight ensembles experienced in polyphonic singing, which is a very tall order.

The mismatch starts with how people see the role of the conductor. The kind of conducting which was established in the nineteenth century is still prevalent, if touched by a more democratic outer coating. Orchestras these days will no longer blindly worship autocratic maestri; nor will they tolerate the kind of ego-driven rudeness and temperamental behaviour which seems to have characterised so many leaders of a hundred years ago. Conductors can be told where they get off in no uncertain terms, as a leading English conductor was recently by members of the Vienna Philharmonic, and there isn't much they can do about it. But people standing on podiums tend to have over-developed egos, and nowhere has this been more evident than amongst choral conductors. It is still a commonplace to go to rehearsals and find the singers shaking with fear at putting a syllable out of place, riveted to their seats, their identities subsumed in the common effort. The obvious analogy is with the state of mind of privates in an army under threat. And there are still choral conductors who like to rant and rave at their cannon-fodder, sweeping out of rehearsals leaving humiliated women in tears, after which it can be the custom to applaud him.

At best the nineteenth-century autocratic hero-figure can produce highly disciplined performances from a large number of participants. But it will have to be the kind of music on which he can impose his will, by which I mean music which requires the imposition of louds and softs, special attacks and sudden diminuendos, holdings-up and rushings forward. Letting things happen unscripted in performance is not an option for such a conductor. Rehearsals will involve many hours of honing his special effects, and they are the principal way by which the conductor will impose his will on his group. After all, he has regular weekly rehearsals for months before the concert, how will he fill them? Let us suppose it will probably not be the first time the piece has been performed; and the music will probably have been chosen with the ultimate capabilities of the singers in mind. It is therefore not going to take all those hours just to get the notes right – and there is always a piano present to make sure nothing catastrophic transpires. Something must be 'done' with the piece: new corners must be teased out of it, new perspectives unveiled, the words inspected for the most hidden of meanings. And in the end, however good the music and whatever the final result, the line of command is clear, from massed musicians who have unconditionally put themselves at the service of the conductor, through the transforming power of his vision to the listeners. The audience applauds the conductor first.

Polyphony cannot be made to work like that because, ironically given its élitist origins, it has a fundamentally democratic style. The equalness of the voice-parts in renaissance music should condition every approach to it, remembering that in the most effective democracies the voters think about what they are contributing to. It is inimical to this idiom that the singers should slavishly obey what one outsider – for the conductor is not singing – chooses to impose on them. A satisfying interpretation of polyphony can only come from a reactive group of people who are listening to what is going on around them, and then, when the music calls for it, adding something of their own. This has serious repercussions for the role of the conductor, the nature of rehearsal, the secularisation of something that was originally sung in church, authentic performance, everything from top to bottom of what it takes to perform polyphony well.

The role of the conductor in polyphony is ambivalent in a number of ways; but underneath it all his problem is essentially how to retain his self-respect while doing a job which of necessity commands instant obedience when there are, say, over 20 people present, yet which requires something rather different when there are fewer. It is my opinion that he must cede a lot of that power to his performers, which may well make him uneasy, caught between controlling everything and leaving the singers to get on with it as a self-directing vocal ensemble. In fact both in the amateur and the professional world the conductor has the apparently menial but actually crucial task of acting as a kind of aesthetic umpire. Groups of singers left to themselves in rehearsal can rapidly fall into argument, since everybody can easily have an opinion about what they are doing when they are asked. The astute conductor will allow discussion, for example about the phrasing of a point of imitation which everyone will eventually have to sing, pick the view which seems, ideally, both the most prevalent and the nearest to his ideal, and impose it. In this way he will maintain a sense of progress where anarchy would often be the only alternative. In the theory of democracy there should be unlimited time to discuss what everyone feels, but rehearsals are of finite duration, as is the patience of people who lead busy lives. In this sense the skilful conductor has a difficult, unconventional but ultimately essential job to do. He must have enough ego to quieten the egos of everyone else present, not because it is his divine right as conductor, but because that is simply his task as the person called conductor. No one else will do.

In the professional world it is a commonplace attitude for singers to want to rehearse as little as possible, not least because they tend to be badly paid. They will know how much a rehearsal is worth in advance and, once they are confident their singing will not be ridiculously exposed in the performance, will want to do the bare minimum once they are at it. Sending them home early is always good for morale, which contrasts dramatically with the point of view of the keen amateur. In the professional climate the conductor needs to make quick and transparently fair decisions, knowing that he will always have the full attention and co-operation of those present, since any other approach vitiates the principles by which they agreed to come in the first place. An academically-inclined singer might well disagree violently with the line I customarily take about any number of issues to do with the music in theory – pitch, tempi, phrasing, scoring – but will only say so in rehearsal if my preferences will force them to give a substandard performance (for example, see the discussion of pitch on p. 212). Otherwise they are trying their hardest to do what is wanted, which should be something stylish and individual with what the composer has given them. In some ways this does resemble what I imagine a nineteenth-century orchestral rehearsal must have been like, with the difference that the whole process of command and obedience has been deconstructed and built up again from scratch. In this version the performers know themselves to be on an equal footing with the conductor, but have voluntarily pooled their talents for the period of the project in question in the service of an artistic ideal. And in this version the audience applauds everyone on the stage equally.

The only disappointment for me in directing amateur or semi-professional performances of polyphony is that the singers often lack the experience to take responsibility for the lines they are singing, and the eventual standard of their performance will depend on how willing they are to acquire that experience. The rank and file chorus singer is probably never going to be prepared to take the necessary risks, and will need to be told everything that is expected of him or her as if rehearsing four-part oratorio

choruses for weeks on end. The problem is that polyphony cannot be prepared like this. It is impossible to attach a dynamic to every note, an exact
contour of phrasing to every point, a reliable scheme of ebbing and flowing
which the habitual chorus member and his or her inevitable pencil can
record in the copy and reproduce precisely in every performance. Anyone
who has tried to map out a detailed dynamic scheme for a renaissance motet
will know how time-consuming and ultimately self-defeating such a process
is. Phrases that look on paper as though they might start loudly and dimin-
uendo before building again to the next set of entries rarely obey such neatness in the heat of the moment. But if everyone's copy says it must be so,
then to some degree it probably will be so, and the result is likely to be forced
and unconvincing. The best answer is to dare to leave just about everything
to the heat of the moment.

The history of publishing renaissance music, incidentally, has reflected
the move towards this understanding. The oldest editions gave a piano reduction and detailed dynamic markings attached to the voice-parts themselves. It is difficult to sing from these editions if one does not intend exactly to follow what Fellowes, or whoever the editor was, felt about the piece,
and one notices how often the very best choirs of yesteryear recorded
polyphony with all the dynamics of the leading editions of those days meticulously in place. The King's College 1964 recording of Palestrina's *Stabat
Mater* and W. Barclay Squire's edition, published by Novello. are a case in
point, and they in turn reflect the enormously influential markings which
Richard Wagner imposed on the piece in his 1848 edition. All of which goes
to show how necessary a new approach to editorial interference had become.
Clearly, in the early stages of the general dissemination of polyphony it was
felt that the rank and file could not be trusted to make interpretative decisions of any kind so that, following tradition, someone in authority must do
it for them. We will never know how justified that rather condescending attitude was, since general knowledge and understanding of this music is now
quite widespread, not least as a result of Fellowes's efforts. At some stage it
was recognised that it is hard to sing anything other than forte when the
copy tells you to, and the markings were restricted to the piano reduction.
The piano reduction anyway had its merits: it could be useful in giving a second reading where the printed polyphony clearly had errors in it; and the
suggestions for dynamic schemes could be useful, or ignored. But even this

came to be seen as extra to requirements (and piano reductions were time-consuming luxuries for the new one-man editor-publishers to produce) and now one buys copies which are completely clean of any such helps. I favour this in principle because it leaves me and my performers to take the risks I am advocating; but I accept that at some level of amateur endeavour it makes the music seem more daunting and unfamiliar. One very simple way a modern editor can facilitate access to the music is to put an accent on the syllables one would stress in speech, throughout the text. This device can make phrases come alive in rehearsal immediately, without the natural lie of every textual subclause having to be laboriously explained by the conductor.

I have been asked, sometimes with more than a hint of irony, whether a conductor is really necessary in the performance of polyphony. Certainly anything resembling a modern conductor standing out in front of the performers, waving his arms around and 'interpreting' the music is anachronistic. The very most the original singers would have had in the way of direction was someone keeping the pulse, probably in an audible form like tapping the stand or the choir-stall with a finger or a roll of parchment. I have already said that in modern rehearsals having someone in control is always going to save time; but in performance the issue is less clear-cut. The tempo and the first down-beat need to be given at the start, but they could be indicated by one of the singers. Since polyphony in theory rarely changes tempo in the middle of a movement there should be no difficulty in the singers directing themselves, assuming they watch each other carefully; and this method, in so far as we understand original practice, would have the merit of being authentic. Indeed the chamber-music-like nature of polyphony would seem to be well served by this way of doing things. String quartets achieve their subtleties by intense listening within the group: small chamber choirs should do the same.

How do I justify what I do on-stage? The self-conducting method has been known to work well, but not with groups which employ more than one voice to a part. I am certainly surplus to requirements on the rare occasions that we sing, as for example the Hilliard Ensemble does, with four or five people in total on the stage. But the moment there are eight or ten standing there, and two singers are responsible for one line, the director gains a new importance. The two ends of the line begin not to be able to hear each other; the two singers performing the same part cannot look into each other's eyes without turning their backs on other singers; the sheer number of people begins to make an on-the-spot consensus about the minutiae of the performance less achievable. It is true that much of the time all I'm doing is setting and keeping the tempo, but there are moments when suddenly the presence of a conductor is absolutely crucial, by which I mean that a conductor not being there would instantly lower the standard of the performance. Although the singers may not always seem to be watching me directly, I have the power, with a single movement of the hand or expression in my face, fundamentally to change what they are doing, in speed, dynamic level or strength of interpretation. An ill-considered gesture can instantly disrupt the flow of the music; a deliberate look or gesture can up the ante in a split second.

Many good singers instinctively think they can do the job I am describing perfectly well without outside cajoling from a conductor, and that there would be a perceptible gain in the chamber-music subtleties if they were left to present the music as a group. Assuming the performing conditions were ideal (which is rare, especially in churches) so that everyone could clearly hear and see everyone else, and that the group were prepared to accept one of their own number as a kind of leader, then some of the time they would be right and I have no doubt some of the results - the phrasing, the dialogue within the music - would be very exciting. The drawbacks are that no one is in a position to comment on the balance of the ensemble, because the leader, while singing, can only ever have a very partial impression of the overall picture; and the 'interpretation', however democratically arrived at, would inevitably be in danger of losing its way. Also I gather, though it is outside my experience, that taking responsibility for one's own line as a singer, as well as for the ensemble as a whole, is almost impossible to do properly.

The most important aspects of my job are: to plan a programme which is singable and not likely to bore the audience; to choose speeds which suit the music, the singers and the building, and keep to them in performance; to predict and take certain fundamental decisions in rehearsal on behalf of everyone present.

It could be said that half my job is done if I manage to choose a programme which really does fulfil the two criteria I mention. A concert which is over-long, or which contains music which is too unfamiliar or technically difficult for the singers to come to terms with in the time given, will prejudice the success of any appearance from the beginning. No half of a concert of polyphony should be longer than 40 minutes unless there is a single work which is longer, which is rare. Most Requiem settings exceed 40 minutes but not by very much – and should obviously not be cut up – and Mass Ordinaries are usually shorter, in fact often an ideal length for a half which will feature a single masterpiece. We used to break up Mass settings, interspersing the movements with motets, which made the sequence a little more like how it would have been originally, but I eventually tired of pseudo-services. Nor have we found that the often tight logic between the five movements of a single setting is overstated by adopting the modern 'symphonic' approach. Only once in recent years have we performed a Mass which really is too long for a single half – Obrecht's extraordinarily expansive *Missa Maria zart* – and had to set the interval after the Creed. In fact we sang it in concert before we recorded it, and initially had little idea how colossal it was. As the rehearsals proceeded I had to telephone the printer of the book of words several times to ask him to delete one item after another from the programme as I had planned it. I don't usually get timings as wrong as that, but there is a difficulty in predicting how long new pieces are going to be, and I probably misjudge most of them the first time. My heart sinks at rehearsal when I realise I have overstacked a half through making inexact predictions, knowing that nothing is gained. The singers will tire at about the same moment as the audience, which is simply a waste. I have almost never offered a half which was palpably too short, which would be even more embarrassing: in that regard one is cautious, preferring to give too much rather than too little.

A single masterpiece in a programme makes good copy for the promoter. After that it is my task to find a satisfying succession of pieces which throw light on each other while offering a varied sound-world: pieces with high sopranos, two sopranos, men's voices only, eight-voice textures down to four or even three (such as Sheppard's *In manus tuas* III). Normally I am asked for complete programmes from the same country of origin, which restricts the repertoire quite helpfully since every tradition can provide the kind of variety I've just outlined. In fact I find it unsettling to do a half of English music and a half of Italian, for example, and rather prefer being restricted still further by being asked to compare just two composers: Josquin and Lassus, or Byrd and Tallis. We regularly do whole programmes of just

Palestrina (with or without the Allegri).

The trick is in how a half unfolds. There are some rules. The two halves of a programme can be very similar in what they encompass, though the beginning of the second half is one place for an intellectual challenge where the beginning of the first is not. The opening of the concert is not quite the sensitive moment one might think – that comes later – though it is important to lay out one's stall without compromise right from the start. Many audiences will not know what to expect and will take perhaps ten minutes to get the idea, during which they will naturally be restless, unsure what to listen for. Two short and fairly brightly obvious pieces should do the job, leaving no doubt what the next hour is to consist of. Assuming the majority of those present have decided to stop struggling after these initial pieces and enjoy what they can, it is then possible to intensify the mood and programme more difficult music, which means longer pieces, certainly more penitential ones, or those with dense textures. In general the real blockbusters come at the end of either half, or at the beginning of the second. Before those the running times should be shorter and the message of the writing more graspable. The blockbusters need to be pieces the performers really believe in as great music, then the concert can end with a penitential work instead of the expected upbeat one. I try to avoid programmes which consist of a succession of pieces lasting three minutes each: it's hard to establish a good level of concentration with constant stopping and starting. This also applies to sharing the stage with other performers, and making spoken introductions: a concert of polyphony is most likely to appeal if one allows an unbroken atmosphere to be established, what I call elsewhere 'a general mood of contemplation'. In this respect a secular concert of sacred music can indeed resemble a church service, especially those which rely on mood, for example those of the Orthodox Church.

If the director can get the sequence of pieces right his job is simplified. However, the actual business of conducting music which hardly ever changes tempo can be surprisingly tricky. By virtue of standing in front of the performers, who cannot ignore what he is doing however much they may want to, the conductor inevitably controls the performance. If I hit the wrong initial speed, for example, the chances of correcting the error without the ensemble audibly suffering (which is when so many audiences start to shift about and cough) are not good. This problem is especially severe in music where the mensuration signs (or time-signatures) change radically in the middle of a piece. Despite the heavy-duty academic arm-twisting that goes on about how these signs are all related to each other – the argument being that the first implies all the subsequent speeds in a movement – I think the modern conductor is entitled to go his own way. Nonetheless it can be dreadfully difficult hitting those mid-term speeds, whether one decides to go in strict relationship with what went before or not, and the crashing of gears which may follow a misreading from me has produced some of the most embarrassing moments on-stage I have experienced. The most testing of all these speed-changes come in the English votive antiphon tradition, where it was customary for the composer to change from triple to duple time about halfway through the composition. At a certain point in history one finds, miraculously, that the tactus can remain the same between the two sections, and therefore throughout the entire piece. This is the case, for ex-ample, in Tallis's antiphon *Salve intemerata*, while in Taverner's not-very-much earlier *Gaude plurimum* there is no single speed on earth which will satisfy the flow of the lines in both the sections; and no exactly proportion-al tempo relationship will provide the answer either. I know this for certain, because inadvertently I must have tried just about all the options over the years.

Very few conductors of polyphony have classically-trained gestures, which results inevitably from polyphonic performances being a subsection of a discipline (choir music) which is itself a little-regarded subsection of a yet larger discipline (orchestral conducting). As I said earlier, there is no for-mal tuition in conducting renaissance music in Britain. My method has evolved over many years simply through experience. My beat has gradually got clearer and more relaxed, but even now it takes by surprise people who are not used to it. Apparently I expect the singers to sing not with the actu-al down-beat, but with the mini-gesture which follows. When I started con-ducting there were stories of the singers being asked by those listening, 'How can you sing so smoothly with THAT going on in front of you?' (re-ferring to my very jerky and tense way of beating). To which an apologist for it said, 'We know what he wants' (i.e., I conveyed my meaning by move-ments other than those I made with my arms). Now I try to indicate the lega-to sweep of phrases while keeping a very strict tactus, two things which do not automatically make easy bedfellows. Originally I just kept a very strict tactus and left the rest to the singers, which gives an idea of where my priorities lie. If I can manage both, so much the better, but the tactus is what I feel I am ultimately responsible for. One of my newer singers recently said that he always knew when he had been singing with the Tallis Scholars because he came away with such a strong beat in his head it took days to expunge it. I took that as a very great compliment. At every opportunity, though, I try to reconcile in my gestures the twin needs of sweep of phrase and strict tactus, which a recent critic (in the *Guardian* of the 14 January 2003), incredibly, was perceptive enough to notice: 'Director Peter Phillips, not a "conductor" in the conventional sense, rarely beat time in the usual manner, and avoided cramming the music into regulated bar lines. Instead, the music flowed like an evolving organism.'

That strong sense of beat is a crucial adjunct to good style in singing polyphony. It means that the length of every note, no matter how short, is being respected. One of the worst solecisms to be imposed on renaissance music from later practice is the notion of *notes inégales*, or interpreting the shortest notes as embellishments. This is, of course, essential to good baroque style, but the earlier repertoires rely on every note contributing exactly its length in a legato phrase. I suppose the baroque inverse of this is not giving any note quite its stipulated length, in an off-the-string, off-the-voice, lightly-phrased dance idiom, in the interests of suavity. Nothing could be less appropriate to the gleaming architectural structures of a composer like Palestrina; and in order to build those magnificent edifices on sure foundations I try to keep an absolutely metrical beat, in the hope that the singers will subdivide it into quavers and semi-quavers with perfect accuracy. This was the instinct which caused me for so many years to make jerky gestures, when I felt it necessary as it were to shout the tactus at the singers for fear they would not understand this. I used to leave the stage at the end of a concert with my right shoulder aching, or even with my right arm briefly dislocated, obliged to conduct only with my left. But the result at its best, and as it usually is nowadays, was a sound which had the metricality of a clock ticking, everything in its place. Almost every piece in the repertoire illustrates this, but none does it more audibly than Tallis's *Loquebantur variis linguis*, which has quavers on every beat, against a minim cantus firmus, from beginning to end. These quavers set up a kind of *moto perpetuo*, which one also finds in Bach's counterpoint, and which requires the strictest rhythmic control in performance to make it effective. I like the metaphor of the clock, incidentally, because it also hints at a sonorous, beautifully ordered universe, connected to the music of the spheres, an image which meant much to the more humanistically-inclined composers of the renaissance period. (This ideal in fact was expressed long before the renaissance period, by Hrabanus Maurus (c. 780-856), when he wrote, 'Without music no discipline can be perfect, nothing can exist without it. For the world itself is composed of the harmony of sounds, and heaven itself moves according to the motions of this harmony.') It is to this end that I still beat in four where most conductors, aiming for a sweep of phrase which I hope to achieve by other means, instinctively beat in two. There is a comfort in those grand sweeps of phrase, which rush over detail to arrive triumphant at the cadence, but to me they ultimately suggest a lack of confidence in the sound, as if it cannot bear very close scrutiny. It is worth adding that for some years the Tallis Scholars allowed a kind of compromise position with baroque practice in lifting the sound off a dotted note. So long as this was done in strict time I had no objection, and no doubt in those lighter and airier days quite liked the resulting lilt. But eventually I thought it sounded mannered and insisted that any dotted note be sung through, legato, to the end of its length.

In my experience the singers who find this ticking metricality of beat most difficult to hear and sing by are not amateurs, nor even opera singers, but student professionals who are training as soloists in baroque music. However much they may admire renaissance writing, they can find it almost impossible to undo the mindset of hearing musical phrases in baroque patterns, especially in the late renaissance repertoires. Byrd's *Tribue Domine*, for example, has some duets and trios involving dotted rhythms which can raise almost insuperable stylistic barriers to singers whose throats seem to have been shaped, as if for a mother tongue early in life, around the two- and four-bar phrases of Bach and Handel. It is almost as if they cannot quite undo a prejudice that such phrases ought to be rendered according to later ideals, and that the baroque masters ultimately knew best. I find this fascinating not least because it underlines the scope of the revolution which Monteverdi unleashed with his *seconda prattica*. But the most extreme example I have ever met of this difference of approach was in hearing a performance of Palestrina's *Tu es Petrus* directed in one (where I beat four), by Paul McCreesh. The music flashed by in a great shout of praise, Palestrina's meticulously-worked turns, which I think to be as much a part of the central frame of the conception as the longer notes surrounding them, presented as superficial detail. In this performance the words were respected but not, in my opinion, the music. However, there are phrases where four in a bar may be too cumbersome. The right speed for the Sanctus of Byrd's Four-part Mass, for example, is as elusive as these things can be. It may help to think of it in two, though if I do this I then find myself beating in four again at 'pleni sunt caeli', which goes at a faster tactus than the section just finished in two. Part of the conundrum of the opening phrase of that Sanctus is the dot in the first note, which requires the conductor to be very precise with the second beat. In any other phrase that starts with a dotted note I would take it as a standard opportunity to set an especially precise tactus, in order to have the following quaver in just the right place; but in this particular phrase, which lies so exactly between the sense of two and four, it doesn't help.

There are moments where a traditionally clear, orchestral-style conducting technique is more or less essential. Obviously, contemporary a cappella writing regularly makes demands which polyphony does not, and I have had to match up to those on occasion, but even in renaissance music there are moments. De Wert's astonishing motet *Ascendente Jesu in naviculam* has such complicated cross-rhythms that really only the most expert beater is going to do anything other than trip his singers up – and it is a measure of how powerful the conductor is that the slightest flick out of place in that piece will cause the whole edifice to fall apart. Those flicks out of place are anyway potentially dangerous things in many circumstances. There may be a strong temptation, for example, to give extra emphasis to an important lead by delaying it a split second. In later more homophonic music such emphases are quite normal, but in counterpoint tampering with the rhythm of one part can only mean it will get out of time with the others, which have their own logic. Since the other parts will not have an emphasis at just that moment, there is bound to be an imperfection in the ensemble, and all in the name of the conductor doing something instinctive. Also instinctive is the habit many groups have of slowing down at quieter passages. One classic example comes in Byrd's *Vigilate* at 'dormientes', where the words and the music suggest that the speaker has fallen asleep and the conductor may find himself fighting hard to keep the sound together just when the music implies relaxation. Obviously it is the job of the conductor to resist this kind of meaningless rubato – like every composer who knows what he's doing, Byrd has made sure that nothing is needed to make the desired effect other than what he has written in the music. Careful explanation in rehearsal, for once, is the best remedy.

What polyphony most requires from its director is the ability to listen into the texture. To do this to a refined degree does take a lot of practice, which is not to say the inexperienced cannot enjoy the music straightaway, but the more sophisticatedly the conductor can manage it, the more helpful it will be to the performance. By this 'listening into' I mean projecting one's ear into the middle of the sound and leading the interpretation from there. I believe it is only from there that the conductor can sympathise as much with the middle parts as with the more audible outer ones, and encourage those middle parts when they have the crowning phrases or the tricky rhythms. Ultimately this discipline depends on shrewd aural selection, especially in music in more than four parts, since it is not humanly possible to keep an ear on everything. But one will stand a greater chance of success by working from the middle outwards.

An equal refinement is for the conductor to look as though he is breathing the important phrases in the music with the singers, and even mouthing the words with them. Many choral conductors are singers by inclination and training, for whom this may not seem on the surface a difficult task. I am not a singer and have had to acquire the knack, but I suspect no one finds this entirely straightforward when it comes down to it, because to manage it well requires complete relaxation with the make-up of the music, to know where the next big phrase is coming from and to show that one is ready for it by body language and by such refinements as conducting the rest before the beginning of that phrase as if it were an integral part of the phrase, while staring straight at the singers about to enter. The increase in impact when the singers realise the conductor is right with them can be great, generating electricity on-stage, involving eye-contact, conveying mutual understanding of the importance of the moment and so on. In fact when the ensemble as a whole is going really strongly everyone will be visibly reacting and moving together, and at that point the conductor will find that he or she can control phrases, commas in the text and cadences by the split-second placings of chords which will make the difference between an inspired reading and a matter-of-fact one, where to rush or for the ensemble to become ragged is to spoil everything. There is nothing more expressive than a body of singers heading full tilt towards a cadence, and then, as it seems by common breathing, defining the final chords as if the group were one person.

Beside all this the technique of taking rehearsals is tame stuff. I have indicated earlier in this chapter how the conductor of polyphony acts as a kind of umpire, both aesthetic and practical. I will add here a few more small items to that list of adjudication. It may be necessary to spell out in words the mood of a piece of renaissance music. Handel is praised in the history books for writing a Dead March in a major key; renaissance composers standardly set penitential or sad texts in 'major' keys, and it can be very easy with our later training for us to forget that major does not necessarily mean happy. Byrd's *Infelix ego*, for example, has as penitential a text as any piece in the repertoire, yet it seems to start in a bright major key. If the conductor says nothing about this there is a chance that the music will be misrepresented and sung in the wrong spirit. Unlike later repertoires, renaissance music does not always hand its mood to the performers on a plate, not least because there is the constant danger of underplaying Latin – either not bothering to translate it fully, or not allowing it to have a full emotional impact because we instinctively think of it as a 'dead' language; it may well need some help. On the other hand, I am a strong believer in not over-specifying an interpretation in rehearsal. Apart from a few words of basic guidance, often to do with the underlying mood of a piece as I understand it, I prefer to leave the subtler twists and turns to the concert. This way there are few arguments about what we are striving for on-stage, and every rendition can be slightly different, which is an advantage with pieces we know really well, or on a long tour. This approach also makes it easier to be natural with the music when we have to sing it in artificial circumstances, as on a recording, time and time again. By not over-stipulating I increase the chances of something lively happening each time we sing the piece. As a result my copies have very few markings, if any. I was recently asked by an American conductor, with whom I was collaborating on a performance of *Spem*, to send him my score so that he could transfer my markings into his copy and follow them. I told him there was no point doing this, since there were no markings in my score. He scarcely believed me, and no doubt wondered what he had let himself in for.

All this begs the larger question of what it means to interpret polyphony. People who play Bach's organ fugues know that there is relatively little that can be done with counterpoint apart from trying to make one's phrasing of it audible. If one speeds the music up or slows it down in a romantic way the lines are distorted; any elaborate changes of registration only distract the listener from the raw strength of Bach's contrapuntal arguments and can seem to trivialise the music. Most players nowadays agree that the best thing one can do is play the notes without much decoration and let the music speak for itself. The same is true for polyphony, except that this 'leave everything to the music' point of view disguises the fact that there are still decisions to be made - they are just less impositional ones than later music requires. Of course, as usual, it took some decades for the interested parties to undo the suppositions of their predecessors, and to some extent the process goes on, but it is generally agreed that a performance of a Palestrina motet which does not have melodramatic louds and softs, rubatos, crescendos, diminuendos and the whole range of operatic expressive device is probably going to serve the music best. The interesting thing is that however clean a modern performance might be, it is not going to be authentic. We do interpret this music, however undemonstratively.

For instance, we create a sound from our singers. In my opinion this basic sound, which is built into the writing, is highly expressive, more expressive than any amount of going loud and soft or slowing down at important words. The essence of pure polyphony is in its flow, and to interpret it effectively the singers need to know how to sing legato both individually and as a group. We have no accurate idea whether the Sistine Chapel choir in the sixteenth century studied all the choral disciplines which bother us so much – blend and tuning being paramount – but there is every reason to believe from the descriptions of what went on there – the absenteeism, the surviving descriptions of just how bad some of the voices were, the cronyism – that the standard was endemically hit and miss.

Then there are the issues which contribute to the style of the performance, and hence to its interpretation: pitch, ficta, tempi and dynamics. Someone has to decide about these potentially contentious things, and in the professional world anyway the hope is that they will not be put up for barter at the first (and probably only) rehearsal, but that the conductor will have decided them in advance. And the interpretation will be influenced as follows: if a high pitch is adopted the lines tend to become clearer and brighter, more floating, but if that process goes too far then the voices may become over-bright or shrill and the piece will be in danger of losing its *gravitas*. The problem for both high- and low-pitch interpretations of polyphony lies in maintaining a good balance between the parts. Creating the optimum circumstances for maintaining that balance is a constant struggle. If too much musica ficta (those sharps and flats which seem to be required by the music but are not consistently given in the manuscripts) is imposed on the music it will be in danger of sounding more modern than it should, even proto-baroque where that is clearly an anachronism; if too little ficta is used the opposite case will apply – the music will sound older than it is – with the added nastiness that it may acquire a pre-Raphaelite flavour, a kind of spurious medievalism. The problem with ficta is trying to find a consistent approach within the parameters of the piece in question. Brumel's 12-part *Missa Et ecce terrae motus* exemplified the conundrum for me: with so many voice-parts and so many cadences, every decision I took about ficta had a thousand repercussions. In the end I washed my hands of just about the whole wretched business and decided the only possible approach was to leave it all out – and duly provoked the faux-medieval criticism. As with pitch, ficta is an ongoing, forever renewable supplier of difficult questions.

Tempi and dynamics, believe it or not, are easier. In theory, as I read the manuscripts, neither should really be an issue at all. There are no tempo markings apart from the mensuration signs, and all those are theoretically interrelated (the triple times should be in strict proportion, which can vary, to the duple and vice versa). All that someone has to decide on is the initial speed, from which everything will follow; and, as a Belgian priest once explained to me, that was always decided by the pulse of a man's hand. And there are literally no dynamic markings. If one believes, as I do, that the writers of those manuscripts were quite bright enough to invent symbols for loud and soft, faster and slower if they had wanted them, the conclusion has to be that an authentic performance of polyphony had only the most subtle ebbing and flowing of dynamic range, and everything went fundamentally at the same speed. I realise that, like ficta, the scribes might not have thought it necessary to write such things down, but at least with ficta a code of symbols had been developed, which was only haphazardly used.

Of course that is not good enough for us. We give concerts of the music, where some of the spotlight is inevitably on variety, entertainment and even comparison with other (possibly recorded) versions of the same piece. A great deal changed when we chose to take formal religion out of the performance of this music, and lined up with string quartets and piano recitals as belonging to the modern, secular world; at that time it became necessary to do something individual with it. Tempi and dynamics are the first tools to come to hand.

To think about what goes on in a conductor's head when he is deciding on the speed of a piece, with every eye in the building on his upbeat and sometimes with only a split second at his disposal, brings me out in a cold sweat. I personally try to imagine a phrase at the speed I want to hear it at, and then plunge in, but often there isn't time for that and the decision has to be completely instinctive. And that instinct will be made up of a number of factors, most if not all anachronistic. Which conductor is not tempted to perform the different subsections of the Gloria, Creed and Sanctus at different speeds, going slower at 'Qui tollis' and 'Et incarnatus est', for example? Why does he not choose a speed at the outset which represents a compromise between the needs of the different sections, a speed which can serve both the positive mood at the opening of these movements, and the more contemplative later sections? The composer may even have helped him by setting 'Et incarnatus', for example, in longer notes, so the music inevitably slows down. But it's no good. We have not reacquired pre-nineteenth-century susceptibilities; and we on the stage need to sell our enthusiasm. At some level the audience needs to be made to feel glad they have bought their ticket. Maybe doing everything at the same speed and dynamic level will one day seem like the new, cool approach to polyphony; but I have so far not dared to go with it, not movement after movement. If I see the words 'et ascendit in caelum' I instinctively want a fast speed and a crescendo as the phrase rises. Call me square, cliché-ridden, boringly predictable and inauthentic, but I've discovered I don't fully enjoy the music if I don't do those things.

So my interpretation is made up of all the very ordinary things I've just mentioned, which would probably occur to any modern musician set the task of conducting polyphony; what may make my version distinctive is the sound behind the fast or slow speed, the louds and the softs. I return to the point of view that the sound itself, realised by the singers from the sonorities in the music, is an essential part of the interpretation. In fact what I'm proposing is that there are now two traditions of interpreting polyphony. The more traditional one is rhetorical – that is, the words are held to be paramount and every note sung is made meaningful by reflecting their meaning – and there is mine, which is sonic. In mine the sound comes first, at times frankly acknowledging that the words are a peg on which to hang almost abstract music.

Here we come to a central point of definition. How important are the words in polyphony? Obviously they have an importance – no one wants to sing this music to 'la' – but how essential are they to what the composer actually wrote and therefore to what we feel about what he wrote? My view is that the rhetorical school is again being influenced by those nineteenth-century preoccupations which assume that every word must have been set pictorially. By the nineteenth century both religious texts and the power of music had acquired a dramatic impact which was unknown in the sixteenth century: the error is to suppose that intensity of word-painting is the only way a composer can convey depth of feeling. This is especially true of religious texts, which may well be trying to express something so profound as to be almost inexpressible in words, and for which an abstract or neutral compositional style is the most moving. The sixteenth century was one of intense religious upheaval, in which the meaning of religious texts was at the forefront of the argument, which did eventually lead to a new kind of word-orientated music on both sides of the religious divide. But the bulk of what the Tallis Scholars perform, with the exception of Byrd's penitential motets, was either written before the trouble had really started (or sunk in) or was written with a religious message attached but in a very straightforward musical idiom. No one can claim that Tallis's beautiful little anthem *If ye love me* is trying to convert the unbeliever simply by making the literal meanings of the words expressive in the music.

 The problem with putting over this point of view is that general knowledge of renaissance music is heavily weighted towards the end of the period, when baroque influences had begun to make themselves apparent. When people think of a cappella music they tend to think of madrigals, madrigalian motet-settings, music that is familiar to them from listening to or singing later composers who found their starting point in the late high renaissance style – Purcell is an obvious example. To people who think this kind of music represents all you need to know about polyphony there isn't much of an argument: you adopt practices learnt from singing nineteenth-century composers, and self-consciously clean them out a bit for Lassus. But I am not talking about this music, and, as I say, we hardly ever perform it. I am talking about the vast majority of pieces written in the renaissance period which have no anticipation of baroque influence, no pre-echo of the 'reforms' of Monteverdi towards verbal expression, and which are for that reason not so immediately user-friendly today. Nor will they ever become so if they are sung with the mindset which Monteverdi and his nineteenth-century successors required.

The centre of this repertoire is contained in the Flemish School before about 1560. What has made the music of Ockeghem, Obrecht, Isaac, Josquin, Willaert, Clemens and Gombert (to mention only the leading names) difficult for modern choirs is that it is founded in mathematical complexity which proceeded from the very unmodern belief that the most suitable way to praise God was to impress Him with one's learning. A composer of the Flemish school was rated by his peers not only by how expressively he set a word or a phrase, but also by how brilliantly he could make mathematical conceits stack up. It is not for nothing that some of this music is referred to as 'the music of the spheres', because God was held to inhabit those spheres, and one way to try to understand him was to apply the sheer mathematics of astrology to musical composition. When it worked well, as in the canon of the third Agnus Dei of Josquin's *Missa L'homme armé sexti toni*, it was expected that the listener would come closer to God, and indeed that movement does seem to have something 'heavenly' about it.

Advanced mathematics do not inform every piece of polyphony up to the middle of the sixteenth century, but the traditional training of every Flemish composer involved solutions to such questions as how best to dispose the chant in a cantus firmus (often involving some kind of mathematical relationship between that part and the others), how to write canons which had the potential to become mathematically very intricate, and in later decades how to write imitative points in as many as eight parts. And even the simplest polyphony is mathematically quite involved when compared with the essentially baroque technique of continuo and solo melodic line. Some of what I describe here is more applicable to late medieval than renaissance music but, as with a good performing style, one does well to remember that when the composers were writing they had no knowledge of the future, only of the past. Clemens might not have wanted to write mensuration canons any more (though his contemporary Willaert did), but what he did write started with mensuration canons and the like as its background. To look at his music as simplified Monteverdi, requiring simplified Monteverdi-style singing techniques into the bargain, is obviously to make a very elementary error of judgement.

I have spent countless hours at choir practices where the conductor has dwelt at length on every aspect of the words – their meaning, their liturgical context, their pronunciation, how they are expressed in the music, how best to extract that last ounce of interpretative meaning from the musical phrase which is always presupposed to be descriptive. I have been asked to write into my copy such things as 'smile with joy', 'cry out', 'sob'. The whole preparation time may be taken up with these methods of expression and no mention made of whether the way one is using one's voice is suitable for polyphony, how well one is blending with one's partners on the line, how satisfactory the tuning is, where to breathe so that a good legato is maintained, how to listen to and react to the other singers taking part, above all whether the overall sound is clear enough for all the contributing lines of counterpoint to be heard in equal balance. These are the real, practical differences between the two styles of interpretation I have identified. The latter sonic method works towards a highly expressive basic sound, which can be applied to anything, not least contemporary music, but is at its most telling in music which does not wear its heart on its sleeve; the former rhetorical method has a quite limited application because no choral music actually benefits from singing which is inherently unbalanced and out of tune, even if the music in question is very obviously word- rather than sound-orientated.

Very little renaissance music can be said to fall within that category. Even in the late period one is confronted with masterpieces like Victoria's six-voice Requiem, or the Byrd Masses, or the contrapuntally involved works of the Portuguese school. Such music was still essentially written in the style of the mathematical Flemish composers, requiring the same ensemble disciplines from the performers to make its impact: there are still no instruments, no solo lines, no resorting to harmonic effects to save the day. The Victoria in particular poses an extreme test of those disciplines on account of its length and intensity of emotion, which in my experience only comes out if the underlying manner is sustained and gentle, a very tall order in the context. It is only in the sacred music of Gesualdo in particular, but also of de Wert, de Rore and in some pieces by Lassus, that the Flemish model is taken to such an extreme that my sonically-based method faces a test which it can not fully match up to. Gesualdo's lines can be so distorted that they minimise the chances of a good legato, good tuning and good blend being achievable, or even desirable. In such circumstances one can do little other than throw oneself at the words, as these few composers did.

Mention of Victoria's Requiem highlights the question of what the words meant to renaissance composers, and by extension how we should interpret them. This work poses the question more forcefully than most because we know how religious Victoria was, both from his biography and from the special power of some of his music. Even if we didn't know he was a committed member of the Catholic priesthood much of his working life, we could assume something of the sort from his music. With other composers there is more room to ask whether they had so totally given themselves over to the Church, or whether they were content to go through the motions which nonetheless would have been God-centred in an age when everyone was assumed to be a believer. And of course, in the sacred music which we espouse, the Church was almost always the employer.

One can establish the extremes. Victoria's Requiem is clearly not dealing primarily in abstract sound for its own sake (and would lose all of its inherent drama if it were sung to 'la'). On the other hand, the Hebrew letters in Lamentation settings ('Aleph', 'Beth', 'Teth', etc.) are completely meaningless as words, offering little more than 'la' and requiring an interpretation which will achieve nothing if it has no abstract beauty. In between these two extremes comes a vast body of music which will veer to one side or the other. Closer to the Hebrew letters end of the spectrum will be the umpteenth Mass setting by a masterly technician like Palestrina; nearer the Victoria end will come those texts which composers of the calibre of Josquin were allowed to choose to set, as opposed to being obliged to set by liturgical propriety, for example his *Miserere*. It is interesting that Palestrina also clearly benefited from being allowed to choose the text (as, for example, in the motet *Tribulationes civitatum*), while Josquin really didn't seem to compose unless he had something to say, which explains why *his* 15 or 16 Mass settings are so unusually expressive.

Should we conclude, then, that on balance Palestrina's Mass settings are not as interesting as Josquin's motets? My answer is 'no'. By adopting an interpretative method which is based in pure sound, which concentrates on what is in the notes as music rather than on the perceptible strength of the composer's belief, or indeed of my belief, as it comes through the words, one may find beauty in what looks run-of-the-mill. Palestrina may have been emotionally cool on occasion, but he was never less than a superb craftsman who was regularly inspired – by the words, by the logic of his lines, by the sonorities he was creating. If ever a composer relished the musical style he inherited and perfected it, it was him, which one would miss if one looked only for verbal expression. The coolness is a mask; behind it is a passionate commitment to music for its own sake.

Perhaps this can be said of every reputable composer, even of those, like Britten, who seem unable to write a note that does not literally depend on a syllable. But the stakes were different in the polyphonic period. The very mathematical nature of polyphony, which would understandably be denounced as élitist during the Reformation and abolished, makes superficial word-painting very difficult. For a long time there was no alternative for a composer but to subsume the obvious meaning of the words in the polyphonic web. What was left was the opportunity to create a much more general mood of contemplation, which could easily seem non-specific. Or at least it can seem like that to us now; at the time there was no doubt in anyone's mind what was being referred to, no need to spell anything out or underline with special effects what everyone knew already. But now the very vagueness of the message, apart from the general mood of contemplation, is helpful. It means we can perform the music to people of every or no religious background, who can hear it on whatever level suits them at the time: as simply beautiful and uplifting sounds, as something which conveys a sense of the numinous, or, if they know the precise significance of the words, as a rhapsodic outer coating for profound meanings which the music itself can only ever hint at.

I have long assumed that the standard modern view of the role of the texts in any church music is that they are of paramount importance, and that anybody trying to claim that the music is effectively abstract is being dangerously subversive. In fact what I have just written is actually tame by comparison with a school of thought in Germany in the early nineteenth century, which was led by the critic and writer E.T.A. Hoffman and the philosopher Friedrich Schlegel. They suggested that the presence of words in church music should be ignored because the music alone was capable of 'saying the unsayable', and that Palestrina in particular should not be heard as combining text and music, but simply as writing pure music. Hoffman wrote in 1814 that church compositions communicate through the 'universally comprehensible medium of music', and 'the words associated with the singing are only incidental'. Instinctively though I agree with this, it is perhaps only fair to quote Palestrina himself on the subject of words and music, from a letter to Guglielmo Gonzaga, Duke of Mantua, dated 3 March 1570, commenting on a motet written by the Duke: 'It seems to me that because of the dense interweaving of the imitations the words are somewhat obscured to the listeners, who do not enjoy them as in ordinary music.' One might have to conclude from this that, in theory at least, Palestrina thought that a close relationship between text and music, and a texture thin enough for the words to be heard, was the goal of a composer of polyphony.

To sum up: I have reached a stage where I need to sell polyphony to myself and the audience by adopting certain inauthentic interpretative devices, such as varying speeds and dynamics, but this need to 'sell' does not run to exploding every word with a pictorial meaning in the singing, or to adopting exaggerated poses and expressive methods, to the detriment of the flow of the polyphonic web. I believe that, like a Bach organ fugue, the meaning of sacred polyphony is in the counterpoint, which needs very little front-line help from the performers, who are no more than the medium through which it speaks. The minimum requirement is 'a general mood of contemplation', which is certainly served by producing a beautiful basic sound, after which it is only necessary that the performers remain in close touch with each other, as they would in the performance of any intimate chamber music.

Perhaps it is this lack of obvious, modern, connection between words and music which makes polyphony more difficult to bring off in performance than the later repertoires. Concert programmes which contain samples of music from every period often fall down in performance on their renaissance content, although on the face of it there is no good reason for this. The actual notes in polyphony are as simple, if not simpler, than anything written later. The problem seems to lie in making them have an effect, being convinced about what they are there for, where they are going. Part of this is stylistic, to do with the legato phrasing I mention elsewhere, but part stems from uneasiness with the words. It cuts both ways that Latin is a dead language. On the one hand, a professional secular ensemble may rather re-joice in the distance which Latin imposes on even the most ardent text: we are not pushing Christian dogma and enjoy the purely sonic approach, for all that we want to know what the texts mean (or meant). On the other hand, ensembles who a little later in the programme will be singing Rachmani-nov's Lord's Prayer (perhaps in English) can find it very hard to find a *modus vivendi* for polyphony. Resorting to pure sound will probably not be an op-tion for them; expressing the words will be their mindset. One quite com-mon way round the problem is for the conductor to try to inspire a kind of false reverence. To me this is the worst of all worlds, involving a gallery of gothic horrors from violent extremes of dynamic (especially heart-wrench-ing triple pianos) and ritardandi at the more significant words, to weeping-madonna expressions on the faces of the performers. This answer to the co-nundrum posed by polyphony is more common than one might suppose, certainly extending into professional performances, and it always trivialises the music. A good performance cannot come out of faked emotion, and ren-aissance music is not asking to be treated like romantic music. It was not written like that.

One potentially unhelpful aspect of how polyphony was written is the al-most total lack of repeating material, which can test a conductor's ability to shape a piece. The standard motet or Mass movement written after about 1520 is made up of a series of imitative schemes, a new set of imitative points required by the next phrase of words: Palestrina's *Sicut cervus* is a classic case. Given that most music, popular and composed, has relied on recapitulation both for its intellectual and emotional effect, how is one to present such a bland formula? Where will the points of contrast be? If there is no recapit-ulation, there will be no sense of building to a repeat and through it to the final leave-taking. One can rely on a very consistent compositional idiom in polyphony, but not on a sense of beginning, middle and end, because there was no attempt to use harmony as a controlling or in any way emotive back-ground force. The harmonic background in polyphony is often as simple as could be, which is why it is such a travesty to sing it in buildings which are so reverberant that all anyone can hear of the part-writing is a series of con-stantly repeating very basic chords. Here again the modern conductor may have his preconceptions challenged.

The clue is to have a good sense of the overall architecture of the music, and to judge each piece precisely on its merits. If the music is straightfor-ward it is useless to pretend it is otherwise. There should be no doubt that every piece of polyphony, however elementary in idiom, can be made effec-tive in performance if the basic sound of the group is involving, though one might think twice about programming simple music on a big occasion. But even the grandest pieces follow this basic plan of a series of imitative sec-tions connected only by the strictly controlled musical idiom; they may ebb and flow with the greatest invention and polyphonic effect, but, unless they have chant cantus firmus as scaffolding, they hardly ever advertise any sense of a journey from an initial emotional standpoint to a subsequent one. Re-naissance music has much more to do with contemplating a fixed state of mind, proposed by the words, than progressing through a sequence of them. Nonetheless the modern conductor will be expected to do something more with his material than create an unvarying sound, especially if the piece in question, like some of the grander English antiphons, lasts nearly 20 min-utes as a single movement. This is where a sense of architecture is crucial. A piece like Tallis's *Gaude gloriosa* would challenge the control of the most ex-perienced symphonic conductor, if the two were ever to meet, because its few cadences all contribute something to the total picture, all of them care-fully placed not only to round off a section, but as stepping stones to the 'Amen' which caps the whole vast structure. I believe it is necessary for the conductor to have a sense of exactly where those cadences are in relation to the whole as he approaches them, if he is to make the most of the explosive final pages. In fact *Gaude gloriosa*, although amongst the longest of these sin-gle-movement pieces, is not one of the more sectional. It is a measure of the sophistication of the style by Queen Mary's reign that Tallis could write something which flows so irresistibly over such a substantial canvas. There are many rather shorter pieces which can seem cut up for no reason other than that the composer must move on to the next phrase of words. Parsons's

O bone Jesu is a good case in point. The placing of the last section – 'Fac mecum' – poses a classic challenge in the repertoire to the conductor. Everything seems to have been said in the music already; the obvious framing of the sections with a homophonic phrase beginning with the invocation 'O' has happened several times, the one before 'Fac mecum' having been particularly powerful. How can one build through this unwanted full stop, especially as there is going to be no help further on through revisiting of old material? The answer is: don't pretend it is anything other than it is, and come to it with an exact sense of what has happened in the music up to that point, and what is to follow. After the big cadence which precedes it one can do no other than withdraw. To try to maintain the intensity would feel false, yet within a page or two one is going to be singing the 'Amen'. I believe the power of that 'Amen' will depend on how well the performers have prepared for it from the very beginning, and not by suddenly remembering it when they come to 'Fac mecum'.

Parsons tests one's architectural sense more than usual in *O bone Jesu*, for all that conductors trained in the more symmetrical constructions of later music are going to find every polyphonic composition testing in this way. Parsons was still writing in the mid-century idiom, and it is true that high renaissance music can come nearer to later and more familiar practice. A motet like Byrd's *Civitas sancti tui* is not architectural in the way I have just described because it so hangs on its text that the logic of the words alone carries us through. One would have to be made of stone to fail to make something of the last section – 'Jerusalem desolata est': it is not necessary to plan for it in the same way as for the Amens in the more abstract style, in that kind of writing where one has been singing a melisma for so long one forgets which vowel-sound one has started with, and has to turn back a page or two to find the beginning of the word. Byrd, like Lassus, was heading for the baroque way of setting words, however obliquely.

Acquiring this sense of architecture takes time, more time for the Tallis and Parsons than for the Byrd (or for Josquin and Isaac than for Lassus and de Rore). This begs some questions about the rehearsal process. Certainly the conductor should try to come to the first rehearsal of a new large wedge of abstract polyphony knowing how he wants to shape it. The problem is that no amount of poring over the score in silence – or playing it through on the piano – is going to tell him exactly what he needs to know. Not only is it hard to hear six or more polyphonic lines in one's head at once, but also, separate from the mood suggested by the texts, most of this music really does have a logic of its own. Trying to explain this logic in spoken words, and transposing it thence to dynamic schemes written into copies, is unlikely to produce anything very organic, and it may take a long time. It is obviously better to experience the music as music several times, before one can begin to claim that one knows it. In fact it is one of the great strengths of polyphony that much of it is sufficiently complex to bear almost endless repetition, and for the performers still to find new perspectives in it. Ideally, then, one would sing the music through repeatedly in rehearsal before presenting it to the public, yet both in the amateur and the professional context this is hardly ever done with profit. A good performance of polyphony will depend on an endless succession of tiny details, the kind that don't want to be drilled into people's heads in rehearsal and exaggerated in performance, even if they can all be remembered. The only way is to feel them instinctively in the singing, which is as much a test of musicianship as of vocal technique. Rehearsals in this way of looking at polyphony rapidly become the occasion for doing no more than establishing that the notes are right (as much in the copies as in the singing), which may mean only going through a new piece once before its first public outing.

In this matter of overall architecture, Mass movements, and especially Parody Mass movements, present a case a little apart. In many polyphonic settings of the Ordinary, quite a lot of material does in fact come round repeatedly, though not exactly in the later sense of recapitulation. The problem for the composer of a Gloria or Creed was that he had to set a long text. One way round having to invent new points of imitation for every subclause of these texts was to rework old ones; and one of the pleasures of conducting a Parody Mass, for example, is to see how an imaginative composer represents this old material to new words. Through this reworking all the five movements of a setting become linked, obliging the conductor to think carefully about relative speeds. Of course originally the movements were broken up between the sections of the spoken service, which certainly took the pressure off dreaming up subtle speed changes; but there is real interest in the modern concert way of singing a Mass setting, movement after movement straight through, as well. I would argue that in the hands of a master, parody technique rather benefits from our kind of 'symphonic' presentation, as a work with five movements. Perhaps, though, it would be more ac-curate to liken this to a gigantic set of variations on a theme than a sym-phony, even though each movement has a character, the Agnus ensuring that the sequence almost always ends with a slow movement.

In this context it is of course a great help if the conductor has a good sense of the overall architecture, this time over five movements. If he has he may, for example, think twice about taking the first section of the Creed at the same speed that the Gloria has just ended with, which in turn may re-flect the tempo at the opening of the Gloria. In the more elaborate settings, making the Creed a kind of mirror image of the Gloria means that many minutes may go by in the performance with substantial chunks of music all at the same tempo (in the case of Morales's *Missa Si bona suscepimus*, for ex-ample, this might amount to 25 minutes of music), which may be throwing away an opportunity. I do not necessarily mean by this anything radical: very slight changes can produce the same sense of a new context as bigger ones. Subtly varying tempi will give new perspectives to old material, which fits in well with the underlying principle of a parody. The question of whether to change speeds in the middle of a movement (for example speeding up at 'Pleni sunt caeli' or slowing down at 'Et incarnatus est') is part of the same perspective-building. To put it another way: the borrowed material may be enhanced as much by being laid out for inspection at different speeds as by having new counterpoints thrown round it (and to have both is even better). In this way the conductor can take a front seat in the creative processes, es-pecially if the composer has not been particularly imaginative (one thinks of Lassus).

I have mentioned my sonic ideal but not the kind of voice which will pro-duce it. As I hear, it polyphony needs bright, strong, agile, straight but not white voices which have a naturally good legato over a wide range. Virginia Woolf's summing-up of Proust's prose style (see p. 14) expresses my ambi-tions perfectly. Other directors who specialise in renaissance music, espe-cially non-English ones such as Paul van Nevel, seem to think it needs quite small voices, closer to the timbre of the recorder than the natural trumpet. This may reflect the kind of singer available locally who, the moment they receive any vocal training and learn to project their voices, does so with vibrato, obliging Paul and his colleagues to use relatively untrained voices;

or it may come from a belief that the clarity of the part-writing is better served by voices with few overtones. I have some sympathy with this view, and have admired van Nevel's very different versions of works we have also sung (especially the big pieces like Brumel's 12-part Mass, Tallis's *Spem* or the Josquin 24-part canon *Qui habitat*); but the overall effect is less thrilling, less brilliant, too fussy. I want a core of steel to the sound, and in trying to create it I believe we have encouraged the development of a new kind of professional singing voice, the kind that projects to the back of the Sydney Opera House without employing distorting vibrato (remembering there will always be some vibrato).

Van Nevel's recordings show that he would support me in saying that the equal audibility of all the parts is a prime consideration in singing polyphony. Not to work towards this is to show scant respect for the very nature of the writing. The necessary clarity can only be achieved by good tuning and good blend. Bad tuning will make the texture muddy as the lines blur, and bad blend will cause individual voices to stand out of the texture, making those lines consistently more audible than others. It follows that I want a singer who can sing with colour in their tone without generating mud; who can listen while singing loudly; and who has the flexibility to sing with sensitivity over the wide ranges which renaissance composers preferred, since for most of the period the modern SATB choral ranges only very vaguely applied. I choose to employ two singers to a part rather than one because I specifically want a choral, blended sound, not the sound which comes from having one voice to a part with all the breaks in the legato which that implies. And I suppose ultimately I would do what the leading renaissance choral foundations did, which was employ the most musically intelligent people available, not just those with fine voices.

Every vocal ensemble is identified in the first instance by the sound its top line makes. In some groups this means countertenors – and very distinctive their different sounds can be – but in our case it means sopranos. There is no doubt that our 'signature sound' has come from the characteristic tone-colours made individually and together by Deborah Roberts, Tessa Bonner, Jan Coxwell, Sally Dunkley and Ruth Holton. It has mattered that in all the voice-parts the chosen singers should come to the group with the same types of voice, but it has mattered more that the sopranos did. And, once there, in order to maintain the ideal, they have had to follow stricter guidelines than the singers on the lower parts, not just in singing two to a part even in eight-part music where the other lines are being sung solo, but in working more precisely in the business of 'staggering the breathing' (see 'Staggering' p. 209, where this is described in detail). There have been times when an audience has not noticed the presence of an unsuitable alto, tenor or bass (though repeated listening would soon give it away); but it is impossible to mask an unsuitable soprano timbre, from the very first phrase. Any idea, incidentally, that these sopranos sound like boys is just proof that the person who thinks it has not listened closely to either party. Certainly these sopranos sound MORE like boys than the traditional operatic soprano, but that is a benchmark so wide of what is being discussed here that it is effectively irrelevant.

It stands to reason that polyphony should be sung in a style derived from the music which preceded the renaissance period, rather than from the music which succeeded it. But however much it may stand to reason, in practice it is impossible to undo the training we have all had in later repertoires; which is just another way of saying that we live in a different era from the renaissance and are entitled to bring music of the past alive to modern ears. Over the years the Tallis Scholars have felt their way towards a balance between singing with voices trained in a modern way and singing in a style which we think suits the music. This is a compromise, but at least it has come from specialising in this one repertoire, and thinking only about how best to put sound to it. The ideal in one way would be only ever to have sung plainchant before approaching polyphony, to know only the kind of legato which that music requires, to feel the way chant melodies flow and build and fall away, never to have been in hock to a bar-line. But the untrained voices of monks, such as can be heard on the historical recordings of the monks of Solesmes, only have a limited impact, which would not have enough purchase in a modern symphony hall to hold a large audience. Our compromise was inevitable and, judged by the strictest standards of what the music demands, its success has been partial. I have never heard a choir trained only in plainchant singing polyphony so that a big hall can be filled by their sound, and I never will. But I have heard countless choirs singing polyphony in mixed programmes with later music and have noted how uncomfortable the early repertoire can sound, hijacked by four-bar phrasing, sudden louds and softs, little sense of where those long, melismatic phrases are going. (The nearest one is likely to get to this ideal is with choirboys, who spend much of their singing lives concentrating on chant in services. Of course they are still modern people, influenced by listening to later music, but I was struck by hearing the boys of Westminster Cathedral sing some nineteenth-century music recently. It sounded almost ridiculous because they had been taught to sing the words legato, as suits the performance of chant, running the syllables together in a smooth continuum quite unsuitable for the boxed-up phrases in question. But for decades now they have been famous for their stylish performances of polyphony, that style greatly aided by their daily experience of chant-singing.)

I never audition singers because I doubt that I shall be able to tell from their prepared pieces – or whatever people bring to these occasions – how well they can sing polyphony. Presumably I would learn something about the type of voice they have and how quick they are at sight-reading, but I shall not learn how well they listen to their neighbours, how instinctively they are prepared to blend with them and what feeling they have for melodic lines which only exist in the context of other such lines. We are fortunate in having a wide choice of candidates in London, and these days I tend to leave the final decision of who will join us to the singer whom the newcomer has to stand next to. That way there should be a meeting of minds, at least, before we start. And just as I may never have heard a singer before his or her first rehearsal with us, I am careful to judge very little on that or any rehearsal, but only by what I hear in concert, and preferably across many concerts. The only fair way to judge a singer who has an aptitude for polyphony is to judge them on an average, both because the demands of the repertoire are varied, and because everyone is entitled to an off-day. I have thrilled to the debut of people who can realise the most perfect high Palestrina part in the relaxed circumstances of a rehearsal, only to wonder what I was so excited about when listening to them sing it in bad acoustics in a concert; or when fate dealt them a part which lay consistently just too low for them (in bad acoustics in a concert). The average is crucial, not to mention the time it takes for a newcomer to get used to the minutiae of our style: the meticulously metrical placing of the shorter notes (newcomers standardly rush quavers and semi-quavers for a good few months); acquiring that desired legato phrasing throughout a whole programme; not half-expecting the music to slow down (and go flat) at the soft passages or speed up at the loud ones.

One of the decisions the conductor of polyphony has to make in advance is what pitch to sing it at. By and large we have adopted the theory articulated by David Wulstan, which is to transpose most of the repertoire up a minor third from written pitch on the grounds that a written note in the renaissance period represented a sound nearly a minor third higher than what that written note means to us. Whatever one thinks of the evidence for this, the results can be very distinctive, especially in English music. I mention this here because the decision whether to transpose or not has serious repercussions for the balance and the clarity of the ensemble. We have been criticised more consistently and with greater reason for our high-pitch interpretations of English music than for anything else. It stands to reason that if the top part (called 'treble') goes very high the lower parts, especially if they include one or more low Tudor countertenor lines, are likely to be obliterated. There are two alternatives: be inconsistent and sing this particular repertoire at untransposed pitch; or shape up to the demands. I say inconsistent because it has long been standard practice to sing the non-treble repertoire up a minor third or more.

I still choose to grapple with the rather exotic problems of the high-pitch solution firstly because I miss the light-weightedness of the sound at written pitch, and secondly because I find that the imbalances caused by the voice-ranges at high pitch are simply transferred down the texture at low pitch. Of course it takes a little longer to notice them, since the highest part is now likely to be less dominant, but sooner or later one wishes the tenors would not have to sing so persistently high, especially with the basses now rather low for younger voices. The altos too can sound uncomfortably high, with the result that the bottom part can disappear, while the middle of the texture is in danger of being overstated and thick. Preferring antiphons to sound more airy than massive, I have tried to produce a treble part which is gossamer-light. This is a very difficult thing to do, and without the exceptionally high-lying voices of Deborah Roberts, Jan Coxwell and Ruth Holton it would have been a vain quest – and anyway it took many years to hone. In the early years of the group there was a constant danger of the singers, and the audience in sympathetic reaction, coming away from the bigger pieces (and they are long) with sore throats. Now, not least in *Spem*, which has eight of these high parts, experience has suggested the way forward. It is possible to float them in such a way as to make them sound expressive rather than demanding, and to go some way towards keeping a good balance with the lower parts.

One way to help the balance is to employ a high tenor on the countertenor parts alongside falsettists. In the same way one can also add a high baritone to the tenor part. The need for these combinations is really only an admission that renaissance voice-ranges do not conform to what we expect and to what is taught in singing lessons today, something which has to be faced up to not just in Tudor polyphony but in most Flemish polyphony too. Singers of this repertoire simply have to be prepared to adapt what they know to the circumstances, and in the case of doubling with another voice-type this means taking over or yielding the line as it comes into or goes out of one's range. At the same time, all the singers on the line need to contribute to the overall interpretation, which requires a degree of sensitivity unlikely to be found in the kind of professional who comes to the job thinking, 'This is what I've been taught to do, this is my voice-type: I'm not prepared to sing in any other way.' One sympathises with, but does not employ such thinkers. (For a further insight into this androgynous world see the section under 'Roving', p. 206.) And speaking of androgyny, it has been a source of strength in the Tallis Scholars in recent years to have employed a male and female alto alongside each other. Originally, when we were still trying to ape the cathedral set-up, it was thought that this was going too far in the direction of a purely secular sound. But it has worked really well, yielding a perfect blend and giving the flexibility of an overall range which can be very wide if the male will sing in chest voice for the lowest notes and the female will fill out the difficult notes for a falsettist, just below the stave. The success of it stands as a tribute to the sensitivity of the singers in question: Caroline Trevor, Robert Harre-Jones and, more recently, Patrick Craig. We have never employed a female tenor, though in theory we would.

These tessituras beg the question what kind of performer renaissance composers did expect to use, since it is hard to believe that throats have changed that much in a few hundred years, or that diet has had quite such a transforming effect on ranges. My guess, which can never be proved, is that once again later thinking has got in the way. It is very likely that in the days before voices had to be heard over orchestras modern projection techniques were not considered. When ordinary vocalists today sing to themselves (or down a microphone if in public) they make no attempt to project their voices, but sing lightly in the throat, head-voice or falsetto as the range requires. Renaissance ranges strongly suggest that this was the contemporary singers' method, implying that we should model ourselves not on Jessye Norman but on Sting. No self-respecting singing academy would charge to teach people what they can do naturally, which would explain why there isn't any evidence of voice tuition until instrumental participation forced the issue. I also take the point that if I am correct I am presenting just another argument which shows that the loud, steely-bright sound the Tallis Scholars make must be far from how renaissance choirs sounded.

Apart from the unfamiliar ranges which Josquin, Cornysh, Taverner and their mid-renaissance contemporaries regularly deal the modern choir, there is the less discussed problem posed by Palestrina. This forms a little area for study all by itself. Where English composers tended to double the countertenor part when writing in more than four parts, Palestrina doubled the tenors. Not only is this inconsiderate in the modern context, where tenors are the least findable of all the voice-ranges, but Palestrina compounded the problem by writing unusually high parts for these tenors, regularly peaking on high A at written pitch. And even if high A to Palestrina and his contemporaries was not what we hear as high A, because of a concatenation of adjustments made necessary by changing practices, the 'tenors' will still be singing a third higher at the top of their range than the 'sopranos' at the top of theirs, which never happened in English music, even when the top part had the 'mean' range and the trebles were absent. It is rare in the Flemish school as well. The regularity with which Palestrina wrote these ranges does pose some questions about which voice-types he really had in mind. Since we know little about the sound the singers of the Sistine Chapel choir made in his time – except that there were no boys or castrati – it is very hard for us to imagine what sound he heard. Presumably there were falsettists and high tenors in abundance, but that assumption in itself does not sort out the practical difficulty of having two equal-range voices towards the bottom of a five-part texture which regularly sing within a sixth of the top part. Palestrina's unique voice-ranges suggest there was no other ensemble with quite the same make-up and therefore sound anywhere else.

Modern editors, wanting to sell copies to the standard SATB choir, have tended to avoid Palestrina's five-part pieces in favour of his four- and six-part ones, a policy which at a stroke has considerably restricted knowledge of his work. The modern need is to find pieces first with two soprano parts, and second, with two of anything else. Five-part Palestrina with two sopranos is very rare, whereas his six-part writing often has two sopranos with two altos or tenors. So it is that there are many recordings of Palestrina's *Missa Assumpta est Maria* (SSATTB) and none except ours of his *Missa Nigra sum* or *Missa Sicut lilium* (both SATTB), despite their outstanding quality. There are many more Masses and motets in this awkward category. What is to be done? Everything points to the unpopular solution of transposing a very great deal of Palestrina's music down something like a fourth, and scoring it for falsettists (or possibly just high tenors) on top, and arranging the other parts between a mixture of low tenors, baritones, basses and low basses. (The problem of the modern collegiate choir having only young voices and therefore no profundi of course did not apply to the Sistine Chapel employees, whose average age in fact was high.) If one were to do this across the board the current view of Palestrina's bright, luminous sound-world would have to be radically redetermined. But although the staff-lists in the sixteenth-century Sistine Chapel suggest this solution, we have other options. If we transpose Palestrina down a tone his standard ranges often become a modest soprano part, ordinary alto, highish tenor and highish bass or multiple thereof. This has been the normal reading of Palestrina since he was revived in the nineteenth century, and looks within reasonable bounds on paper. The only problem is that the tessitura of the tenor and bass parts remains high for older singers, the tenors in particular finding a whole mass (and especially the *Missa Papae Marcelli*) at this pitch extremely hard work even though they never sing above G.

Ficta is the one area of performance practice which leaves me cold, though I feel it should not. After all, a piece can be transformed by its ficta. The English repertoire would be quite undone if those famous clashes, most of them created by ficta, were disallowed. Gombert's music would have been hailed years ago if he had been allowed the same ficta-rights as the English all along. But although certain basic requirements have not changed in my

ground-plan for performing polyphony these thirty years – such as ignoring all the nonsense about contemporary regional pronunciations of Latin,
English, French and the rest; finding just the right voices to suit my aural
vision – ficta finds me fumbling and weaving, changing my mind every few
years.

My craven hope is always that the editor will have been reliable in taking the necessary decisions, that those decisions are good ones, and that
there is not going to be any argument about them in rehearsal. I would
rather not be asked what my preference is, but if I am, my answer until about
ten years ago was to cut the whole lot out (witness our recording of Brumel's
'Earthquake' Mass, which is a monument to the pre-Raphaelite approach)
in the interests of consistency. Since then I have proceeded by degrees, from
putting in sharpened leading-notes at cadences, to putting them in more
widely, with every variation in between. I have finally been weaned from the
faux-medieval sound which was installed in me by the editors of those
daunting Complete Works/Opera Omnia editions published from the
1930s onwards; but I have not yet fully embraced the hard-line melody-only
argument which says that when the leading-note leads to the final it should
standardly be sharpened no matter what the harmonic context. Nor am I always swayed by the avoiding of the tritone as a reason for adding ficta. Let
them sing diminished fifths if the impact of the music benefits from it. And
I am so used to Cornysh's *Ave Maria* without any ficta at all that I find the
music means almost nothing to me when ficta is added, against all my current instincts. Ironically I may be being uncharacteristically authentic when
I consult only my own predilections in the matter of ficta: there is good reason for thinking that was how it was for the original scribes. The problem
is that there is so much choice, and so little in the way of certain guidelines.

At the end of such a discussion one may fittingly invoke the quotation I put
at the head of the Introduction to this volume (p. 9). The architect and the-
oretician Leonbattista Alberti did more than anyone to define what renaissance humanism was about. In around 1460 he defined beauty in building
as 'a harmony of all the parts, fitted together with such proportion and connection that nothing could be added, diminished or altered but for the
worse'. He may have lived and worked rather earlier than the composers we
associate with renaissance music – he died in 1472; but music has always

brought up the rear in following the defining philosophy of an era, and Alberti's buildings, along with those of the next generation, represented by Brunelleschi, are the perfect expression of what I hold to be typical of all renaissance sacred music, whether of the 1510s by Josquin or the 1570s by Palestrina. Standing in the Pazzi Chapel in Florence, or the Tempio Malatestiana in Rimini, one can see what can also be heard in the music: that if the overall proportions are well-calculated, sheer size does not matter. With sound mathematics underlying the structure one can have all the sense of harmoniousness, spaciousness and luminousness one could want, without a feeling of being dwarfed by massiveness for its own sake. And there is the advantage that on this renaissance human scale one can be closely in touch with the detail which goes to make up the whole. Alberti's idea that the whole was greater than the sum of its parts, but that the parts should be perfect in themselves, underlies all renaissance thought. There is no better definition of polyphony or how to present it.

4

AT HOME AND ABROAD: THE SPREAD
OF INTEREST IN POLYPHONY

Any attempt by me to claim that we were the first to do any of the things we do is sure to be met by someone somewhere (possibly in New York or Ghent) with snorts of indignation and copies of programmes from the late 1960s, which show that whole concerts of polyphony were commonplace long before the start of the Tallis Scholars. In fact I know that much, since I sang in the Clerkes of Oxenford (twice) whilst worshipping them, well aware that they had been singing concerts and making records of this music in the 1960s. I had also collected the discs of the Renaissance Singers, Cantores in Ecclesia, Schola Polyphonica, Scuola di Chiesa and the Choir of the Carmelite Priory, not to mention those of the choirs of King's College, Cambridge, St John's College, Cambridge, and Magdalen College, Oxford, and although I never attended any of their concerts I imagine they regularly performed polyphony and possibly nothing but polyphony.

So what do I claim? What profile is it that groups of singers in widely diverging countries have noticed and imitated? The idea of fielding a team of about ten singers as the optimum number has caught on, though I am always quick to point out that it was not so much the choice of ten that was important as the underlying principle that there should be two voices on each vocal part. And I think it has been generally recognised that this scoring produces a particular sound – as flexible as when there is one voice to a part but with greater sonority – which is the ideal to be aimed at; and the Tallis Scholars have come to epitomise that ideal.

Having said that, I cannot think of a single group that invariably turns out with ten singers. To state the obvious, they either have more or less. One or two have only had eight members (or even six – A Sei Voci trading on the fact), which means that they either sing nothing but four-part music with two voices a part, or they are obliged to move in the direction of sounding like a vocal ensemble rather than a choral one. To my ear the moment the top part (usually soprano but on occasion alto) has only one singer on it something radically different enters the aural frame, and 'the sound' leaves the realms of what I am trying to achieve. Ideally I would always put two singers on each part in every piece, but the Tallis Scholars have had to compromise. It is too expensive to have singers on tour who may only sing in one or two pieces, which means that unless we only sing eight-part music and have four each of sopranos, altos, tenors and basses – which would cover almost all eventualities – there would be unacceptable wastage. Our compromise is to try to ensure that the top part(s) always have two singers on them, which may mean in concert that some of the lower ones have only one. By and large the required sonority is preserved in this arrangement, though it will be observed that on our discs we have always used two singers throughout the texture no matter how grand (except in *Spem in alium*). Since the original idea of ten singers was modelled on Tudor music with its two soprano parts – one high, one low – our repertoire has tended towards music that is scored for SSATB (or TrMATB), though recently I have felt free to interpret the ten as involving only two sopranos but, say, four tenors, which has given a considerable extension of the available repertoire. Gombert's Magnificats come to mind.

Most ensembles singing polyphony tend to number slightly more than ten. Sixteen would be the maximum if one were to follow the layout as I have just described it, assuming music in no more than eight parts, but usually there are nearer 20 singers, and most lines most of the time are sung three to a part. If I am conducting one of these groups the hope is that I shall be able to form from them a sound something like that of the Tallis Scholars, without adopting one of our founding principles. We may have to sing music with only one to a part on occasion, but we have never sung with three. In the event I rarely insist on two when the three are there for good reason: they sing later repertoire like this and are used to each other. To take one away would expose the line in an unhelpful way, possibly making it uncertain and probably reducing the overall sonority. With the time constraints that usually apply, I prefer to make the most of what people are used to rather than start from scratch; but ultimately it remains the case that three singers on a line cannot at all easily phrase together, or even place final consonants together, because those on the outside will not be able to hear each other clearly enough, or be sure of being able to react to any other line. When the sound is going strong, the only voices a singer can hear are the ones next to them. Standing in a semicircle on-stage, rather than in two rows, is a presentation which can only work properly when every singer present is both in aural touch with the other singer on their line, and with the line next to them. This will automatically happen with two to a part, and cannot happen with three.

The most influential aspect of the Tallis Scholars' performing style is the sound itself. In essence this was not my creation either, since I first heard something very like it made by the Clerkes of Oxenford in 1972. David Wulstan got 'the sound' first, and he did it not least by sticking to his guns over the use of high pitch in Tudor music. I would say I have been trying to recapture the sound of the Clerkes ever since I started to worship them and their music-making, with the disadvantage that I cannot exactly remember what that sound was. Has it improved in my memory as time has gone by? Could it possibly have been as beautiful and effective as the sound we make now, with all the practice and effort that has gone into it? It seemed at the time, especially in English music, to be flawless, like a gem, something made possible by using young untrained voices and quite a number of them, certainly not ten. Normally the small-voice approach doesn't really work, since the ensemble can easily lack impact: as a general rule I try to avoid soft singing no matter what the context. It seemed to me that the 1972 Clerkes were never exactly soft or lacking in expression, yet they stood in two rows, had as many as four to a part and blended by virtue of having mostly small voices. The expressive element to me was their astonishing sense of line, sung with a perfect legato and excellent tuning; and I am tempted to say that what there was of sheer impact came from this tuning, since their sound had a ring to it, heightened by the acoustics of Magdalen College Chapel – they were a quite site-specific group – which didn't need loudness to make its effect. That to me was a definition of subtlety; and the scope of it increased as I slowly began to understand the quality of the music this sound was being applied to.

Since sound vanishes the moment it is made, and recordings can be misleading, it is quite possible that the prototype has been buried. What has been left in me is the desire for the same feelings when listening to polyphony as I had when I first heard it. This much I have certainly had, and I have discovered that there is a surprisingly wide toleration, within basic limits, of what sound may be produced to allow these feelings to flow. After all it has not been a question of trying to recapture a very precise sound-world created years ago – though that has been haunting – but of encouraging the people present to express the music as it occurs to them. This has equally involved not trying to turn other groups precisely into the Tallis Scholars.

One thing we can unquestionably claim as our own achievement is the extent to which our recordings have travelled round the world: no group in our line of business has sold so many copies of their discs in so many countries. The result is that knowledge of our sound, and by extension of our branch of the British choral sound, is very widespread. British singing in its different guises must have been one of the most influential exports the country has produced in recent decades, and it has led to many imitations. These have come in all shapes and sizes. At one extreme are directors like Renaldo Alessandrini, who told Gimell some years ago that the British sound had provided the building-blocks out of which he created his own edifice, which at the time was a remarkable thing for any Italian to say since the raw material simply didn't seem to be there. Concerto Italiano was the first sign to me that the northern hegemony over stylish polyphonic singing was about to be broken; and similar breaches have been made by quite a collection of other southern European groups since, some of which I have directed (see p. 152). Then there are the English groups who pay lip-service specifically to us, but always add in the same breath that they mean to do something 'more human' with the music, thus hoping to gain acceptance twice over. Finally there are the groups which more or less openly want, at least for the length of a project, to recreate as nearly as possible what they have heard on our records.

This process started as early as 1988, in Washington D.C., where a group called Vox formed by Pamela Berkeley invited me to direct them in a concert of Sheppard, Tye, Tallis and Tomkins. They were bold enough to tackle Tye's colossal motet *Peccavimus cum patribus nostris*, which showed me that there was a tradition there already. They were my introduction to the choral scene in the US, which has since supplied me with countless master classes, seminars and courses, and three first-rate ensembles to give concerts with: Vox, a descendant of the original group of that name, now in New York under the direction of George Steel; the Woodley Ensemble of Washington, D.C., currently directed by Frank Albinder; and The Tudor Choir of

Seattle under Doug Fullington. What has struck me about almost every en-counter I have had with young American singers who are interested in singing polyphony is the similarity of the voices, and the similarity of the circumstances in which the groups make music, to those I knew in the first ten years of the Tallis Scholars. Hovering between being paid (a little) and being amateur, with easy-going voices of real ability which are very often nurtured in church choirs and may well be untrained in any formal sense, content to range a little more widely than we ever did over the unaccompa-nied repertoire, but with renaissance polyphony as a focal point, these groups give concerts of the highest quality to larger audiences than we ever had as amateurs.

I wonder what their ambitions are. As if by instinct, these groups make the same basic sound the Tallis Scholars made before 1983, which other choirs in the English-speaking world, for example in Australia and New Zealand, make, and which experience suggests is potentially very mar-ketable. Obviously something in the language, culture, religion, in the Anglo-Saxon mentality is responsible for this. Unfortunately something in the Anglo-Saxon mentality is also responsible for the fact that public bod-ies tend not to pay for such delights. This is what distinguishes these careers and those of similar endeavour in France, Belgium, Holland, Spain and one or two other continental countries. There is nothing fundamentally differ-ent between the way these American groups were formed, and how, for ex-ample, the Collegium Vocale of Ghent began: young, talented amateurs who fell in love with singing in chamber choirs, who put themselves to con-siderable personal inconvenience, amounting at times to living a bohemian lifestyle, to join in; but the Belgian group was nurtured in an atmosphere of official support, from singing in festivals underwritten by public money, to eventually having a sizeable part of their annual budget paid for by the local council direct. Of course there are drawbacks to coming to rely on public handouts – like what do you do when there is a change of official policy and the money is withdrawn again? – but in fact in the broader view it never is completely withdrawn. It is deeply ingrained in these continental countries that culture is something everyone should pay for: and not just familiar es-tablished culture like opera houses and symphony orchestras, as their sup-port of singing polyphony goes to show.

The practical difference is that the administrators of the American

groups will spend much of their time looking for support from a wide spectrum of likely donors in order to put on a concert or a series of concerts
themselves, while the administrators of the European groups will spend
their time looking for already existing concerts, dealing directly with festivals all over the continent. Collegium, which was established in 1970, had a
hundred concerts in 2003; I doubt the American groups will put together 30
between them, a discrepancy which certainly does not reflect the relative
standards of the performances. The problem for an ensemble with only a
handful of events is how to form and keep a loyal core group, who can mature as performers together. Only giving concerts, preferably in diverse
places, will convince musicians of the kind needed in these specialist choirs
to give up their safe jobs and adopt the challenging and disruptive lifestyle
of itinerant singers; and only concerts (not rehearsals) will form their sound.
The next step for these American ensembles is a very difficult one. They are
where we were in 1983, and although we never had a penny of government
money, we had more opportunity for concerts because our cultural centres
– London, Oxford, Cambridge – are geographically closer together than
theirs. It is not clear yet how they will break out of their respective areas,
should they want to, but they can take heart from the fact that in the renaissance period alone there is two hundred years' of music to sing, almost all
of it unexplored. There is a public for it; the era for independent record labels seems to have dawned; editions can be made easily and cheaply. They
are potentially in demand.

As I say, the continental European countries tend to be more generous
with public money in support of private cultural initiatives than Britain or
the US, where such initiatives are allowed to sink or swim according to the
dictates of the marketplace. The Tallis Scholars have only ever received tax-
payers' money through such bodies as the British Council, who will occasionally contribute to our costs abroad if we are advertising British culture,
and the Arts Council, who once or twice have given us unbelievably small
sums of money in the hope of kick-starting a project in the provinces. We
have never received a regular annual hand-out, which has meant that the initial stages of setting up the group were more perilous than they might have
been, but that, once established, we had not come to depend on outside assistance, a state of mind which can destroy otherwise healthy organisations.
Nonetheless, two of the best continental groups I have worked with owe

their continuing existence at least in part to government support, though I suspect there is never enough of it for them really to break out and realise their dreams. These are Bo Holten's Ars Nova of Copenhagen, and JanJoost van Elburg's Lelikoor of Amsterdam, whom I worked with in 1989 and 1999 respectively. Both Bo and JanJoost are highly experienced polyphonists as well as experienced conductors of a wider repertoire, so it came as no surprise that their groups were receptive to the music I wanted to do with them. The main problem in rehearsal was my idiosyncratic conducting method, which in Amsterdam reduced one participant to tears – a salutary lesson all round I felt. In addition to benefiting from the opportunity to work with their groups – which I have never offered them or anyone else in return – I have learnt some of the most useful lessons about my work from these two men. It was Bo who introduced me to the music of Nicolas Gombert, telling me once that it had a quality which made one want to hug it – a description I have never bettered – and giving me an edition of his eight-part Credo that had such wonderful ficta inflections added by Bo that I still cannot bring myself to remove them. Similarly, to JanJoost I owe many hours of discussion over the whole range of renaissance music, as well as insights into how to get the best from one's singers. However, some years ago Ars Nova offered an interesting lesson in what can happen when democracy gets out of hand. Because the group had government support its members automatically acquired certain legal rights over the organisation. One day Bo found that he had been voted out of office by a majority of his own singers and there was nothing he could do to stop them, even though, like the rest of us, he had set the group up from scratch with his own money. I nervously fingered my neck when I heard this story, more than ever determined not to ask outsiders for assistance. In the end Bo simply started another group – Musica Ficta – with some of the same people and rather less government involvement, which continues his good work to the present.

The other side of the public sponsorship coin are those groups which were set up by an official body, like a radio station, to act as in-house ensembles with unlimited financing. My experience with these has been very mixed, and the first of them I was too inexperienced to cope with. In 1985 I was invited to direct the Netherlands Chamber Choir, the only salaried choir in Holland outside the opera houses. The difference between them and what I had been used to in England from the amateur days was total, and bewildering to me. Where talented amateurs with light voices very often have the technique to manage the demands of polyphony without serious trouble, and will rehearse long hours as necessary for the pleasure of it, the Chamber Choir singers were highly-trained professionals of wide experience in choral singing, whose sights, more or less realistically, were set on a solo career. The style of polyphony did not come easily to many of them, not least because there was a sizeable element in the choir which actively disliked the music. Being in effect civil servants, they had carefully articulated, highly-politicised, working conditions which obliged them to rehearse according to an immutable pattern: between 10.00 and 1.00, never in the afternoons or evenings, with an exactly timed break and the fine of a guilder for every minute anyone was late. These conditions also gave them generously paid leaves of absence in case of illness. I have never known a small group of people to be so ill. Nor have I felt such an unco-operative spirit in the guise of a co-operative one. Even the music, which once had seemed so fluent and easy, now seemed to be riddled with technical traps and difficulties, which I was made to understand was demanding more of them than some thought reasonable. There was nothing I could give them, and I have not been back.

Frustrated soloists who spend their working days singing a lot of very taxing contemporary music – for this is what these official choirs tend to end up doing – are probably not in the right frame of mind for polyphony anyway. At least the sheer difficulty of much contemporary writing keeps their minds engaged; polyphony is at once too easy and too communal. The actual notes in any polyphony that is not by Gesualdo must be the easiest things to read in the entire choral repertoire, though I realise my insisting on the pinpoint tuning of them may muddy the waters; but the real barrier is the need for the sound to be choral. No individual voice should stand out in the ideal performance, only a line can, and that line will have at least two singers on it. These singers need to work as one, burying vocal foibles and projecting personalities to make a unanimous interpretation. Perhaps the chance of success operates in inverse proportion to how much each singer is dying to have his or her own name in lights, but in my experience some of these more formal choirs have tamed this instinct far enough to make it a pleasure to work with them. The Finnish Radio Choir, which I conducted in November 1989, was a good example, singing Spanish music as if the outside temperature was something warmer than minus 20°. And in May 2003, finally after a number of stand-offs, I was invited to conduct the BBC Singers.

I was nervous about this, not least because the Singers had become something of a football in my seemingly unending spat with the BBC hierarchy. I was nervous also because I knew that this ultimately professional ensemble was not going to be converted to polyphony wholesale, no matter how persuasive I was. Some of their voices are not formed for 'early music', as they are quick to call polyphony, and those that are fully relaxed with the idiom would not have an interest in preferring any one kind of music over another as a matter of policy. We could all do our best, but it was in the nature of the make-up of the Singers that there was no question of a tearaway readjustment of thinking on their part, such as I am describing with some of the other more impressionable groups here. I knew all this, and yet I was surprised. For a start, nothing had prepared me for the intensity with which a full-time professional ensemble of this calibre works. When I made my points – provided I didn't waffle – there was total silence. They would then do what I asked exactly and immediately, with perfect understanding and commitment. I could ask for whatever I wanted. It was a kind of fairyland of opportunity with no limits. If I had the imagination, they had the technique; and since sound is the currency I deal in I had no problem at all with the size of the sound they could make. My job was to shape their singing in the service of the music, just the same as usual, but with the perspective element, the range of available sonorities and colours, greatly increased. The results weren't like those of the specialist ensembles, but they were stylish within the terms we had set ourselves, and infinitely flexible in interpretation. The main onus on me was to show consistently and clearly exactly what I wanted, otherwise, with so many other influences on them from yesterday and the day before yesterday, the members of this superb instrument would quickly go their own way.

Ironically it has been a choir made up in part of opera-chorus singers which has produced some of the most moving music-making I have known outside the Tallis Scholars. One might have thought that such people would be too close to the ethos of vibratoful singing to want or be able to fit in with what I have been describing. But then the circumstances of their lives are not normal. Living in Novosibirsk, Siberia, they are more cut off from the standard concert-giving circuit even than West Coast groups in the US and Canada.

If I've got the story right, Markell's Voices was set up by a Georgian from Tblisi, Igor Tjuvayev, on the model of the Tallis Scholars, to sing mostly renaissance music. The choice of repertoire in itself was remarkable. Whereas Germany produced few renaissance composers of any repute, which has caused the natives of that country to take more interest in the baroque, Russia had no renaissance period of any description. Instead they have their own church music, which is sung in a very different way from polyphony. To find a group like this with a public following in such an isolated place defies all the rules of probability. Igor's information about how and what we sang must have come from pirated copies of our CDs with their characteristic photocopied booklets – I have now seen many of them – because we have never been able to sell our discs in Russia due to the weak currency. I knew nothing of Markell's Voices until 1999 when, to my astonishment, I received a fax from Igor inviting me to go to Siberia and give two concerts with his group. When I arrived I found about sixteen singers sitting in our characteristic semicircle ready to perform movements from Taverner's 'Western Wind' Mass (not an easy piece) alongside music by Gibbons and Victoria. They were singing from copies which had been made by photocopying a single original, cutting out each voice-part separately and sticking the individual lines onto one page and photocopied again, in order to reduce the costs of making a complete set. This was less than ideal because the cutting and pasting had inevitably obscured things, and no one present except me had the whole score in front of them. The old part-book format had returned with a vengeance.

I soon discovered that with perfect authenticity these copies were only being used as aide-mémoires and that the singers had come close to learning the music off by heart, in part by listening to our recordings. I was thus presented with more or less perfect versions of interpretations I had mongered anything up to 15 years earlier. The problem for me was to undo the thoughts I had had in the meantime. With sign-language and goodwill various compromises were effected and I began to hear a radically different view of how polyphony can sound, a sound which was made dramatically apparent at the first down-beat of my first rehearsal, conducting Victoria's *O quam gloriosum*. On those arresting opening chords first the altos and then

the basses gave me a taste of how resonant well-produced straight low voices can be. The bass entry was like driving a sports car full throttle up the fast
lane. I got addicted to that ensemble sound, and have been back several
times to repeat the experience, despite the lack of money and the extreme
weather. I felt from the start that if highly-trained singers cobbling together a living in a provincial opera chorus, or busking in the local Mexican
restaurant (yes, there is one) wanted to sing polyphony I was the person to
encourage them. In return I have had the experience of coming to grips with
daily life in a most unusual place.

Novosibirsk is situated in the fourth of the seven time-zones across Russia, going east. Japan and Taiwan are further east still, yet interest in European renaissance music has not been confined to Europe and its remoter
outposts, of which Novosibirsk is just as much an example as Seattle, Sydney or Wellington. I was once asked where I thought the next Tallis Scholars sound-alike would come from, and I unhesitatingly replied Japan. This
remark was based on the ability of the Japanese to imitate what they hear
and see; and I reasoned that although there are quite a few sound-alikes
nearer home, at least the Japanese would not be pretending to be something
else, but would rate their success according to how precisely they did manage to copy us, rather than the opposite. So far I have not led a Japanese choir
in a full-blown, week-long project with a concert at the end of it; by contrast, the Taipei Chamber Singers in 2001 invited me to do just that, the
week's rehearsals culminating in a concert in the incomparable Taipei Symphony Hall. I have long admired the sound in this hall, as much for the fact
that it rivals the acoustics of Russell Johnson's spaces in Lucerne and Birmingham as that it dates from several decades ago, long before the kind of hi-
tech, computer-aided calculations Johnson can call on were available. It
must count as something of an acoustical fluke, easily outclassing any of the
much more modern Japanese halls I know, though I think the highly-pol-
ished redwood panels which hang throughout the interior must have something to do with the way the sound carries in there. Anyway, inspired by this
prospect, I asked the singers to undertake a really big programme, one the
Tallis Scholars might think twice about doing every night of a tour, forget-
ting a little that the Taiwanese might not be fully fluent in the polyphonic
idiom. The rhythms in Josquin's motet *Praeter rerum seriem* caused them the
most difficulty; but after a strategic pep-talk just before going on their con-

centration was at the sticking-point and nothing went astray. I'm sure the results sounded beautiful in that hall; and the audience numbered over 1500 people. The Tallis Scholars have been listened to by similar numbers both there, in Hong Kong and in the Symphony Hall of Seoul, South Korea.

Differing national characteristics can prepare people differently for polyphony. Something in the make-up of the lives of the Siberians gives them a natural facility for dark sounds in the context of unusually low notes (one speculates about vowel sounds in their language, their physical size, how much they smoke or drink vodka). The altos were as adept at this as the basses, while the upper voices seemed to need to import a foreign training (from Italian opera) to be able to manage the higher tessituras, which subtly affected the ease with which the different lines were realised in the ensemble sound. The Spanish singers I have worked with in Musica Reservata of Barcelona also naturally produce dark sounds, but in higher-pitched voices, yielding an ensemble sound which is different again and peculiarly well adapted to the music of Victoria and his contemporaries. Spanish music (and art in general) has a reputation for being 'darkly' passionate. Michelangelo noticed some aspect of this in the renaissance period itself, when he advised the Florentine painter Pontormo to 'show much blood and nails' when working for the Spaniards; and those are attributes one can almost hear in Victoria's Responsories for Tenebrae. Musica Reservata, started by Jordi Abelló and much encouraged by Bruno Turner over the years, is one of the pioneering groups, alongside I Cantori di Lorenzo in Florence and Officium in Lisbon, which has begun to show that singing is not all opera in the Mediterranean countries, and, more than that, has chosen to specialise in polyphony. It is often too easy to say that singers from a particular country are the best equipped to sing their own music, but in the case of these Spaniards there is clearly some truth in it, since their unusually plangent tone quality, driven by the dark vowel-sounds, seems to fit Victoria's music like a glove. And not only Victoria. Their rendition of Guerrero's *Hei mihi, Domine*, with its sustained dissonances, or of Lobo's *Versa est in luctum*, was a revelation to me.

Clichéd though the thought may be, I have always wanted to hear Palestrina sung by Italians. I have always supposed that the English view of Palestrina – gleaming, pristine, the ultimate technical challenge – could only be part of the story, and that something in my make-up prevents me from understanding further. I reasoned that the Italians of all people should be able to bring out the innate warmth in his music and so revise the image we all have of him as a daunting pedagogue. The work of I Cantori di Lorenzo under Filippo Bressan has not gone far enough yet to prove this point one way or the other since it doesn't help anyone performing Palestrina that he really does demand a technical control which only years of specialisation can bring, and this is a young group; but even in our first project together I was struck by how my English ways did not completely turn the music of this Roman into something from the north. In the first place they had a fluency with the Latin which immediately removed a difficult area of interpretation. There was never any doubt about how the texts should be pronounced, or what they meant, leaving me free to proceed straight on to the business of constructing a sound in which the language was completely secure. Palestrina's Italianness has always struck post-eighteenth-century outsiders as an uncertain quantity, hard to place; but if one thinks of the style of the painting which Italy produced just before Palestrina reached maturity – especially in the religious work of Giovanni Bellini and Botticelli – a different facet of 'Italian' comes through. Instead of the tiresome sob in the throat and the dreary white handkerchief at the ready, one finds gentleness, innocence, a natural emotional distance and a technique unsurpassed in design and (colour) sonority, beside which Palestrina sits perfectly, making me wonder whether the sheer power of northern polyphonic singing can ever quite capture what is ineffable in his music. Since the Italians I know tend to have more of this gentleness and innocence in their natures than the inclination to allow their lives to be dominated by the routine emotional scenes popular culture assigns them, it came as no surprise that I Cantori were able to show me what the way forward for me with Palestrina might consist of. I had the same opportunity during the new annual course in Rimini, set up by Andrea Angelini in 2002 on the Oakham model to encourage Italian interest in polyphony. I have noticed amongst the participants there exactly the same affinity with Latin, the same delight in Palestrina, and even a solution to one of the problems posed by Palestrina's scoring (see p. 137): there are standardly more tenors taking part than any other voices.

Whether nationals of one country are the most qualified to realise something important in their own polyphonic repertoires depends as much on the music having an individual sound as on the talents of the people themselves. The great Portuguese school of polyphony is interesting in this respect because to my ear it doesn't have a distinctive sound-world. It is unquestionably individual, but this individuality is expressed through harmony, not counterpoint, and distinctive sound-worlds in polyphony are created by part-writing. Counterpoint can also accommodate unusual harmony – one thinks of Gesualdo – but to rely on harmony is not enough. In fact the Portuguese didn't rely on harmony, despite writing their music so late in the history of the renaissance period, and despite some astonishing augmented chords in the music of Cardoso; yet one still looks in vain for something to single out as specifically Portuguese. This is not so true of the other schools of composers, even in the case of their minor figures. The Portuguese use of augmented harmony though, alongside some rather fusty examples of double counterpoint using inversion in the imitative part-writing, does suggest a mature, almost 'noble rot' approach to the style which at its best can produce wonderful additions to the vocabulary in its own terms. Much of this repertoire is unquestionably great music, and I am proud to have brought this fact to the attention of a wider public by recording Cardoso's Requiem. That Requiem, alongside Cardoso's six-part Lamentations and Magnificat secundi toni can rival anything to come from Spain in the period from 1620 onwards.

Even the Portuguese find it hard to make something distinctively their own of this repertoire, despite the fact that in speech they have one of the most unusual sound-worlds of all the European languages; and indeed in the only project I have done so far with Officium of Lisbon we sang an all-English programme at the request of their founder Pedro Teixheira. Nonetheless they are justifiably proud that a small country such as theirs should have produced such a distinguished and prolific school of composers. Some years ago this encouraged Helena Zuber to start a course in Evora dedicated only to music which was written in Evora, or at least by composers associated with the cathedral there. To spend weeks concentrating only on the compositions of a single town is unique in my experience of singing courses; not even the Flemish have tried it. Add to that the fact that all the music in question is unaccompanied polyphony and that knowledge of this repertoire and style of singing in Portugal can hardly be described even now as being deeply established, and one begins to grasp how idealistic this initiative was: idealistic and tenacious, as it has turned out, with whole choirs coming to join the

Portuguese attendees on the course – from Kosice, Slovakia, one year, and from Sicily another. Whether or not these foreign choirs knew exactly what they were heading for when they set out in their buses across Europe to get to this remote place, hundreds of people have now spent many days studying nothing but Cardoso, Duarte Lôbo, Magalhães, Martins, Melgas, de Brito, Morago and the rest. Portuguese baroque music with instruments would have been easier, and better guaranteed to give instant satisfaction to such a wide constituency of amateur musicians, but the polyphony is unquestionably the greater music and Helena was not to be distracted. So she has given us all the unique feeling of standing in a building – Evora cathedral – once a year to perform music which was written only by people who had stood exactly there centuries earlier. The Jornadas Internacionais of Evora are a powerful example of the new more generalised interest in polyphony.

I am not going to talk here of the Englishness of English music, and whether we are best equipped to bring it alive. I am sorry that the perceived British hegemony over polyphonic singing seems to have scared so many non-British groups away from this repertoire, because this has only gone to heighten an impression that it is an art apart. Of course it is not; the English repertoire simply contains some of the best and most individual music of the whole period, individual because it was less influenced by the Flemish than most national repertories. For this reason any concert programme which sets out to compare different settings of the same text will benefit from having some English examples, since they do tend to conjure up their own sound-world. But at the very least it is not an imperative that the English must sing them. We have nothing in our throats which other nationals do not have: countertenors are everywhere these days; the high pitch theory does not have to be adopted; and of all the European languages English has probably changed more in its pronunciation since the sixteenth century than any other, so we cannot even claim primacy in the ticklish business of the vowel-sounds. All that has happened is that the English have been performing their own music very well for some time, lending it a sound which is now widely regarded as being in some way authentic. I do think the light, bright legato sound we make suits the long lines of Taverner and Tallis, but there is every reason for thinking this is a modern construct. Let other minds and throats come to bear on the subject, otherwise the world will tire of this music sooner than it needs to.

Exactly the opposite is the case with the Flemish repertoire: every group interested in polyphony wants to sing it, for good and obvious reasons. The music is of the very highest quality, the greatest there is, and at the time it was seminal in a way other national schools were not. Whatever the theme of the festival or concert one is planning for, it is very hard not to include some music by Flemish composers, because they travelled just about everywhere and led the way in every significant compositional endeavour. Yet the fascinating aspect of their story is that although they went everywhere, it was not until the high renaissance compositions of de Wert, de Rore and late Lassus that their music started to lose its Flemish flavour. For nearly two centuries their training, their instincts for music, their aesthetic make-up held Europe in thrall.

Yet despite the consistency of their native technique, which was based in solid mathematical principles, the leading composers of the Flemish school inevitably acquired an international dimension in their writing. Between them, men like Josquin, Isaac, Ockeghem, Dufay, Rogier, Gombert, Willaert and Lassus must have travelled as widely as anybody in the renaissance world, and some of the music they found on their travels, especially in the secular repertories, rubbed off on them. The Flemish wrote chansons, madrigals, villancicos, villanellas, rondos, ballades, alongside their own souterliedekens, with the best of the local writers; and as they allowed their own rigorously constructed sacred edifices to become less formal during the sixteenth century, one could say that sunnier elements also eventually found their way into the heart of the Flemish style. The question here is what modern Flemish performers make of this colossal achievement. Are they in a better position than all their many competitors to understand and interpret it, especially given that from as long as anyone can remember the 'sound' in Flemish music has been formed by groups from all over Europe and America, of differing sizes, with widely differing modus operandi?

Collegium Vocale of Ghent, founded by Philippe Herreweghe in 1970 to sing Flemish polyphony, goes about providing an answer to this question in an unusual but appropriate way. It was founded with Flemish singers, but standardly employs a mixture of foreigners alongside them. When I worked with them in March 2003 there were 15 singers of whom five were Flemish, four German, three English, two Dutch and one Latvian. I was thus presented with the inverse of what I am used to in England, where we tend, like an army unit, to put our trust only in people who have been brought up like ourselves speaking English in the same tradition, by which I mean the English cathedral choral tradition. Yet there is a neat equivalence here between the make-up of the Flemish and English groups in question, and the way their renaissance composers went about their careers: the Flemish international, multi-lingual, adding outside ideas to their own cultural identity; the English isolated, mono-lingual, cultivating the only style in western Europe to remain *sui generis*, at least until the internationalising influence of the Reformation came to bear on it. The only issue which remained to be decided was whether I, with my background, would be able to form a coherent ensemble sound out of such disparate material. If I was ever worried I should have remembered that the Flemish are past masters at making undertakings of this sort work; indeed, being a small nation at a geographical crossroads, who have had to accept all kinds of infractions of where they belong, including at one time the abandonment of their religion, they have had little option but to make such things work, for many centuries. They do it by being accepting, relaxed, organised and determined. They would have known what made Josquin and his colleagues tick as people; and, given more time to study the repertoire in depth – they seem to spend their days singing foreign baroque music – I believe their mindset would be ideal for understanding why Josquin wrote as he did.

If ever I saw Voltaire's smile of reason, it was on the faces of some of these Flemish singers as they performed polyphony, which brings me to an interesting point of definition. The Flemish school of composers has always been referred to by academics as Franco-Flemish, unlike the Flemish school of painters from the same epoch and territory which is much more accurately called Netherlandish. There is no good reason for the use of the term Franco-Flemish. Although some of the composers in question have French-sounding names, they all came from a narrow geographical area which had historically been part of the lands of the Dukes of Burgundy: the word Netherlandish neatly includes the residents of what later became northeastern France as part of that different tradition. As I far as I'm aware not one of the great polyphonists came from what was France in the years before Burgundy broke up, even though they may have had French as their first language, like Josquin. Brumel, Compère and Févin – not of the first rank – were properly French by this definition, yet even they came from the north-east. Where were the polyphonists from Bordeaux, Montpellier, Toulouse, Poitiers, Brest, even Paris? I insist on this a little because, if this national identifying is to be done properly, a sharp distinction needs to be drawn between the Flemish and the French, then as now. The French attitude to polyphony has always been one of intelligent interest tempered by unease. It is well known that in every epoch the French have instinctively turned to the more decorative elements in music, most notably dance music, and Flemish polyphony does not readily accommodate decoration. There is a rigour in it, and a lack of rhythmic life, which properly-French renaissance composers like Janequin and Le Jeune obviously found uncongenial. The history of Collegium Vocale curiously reflects this contrast. For years they were linked to the Chapelle Royale of Paris, also started by Philippe Herreweghe. I conducted the Chapelle in 1985 in a programme of largely Flemish polyphony written for the court of Prague – music by de Monte, Regnart, Vaet and the Slovenian composer Jacobus Gallus – when the ensemble was very roughly half Flemish and half French (with one Briton, Angus Smith). Nothing much was said at the time, at least to me, but it was obvious that the two halves of the ensemble were not thinking along the same lines. To over-simplify, the Flemish attitude was familiar to me from home: fluency with the notes, an understanding that the effects in the music were cumulative, that legato singing through the phrases to the cadences would provide all the shape the lines needed and that the words were often just pegs on which to hang abstract sounds. By contrast the French singers, all conservatoire-trained, started with the words, approaching the music as if every note had a special significance and almost as if it required a special vocal effect. In a sense they wanted to put too much weight onto each individual note, which, given that every singer in an evening of polyphonic music must sing several thousand of them, is going to need years of rehearsal if it is to be done properly. The end-result was a ponderous and yet tentative sound, constantly at war with itself as the two blocks tried to get to grips with what was an unusually esoteric programme.

It was inevitable that the two elements would go their separate ways, which by 2003 at least was what had happened: there were several European nations represented in Collegium for my project, but no French. In fact all these representatives came from northern Europe, which, given how homogeneous the results were, suggests something important about the nature of polyphony and the cultural differences between north and south, and begs some questions about what the local composers in the Mediterranean parts of the Flemish musical empire really thought of polyphony. One notices that the excellent French groups that specialise in renaissance music – A Sei Voci, the Ensemble Clément Janequin, the Ensemble Gilles Binchois – tend to sing it one voice to a part, in a more rhetorical tradition than is the case in other places. Sonic as opposed to rhetorical might be the too-neat slogan to describe this difference, with the best advocates of the rhetorical approach achieving interpretations of the greatest subtlety. But when it comes to sonic, with all the implications of mathematically-based abstraction that word implies, I have heard little to rival Collegium. Its full sound is softer-edged than the Tallis Scholars', slightly more diffuse, yet capable of being just as loud. By comparison the Tallis sound seems more directed – super-focused – and impressive by its sheer resonance. The English way is to compel people to listen, fascinated; Collegium is more beguiling, wrapping its listeners in sound rather than propelling it at them.

It was in order to introduce students of all ages, nationalities and backgrounds both to the members of the Tallis Scholars themselves and to the possibilities inherent in the performance of polyphony that Juliet Allan, David Woodcock and I set up the first Oakham course in the summer of 2000. For years as a young man I had had a romantic vision of setting up a centre for renaissance singing in a chateau somewhere in rural France, a building that was miraculously going to come my way just like that. This dream-castle was going to have a gothic chapel where all the Offices (Anglicanised) would be ritually sung every day and night, a fine library which would hold all the editions we would need, and a cloister around which we could walk in moody contemplation, in the best Horace Walpole tradition. Oakham School is not quite the model of my imaginings, but it does have everything we need including both a chapel and a parish church. It is true it does not have a cloister, but there is enough sentiment lying around the place without the encouragement of monks' cells to fire our feelings, and anyway the workload is so intense that no one has time for contemplation, unless it is at Compline. The only abrupt sign that we are not in France is the food.

Like every music course I have ever been on – I used to attend them as an oboist – the idea is to make as much music as is physically possible, so that everyone goes home at the end of the week exhausted, yet happy to be exhausted. The only difference between this course and any other is that every note to be heard on it was written in the renaissance period, and is performed unaccompanied. Although Ghislaine Morgan, Andrew Carwood, Patrick Craig, Philip Cave and Deborah Roberts over the years have offered one-to-one vocal tuition, the focus of the work is on ensemble singing, whether in small groups one to a part or in larger gatherings. The larger gatherings, conducted by me with the help of David Woodcock and JanJoost van Elburg, make up the more formal end of the activities, with a public concert at the end of the week featuring at least one big masterwork, like Lassus's *Missa Bel'amfitrit'altera*. The small groups, under the eye of Francis Steele, have already ranged very widely through the enormous repertoire at our disposal, a process of experiment which has been greatly facilitated by the availability of cheap computer-made editions. To do such ranging was always my idea of heaven; in fact it was the reason that I set up my own group in the first place. There are now plans to open our doors in other countries. Who needs a chateau in rural France?

One of my self-appointed missions in life is to show that serious music does not have to consist only of the Germanic orchestral tradition and evenings at the opera. The durability of these two things in the minds of most music students and music-lovers is quite remarkable, a real hegemony, maintained by educational establishments throughout the 'western' world to this day and reinforced every time a concert-promoter decides to play safe and once again stages a symphony we all know backwards. It didn't have to be so narrow and predictable: the other arts in the last hundred years have been much less tied to one tradition than music, with the result that their more recent achievements have been more generally accepted and enjoyed than modern music has been. Contemporary music has suffered badly at the hands of this straightjacket; but so also have all the repertoires which have been considered marginal. Believing that polyphony contains music as powerful as any from the periods officially sanctioned in the popular view, I have hoped to prove this point to as many people as are prepared to give it a chance. One way was to tour widely giving concerts, and make records which would go even further than we could in person. But the best way was actually to involve students in the singing, hoping they would come from far and wide and then go home and perform the music there. Slowly the Oakham course has built up the kind of following I hoped it would, encouraging people from all over the world to come there for a week and do nothing but sing polyphony. On the 2002 course one of the small groups which by chance got itself together came to exemplify this hope. They decided to sing the six-part *In paradisum* by Juan Esquivel, which in itself pleased me since I knew nothing by Esquivel and so had missed this miniature masterpiece. But better still was that they were all under the age of 25, and multinational. Of the eight people taking part, there were two Britons, an American, a Canadian, a Dutchman, a Czech, a Pole and a Swede. What struck the listeners was that, despite the variety of backgrounds, of musical traditions and presumably of training, these singers had had no indoctrination as to how this music should sound. This enabled them to come to it from the same starting point and make an interpretation cohere remarkably quickly. We reckoned that with any later repertoire they would have had much more difficulty, with conflicting ideas about phrasing, ornaments and how much vibrato was appropriate.

This performance, and others like it in Oakham, has shown better than anything that interest in polyphony is spreading, and in doing so helping to undermine the notion that concerts must have instruments in them (what people until recently have called 'the music' played by 'the musicians', to distinguish them from singers) to be taken seriously. It is one thing for the Tallis Scholars to be paid to go to sing polyphony in unlikely places like Beijing; it is another for people to pay to come to a distant and rural town to try it for themselves. Twenty or so years from now should be an interesting time in the concert-giving world, when all this energy has begun to hit its mark.

5

ON TOUR

Music is like a drug. Whoever acquires the habit can no longer devote himself to important activities ... We must completely eliminate it.

(Ayatollah Ruhollah Khomeini, reported in the *New York Times*, 25 May 2003)

Ever since our first concerts in 1973 we have been judged not only by the quality of our singing but also by our perceived status in the musical hierarchy. For the first ten years or so we were indeed amateurs; but it was noticeable that even after we had made the costly and dangerous move onto the professional circuit nothing much changed in most people's attitude towards us – and in some quarters it still hasn't. Our experience shows how uneven the playing field can be for what the establishment thinks to be alternative repertoires (and whole concerts of polyphony were seen as being very alternative indeed), which makes life awkward in one way, though in another it did no harm to acquire the skills and wiles of the pioneer. We all actively enjoy having to convince our audiences that what we believe in might come to mean something to them too. But even when a concert or a disc has finally been enjoyed, there remains the possibility of a whole new area of misunderstanding: what it takes to be standing there at all.

For people who are employed in an office which they are obliged to attend between set hours every day, for the housewife who is tied to her home and children – particularly but not only for these people – the life of the travelling musician must seem glamorous. The idea that there are no set hours, no routine, but that when one is working one is doing something creative, fulfilling, and one is doing it intensely with like-minded colleagues; the idea that one travels to all manner of places, not only with all expenses paid but with spending-money in hand and a fee at the end of it, in order to become something of a star, someone special, out of the ordinary: these concepts must seem very seductive. Indeed to those who are not used to them they must seem almost incredible, to the extent that I have been confronted by people (mothers waiting in the school playground at the start of the day are representative) who clearly think I'm behaving irresponsibly. If they are minded to believe any of what I tell them they assume I've hit on some unheard-of way of going on an almost perpetual holiday, and often part from me with the words, delivered in an ironic tone, 'don't work too hard'. Often there is no understanding that one can pursue a career doing this, and so make a living.

The assumption is deeply rooted that anyone who is travelling abroad to sing must be an amateur. Perhaps instrumentalists are not so prone to this blanket view, especially if they are travelling with an orchestra. It is more widely recognised that an orchestra is a professional outfit and that its members must have trained for long years at a conservatoire in order to qualify to be in it. Singers are known to train too, but that kind of singer shows his or her training by singing with vibrato. There is never any question in the popular mind that a named soloist in a performance of an oratorio in the local town hall or church is doing it for a fee. Opera singers even more so. But the kind of singing we practise reminds many people across society of an amateur context which at some point in their lives they have rubbed shoulders with – choral society, church choir, television or radio choral competitions, barbershop at university. To grasp the truth of what we actually do is simply beyond some of our listeners, a difficulty which has caused some appallingly awkward moments.

To ask a professional singer 'what do you really do?', by which is meant 'what do you do to make money?', is surely the most deflating question you can address to him or her. It is the educated version of 'don't work too hard', with the added injustice that one feels the questioner ought to have heard of one's efforts. I have come across it most frequently in the mouths of businessmen who have had difficulty understanding that any grown male can survive without buying and selling. The most demeaning context has been with members of the British establishment whilst making polite conversation. The classic instance was after we had sung in the Auditorio Pia in Rome in 1994, some months after the filmed performances in Santa Maria Maggiore and the Sistine Chapel. This concert had had its own hint of high-level professionalism in having been broadcast live by RAI Tre and been sung before an audience of two thousand people. Amongst them was the British ambassador, who was kind enough to invite us to the embassy for a reception in our honour after the show. The British embassy in Rome must be one of the grandest buildings of its kind in the world: a palace, seized by the allied forces at some stage in the last war, in the main reception room of which Mussolini once shook hands with Hitler in a gesture of eternal friendship. It was in this room that His Excellency, surrounded by a group of us sipping champagne, popped that question which we hadn't heard for some years and thought we might have done enough never to have to hear again. We were outraged and I recall a moment of barely-suppressed violence in one of the tenors present, who pointedly turned his back.

If a concert in a church doesn't immediately support the idea of a properly professional activity to some bystanders, the music itself is another problem. 'Early music' in general still sits uneasily with the concert-going public, despite the advances of recent years. Period orchestras have generally won the fight for acceptance, even if few of them indeed are funded from public money as their modern-instrument peers are. And they tend to play music which was always part of the core tradition. Palestrina, Lassus, Victoria and Byrd may have been acknowledged masters for the last hundred years and more, but they have not been familiar as concert composers. For a professional ensemble to stage a concert of music by Palestrina in a church is to present something of confusing status, even to those who love that kind of event; to those who look down on it, perhaps from the great height of the operatic world with all its glamour and stars and state subsidy, the combination of location and choice of music is further confirmation that it cannot add up to the genuine article. Something of this confusion is cleared up when we sing in a concert hall, preferably in a chamber music series surrounded by leading string quartets and Lieder singers; but then, as I have noted elsewhere, we sail into a whole pack of other preconceptions.

These prejudgements die hard. One of the most persistent is that when we sing we are not singing like properly-trained singers (or, to take it a step further, successful singers) but are trying to emulate the ideal church choir by being modest, or holy in some way. It is true, of course, that we deliberately suppress excessive vibrato and that polyphony of its nature requires restraint much of the time, but these are straightforward stylistic considerations. Nothing takes me more aback than to hear members of an audience or the press continuing to refer to the boy-like tone of our sopranos, and the completely vibrato-free sound of the group (which of course is what they want to hear), following a performance which has made the building shake with noise. It is physically impossible to sing as loudly as the Tallis Scholars sometimes sing without some vibrato, and it is constantly there for anyone to hear, coming and going with the decibels. Yet plenty of people would swear blind that we *never* sing like that.

To parade these issues of public perception – or which pigeonhole to stick us in – as problems can easily come over as special pleading. For the lifestyle which constant touring gives us can indeed be attractive. If it is true that no one on their death-bed ever wished they had spent an extra hour in the office, so it may be true that I on mine will wish I had visited one of my favourite haunts just once more – or given just one more performance in that ideal venue. There is a world of difference between doing a job because it provides security and doing a job which fulfils a talent and in the process provides very little security of a material kind. One feels on a different planet from those besuited salaried people who look so anxious in the street on weekdays; one feels entitled to squeeze every last drop of enjoyment out of what one does – because there is a risk in purveying this beauty. The bohemian life is seductive and self-justifying; and if one is not very aware of what really makes it up it will turn into a trap which will bleed its victims dry.

No one I know who has made even half a fist of being self-employed has longed to don the suit of the businessman, though he may long for the businessman's salary. This means in effect that there is nowhere to escape to from the bohemian life, and since it is seductive one tends to go further in, weaknesses playing on strengths. The vulnerability that self-employed people feel can be imagined, especially by employees who have gone the salary route just for the security of it. In fact singers suffer from a sense of exposure more than most because of the fragility of the voice and its very personal nature. A musical instrument is detachable from oneself, the voice is not. And bound up with these insecurities are the inevitable worries about one's talent and whether it is wanted, whether other people are better or more in demand than oneself, a constant anxiety about one's position in the pecking order. Running parallel with these professional concerns will be financial ones, caused by the lack of a regular pay cheque. Every self-employed person knows lean months, and knows the repercussions of these not only for mortgage and pension payments but also for morale, the ever-present feeling, suppressed at times of triumph, that one may not be good enough at what one does to survive. To entertain that horror is to confront defeat in the most personal terms. No one can help; in this matter one is completely alone.

The obvious antidote is to seek more work. Work means that people want you, which helps to deal with the green-eyed monster; and one is being paid. Work means status and security, being more relaxed with one's existence whilst at the same time doing the thing which gives one the greatest pleasure: indulging oneself through one's talent. Under the guise of necessity coupled to artistic endeavour the performer is giving himself licence to be persistently selfish.

The performer thinks twice about turning down work, with the result that it can rapidly take precedence over every other activity in life. Where the salaried employee might be only too pleased to leave work to tend to a sick member of the family, or indeed take a break at the slightest twinge of a headache, the musician on the contrary feels obliged to be forever available, easily reached by answerphone or mobile, and, when invited, on good form. Illnesses are made light of, inconveniences in the arrangements swallowed without comment, antisocial hours tolerated as a matter of course. The worst of it is the effect of this mentality on one's dependants. Very little is sacred in family life when a self-employed person is offered work. Babysitters are found, elderly relatives pressed into service, the bedtime story goes missing, niceties like a family Sunday lunch are not even registered, since weekends as time off don't enter the equation. Even if one has no immediate family to consider, the effect of a completely haphazard touring schedule is just as disruptive to one's friends: they always expect you to be away and so give up trying to stay in touch.

Glamorous? In a way. One is one's own master, and however difficult it may be to round the circle at home the going is more or less justifiable, just as long as nobody says 'you shouldn't be doing this job', which they rarely do when it comes to artistic endeavour. The musical tourist is therefore doubly fortunate: close friends and relatives do as a rule try to facilitate the pursuing of the insecure career (not least because there may be reflected glory in it); and, once free to go, one enters the kind of charmed world which I have already described. For a while one can concentrate exclusively on the travel and the performance in hand.

Of course the glamour will wear off through excessive repetition. Paul Theroux once wrote, 'Travel is glamorous only in retrospect', which suggests the glamorous side is always a hoax at the time; but when is the point of excess reached? And how does the freelance musician recognise that the way he makes his living has become excessive? A salaried person is very happy to receive more money for putting in the same number of hours: to get a significant rise in earnings, The rank-and-file musician will simply have to work for more hours. They may be lucky at the beginning of their career to join an ensemble – perhaps an orchestra – which is already very well established and can guarantee full-time employment; but it is more likely, as with the original members of the Tallis Scholars, that the participants will begin with very little work, which slowly builds up. Since the process of gain could reverse itself at any moment, nothing is refused until maybe twenty years on when, after endless fluctuations of fortune, one is forced to confront facts which may hint at excess: there seems to be no time for a summer holiday, one is working on Christmas day, the number of trips which last more than a fortnight has increased, or the number of trips to eastern Europe, where the pay is bad, has increased. The signs may be many, but even in the face of such evidence the argument will still run: if I refuse the work this time, the year after next I may have months of unpaid summer holiday.

For many musicians excess is finally acknowledged when they are confronted by the reality of persistent illness (the strain of this kind of travelling is enormous), loss of form coupled to general lassitude (or exhaustion), or the realisation that their children are growing up without them (i.e., they are being useless parents). But there remain those few who never get ill enough to stop them in their tracks – or who are sufficiently out of touch with themselves to notice that they are ill – and who are probably hooked on the travel and the concert-giving and the lifestyle as on a drug. It may be that these single-minded people don't actually need to travel so much to make ends meet, that they are assured of work and anyway live alone incurring relatively few overheads. I do not live alone, but I am one of these people.

Having hardly travelled at all before I went to university, the discovery of abroad hit me as if I had suddenly been made party to all three dimensions of living, where one had sufficed before. My sense of where I belonged in the world – and where Britain belonged in it – was violently changed. And because my family had never provided me with a strong sense of being rooted anywhere, not least because I was sent away to school for the greater part of the year between the ages of seven and eighteen, I was perfectly available for the kind of gainful wandering I have outlined. In feeling that where I had come from was at best only a fraction of the story, and at worst was an impoverished place, I eagerly travelled almost anywhere, not minding if the next visit was to somewhere I had been fifty times already (literally true with Venice, Paris and New York). I have taken delight in trying to learn other languages, and although I am not a talented linguist – this is not false modesty – I am at least an experienced one with a musician's ear, quick to catch meanings through inflection of the voice if not through the words themselves. To take English for granted around the world, although at times crucially useful, has not to me been acceptable in its implications. If I can't find a meaning in English, perhaps I will be able to find one in other words, or sets of inflections and expressions, which means doing everything in my power to go visiting without preconceptions or an agenda. I realise, of course, that this search will never end.

Quite apart from whatever qualifications I have to ply my trade, I am the ideal touring musician. I want to give the concerts, I want to travel and I have come to rely on many aspects of the lifestyle which such constant touring promotes. I travel as the ultimately deracinated self-contained unit, sustained by straightforward portable things such as a short-wave radio; a reading programme which can run to long series of books, such as all of Shakespeare; and a never-ending programme of writing on my own account, from a journal of the Tallis Scholars' activities (now in its 56th volume) to my column in the *Spectator*, which I've done for 21 years; and all that the local scene has to offer – architecture, paintings, cuisines, wines, acquaintances across the world.

Obviously this life is seductive. The attraction starts with that easy assumption most people would make on first hearing about it: paid-for holiday with work which doesn't seem like proper work; and then for some of us the seductive element deepens and becomes more powerful. Eventually the point is reached where travelling becomes normal, and home-life abnormal. The question then is what kind of balance one is left with when it is frankly admitted that in effect this amounts to constantly running away from home. One day there must be a reckoning.

I have already described in part how the justification goes: this is the

only career I have and I need to pursue it both for financial reasons and because it is in itself good and useful work. On the face of it this is irrefutable,
but allowed to continue unchecked it may mean that a musician in demand
is on the road for more than half the year. In a record year – 1992 – I was on
tour for nearly nine months. For people who imagine that concert-touring
is essentially holiday it follows that being abroad is not real life. In almost
everyone's definition of reality, things like paying bills, making the beds,
doing the shopping are the ingredients of real life, alongside the quiet pleasures of routine and family. Yet there is a case for saying that if one spends
more than half one's time in hotel rooms they have become as much part of
reality as one's bed at home. And similarly all the other things that go with
them form a new reality, potentially enjoyable or not: airport buildings,
check-in times, taxis, packing, currencies; so that reality for someone like
me can be as much trying not to be ripped off by bureaux de change as remembering to pay the council tax. What makes touring as a musician seem
so little like commonplace normality is that every mundane responsibility is
taken off one's shoulders so that one is free to concentrate on the only thing
which the paymaster wants from you – to perform to your best ability. Part
of the seduction of touring, then, is that this new reality means no imposi-
tions except making music. One can actually save money on normal expen-
diture because, quite apart from the fee, there are no bills. Why not do it the
whole year round?

At this point everyone must shudder. Perhaps everyone except me has
been shuddering for some time in reading the above; but even I feel nervous at the prospect of so much carefree pleasure. Where does it end, since
end it must?

The consequence of having no roots – or rather replacing the normal
way of sinking roots deeply in one place with planting shallow ones in many
places – is that nothing grows outside oneself. The first casualty is personal
relationships; the second a proper sense of belonging to and contributing to
the life of a community. Of course whether one is staying in one place or
travelling widely one has to take the rough with the smooth – in the touring
existence there can be plenty of rough – but it is the rough of no ultimate
accountability. The experience of travelling for many hours in foul air in a
space three feet square (with a constant supply of substandard food and
drink at one's disposal) is very unpleasant, but it only touches on life-

sustaining issues if it prevents the musician from performing well at the end of the journey. In my experience the essential support systems on tour at worst are kept just above the level which would lead to a bad performance in the immediate future, through tiredness, or illness, or gross disaffection – and so the show rolls uninterruptedly on. The professional soon becomes entirely competent at ensuring he or she is presentable for the evening's gig and for the rest of the time either internalises his experiences or carries on a series of superficial relationships with his colleagues or anyone else he might meet, who may well also be in the same almost-perpetual state of limbo. I have found it is difficult to cultivate profound friendships in limbo, and the very experience of limbo makes it difficult to settle down to long-lasting relationships when not on tour.

The practicalities of being constantly away from home are slowly insidious. At the beginning of a touring career it is likely that the musician can combine the best of both worlds: the excitement of going regularly away whilst being in circulation at home reliably enough to fit into a fixed social pattern. Gradually, as the years pass and the logic of making money in combination with a disinclination to prefer mundane responsibility over jetting away from it establishes its own routine, it comes to be assumed that one is never around, even though one may be. This is not in itself a disaster since it only takes a phone call when home to arrange a meeting, but across the spectrum of one's friends and family this represents a shift of balance which may have serious repercussions. In effect it means that, on returning home, possibly only for a day or two, the travelling musician has not only to deal with the accumulated post, fax, answerphone and email messages, which tend to be more demanding than personal, but then, in order to revive his personal life, has to make a series of phone calls and find slots in his diary when he may be available to meet his friends. And when they do meet, after the initial interest in where he has just returned from has worn off (and it wears off more and more quickly as the process repeats itself) it may be found that the roots on which the relationship was nourished have inevitably withered. The problem has simply been that when the friend felt like ringing the traveller he found him always to be away and so, if he was in need, turned elsewhere. What is left to them is a growing inequality: one has an endless succession of experiences from which the other is excluded, while the other builds up a stock of more average experiences from which the first is increasingly excluded, though he may have had some knowledge of them once upon a time. If the traveller is tempted to look down on stay-at-home life, or even be glad that he can escape it, the gulf between the two will become serious. Anyone can tell you that a flourishing relationship must be between equals. In what I have described here everything is done for the convenience of the traveller who, because he is an artist, is likely to retain the admiration of those who know him, and with it the veneer of friendliness. With this in his back pocket the traveller may feel he can constantly go away, with impunity. Yet every time he goes he ensures that those connections at home become that little bit more superficial. As they do so he may feel – his career being what it is – less and less equipped to manage anything more demanding; and so a vicious circle is established. In time he effectively becomes alone: initially with the admiration of his surrounding world but ultimately, as the impressiveness of what he does winds down – it is dreadfully easy for a performance style to become unfashionable – without it. Nobody knows him any more as an individual who happens to be a musician.

Many of my colleagues reading this will be able to say that it doesn't really apply to them. Of course it doesn't *really* apply to me, since I have made common cause with someone who is in the same position as myself, which is to say my wife is in the group. This is one of the options available to us; others include having a very understanding partner at home who, along with helpful close relatives, takes care of the children; or just having a very understanding partner; or living alone by choice; or living with one's parents (very rare in our world but perhaps not such a bad idea given the real nature of what one is dealing with).

Yet still, deep down there is a panic, which is constantly at war with the incentives of money, career, pleasure, knowledge through travel. This panic is inevitably fuelled by meeting fellow-musicians who are in a worse state than oneself. These people tend to announce themselves by ringing up out of the blue (*they* must be in a worse state if they are ringing *me*) and saying what a shame it is that we haven't met for so long when we used to meet so regularly, and what am I doing in the next five days? If I'm around the conversation proceeds to an hour-by-hour chart of the friend's availability, always constrained by his (it is usually a man) need to rush from one engagement, rehearsal or meeting to another, leading to summaries which are rounded off with phrases like, 'I could make that if I just ring so-and-so. I'll get back to you.' Presumably a little later in the process one has oneself been moved, and not rung up, because these meetings almost never take place. No one is particularly put out by this failure; indeed in a sense – because ultimately we're all in the same boat – it leads to a greater desire to try again, maybe months later, until the meeting is finally effected. When it does happen it is often remarkable how long the session can last: half a day, all night, hours disappearing without moment. All that has happened on the previous occasions is that just one of the many options for the man on the phone has come good, and that, along with copious supplies of alcohol, has put paid to any further desire to rush around that day. When parting, with heartfelt expressions of wishing to re-establish a proper closeness, the friend disappears without trace for another nine months. He may have time to keep about ten people in play like this. He is very unlikely to have a long-term partner and even less likely to have children he is regularly in touch with. He may well be a past master at telling jokes.

It sounds wretched; but although no one in my line of business is ever prepared to say straight out that they are happy, the people I am now describing very often pay tribute to how lucky they are. They may have no property and little sustained contact with others back home, but they do have this lifestyle. Invariably they are aware of its shortcomings, often speak of giving it up and becoming a writer, wonder how it is going to be for them, rootless still and doing exactly the same work, in ten years' time – ironically, never a prospect which seems to give anyone any pleasure. Yet there is often no real attempt, and no real desire, to give it up and stay grounded. This is not just because the training to become a singer or instrumentalist at this level is really a once-in-a-lifetime activity and these professionals are not qualified to do anything else: it is because they cannot sustain the idea of slowing down. They look at other people's lives and feel relieved they are not in their bind (for example: imagine if the only trip abroad every year was the family holiday – assuming the family holiday is taken abroad); they favourably compare giving concerts with adding up figures in the office; above all they want, possibly need, to keep moving. Long after the initial excitement of exploring new places has worn off they want more new places, more travel, more experiences.

These are musicians of a particular kind. They are not exactly what are called session players, who tend to stay in one place and freelance between *ad hoc* groups, working regularly in studios. Nor are they part of the very small élite who can command sufficiently high fees only to have to work occasionally. These latter have a rather different life, and presumably different expectations from the context of music-making, to what I am describing; as do the members of a full-time organisation like an orchestra who can only travel in strictly controlled circumstances. These, either by choice or professional opportunity, will not have experienced the constant repetition of travel, the regular offer of work in glamorous places, the building up of the addiction. The musicians I am describing are freelance players and singers who are at the top of their professions as ensemble members (i.e., named in a list with their colleagues) and whose only hope of significantly increasing their income is to make, if possible and if wanted, the leap to becoming a named soloist. It is probably assumed by the outside observer that every conservatoire student wants to be a big star – certainly the training itself assumes this – whereas in fact many first-rate musicians do not want this. The pleasure for such people is to subsume themselves within a group activity, to contribute to the music-making as it were democratically rather than as a dominator. Although in this description I am not referring specifically to the members of the Tallis Scholars, about whom one would generalise at one's peril, the most likely exemplar of the type will be someone in a group which is devoted to the performance of 'early music', since this repertoire calls for a high degree of virtuosity from a small group of participants, in a sense featuring several soloists at once, and was written in an era when there was no vehicle for the cult of the star soloist. Indeed it is probably not too much of an exaggeration to say that the state of mind I am concerned with has only become widespread since the appeal of early music has spread throughout the world – for instrumentalists since perhaps the early 1970s – which has coincided with the availability of cheap air travel.

Something of this addiction is in me, and in varying degrees must be in the singers and instrumentalists who staff the many British ensembles which for some years now have been such a feature of concert series, whether specifically dedicated to early music or not, all over the world. When asked, I have rarely heard them say that they wished their professional lives planned out like those of actors, who stay in the same, usually English-speaking metropolis night after night. In the first instance they will speak of the delight of performing the music they specialise in, in groups which are so expert; often they give the impression that they would go almost any-where to practise their art. If they are pressed on the subject of travel, reference is always made first to the practicalities of getting to these concerts – the hours spent in foul air in aeroplanes, the characterless hotel rooms, the overwhelming physical discomfort that only a wide-eyed novice would fail to notice represented the routine and cynical overlooking of all but the most elementary human needs on the part of airlines. If they are pressed further one may hear some appreciation of the venues themselves, though often it seems to me only partially acknowledged and never expressed as a distinctive pleasure, as something to be looked forward to with delighted anticipation, for example on the tour after the next one. Yet I cannot believe that sane people with a marketable talent would volunteer themselves for the awfulness of constant travel (as distinct from the quite different experience of constant arrival) unless something of what I think to be in me were not also in them. The singers I work with, for example, are not obliged to work abroad; there is plenty of good work for such able performers in the home market, work which is quite possibly better paid than what I offer them, yet they choose not to do it, or not to do it all the time. There are only two reasons why this might be: that they like this kind of work, or that they like travelling (or both). Very tentatively I would suggest that no amount of beautiful renaissance polyphony would coax someone who loathed travelling to tour the world (though an avid traveller might well overcome a lack of interest in renaissance polyphony to join in).

To anyone who has put down deep roots in the place where they live, the long-term effects of constant travel produce a clutch of distortions. I realise that this means that what I am about to describe makes my view abnormal and, despite the glamour, ultimately undesirable to the great majority of people. Yet, either because it is a harmful drug leading to addiction, or because there really are unmatchable experiences on offer which few outsiders can imagine (not in travel but in *constant* travel) I still want more of it; and I present these details not – to me – as distortions but as a potentially desirable alternative way of living, always bearing in mind that if it is true that I am running away from something, the idea of the opposite of travelling – staying in one place – carries the connotation of vegetating. The thing which most profoundly affects the rhythm of life is the inability to establish a profound sense of belonging in one place. Of course many of my

colleagues have managed to do this, possibly before embarking on their careers, and so travel within the context of returning, one eye continually fo-
cused on what is going on at home wherever they may be. These people are
regularly on the phone or emailing back to England, often not relaxed in the
places they visit, enjoying the music-making, earning the fee, but always anticipating the end of the tour. I, on the other hand, have tried to spread my
roots, of necessity shallower, across the world. I may well leave London
reluctantly at the beginning of a tour, anticipating discomfort, but will leave
Rome or New York or wherever it is after the concerts with just as much
reluctance. Arriving in these favourite places will be as if I have just returned
home and now, sometimes after only a day, am obliged to leave again. The
feeling of being at home is obviously more intense in places I know well –
indeed in Paris I have long had an apartment; but it is the knack of the long-
term traveller quickly to become acquainted with a new place. By long
experience he will know what he is looking for, where to find the nourishment he needs, whether this be cultural artefacts, conversation, or food and
drink. With a quick eye he will appraise streets, buildings and restaurants
for the signs of what characterises the place, and how what he finds may be
enjoyed, understood and assimilated.

It is a precondition of this state of mind that the traveller be completely absorbed by the place where he finds himself. It is true that there will
always be the sense at the back of his mind of eventually having to move on,
but this helps the absorption. In knowingly spreading one's roots shallow
and wide, one is able to cultivate the sensation of being in a place all the more
intensely for the brevity of one's visit there. The person who lives only at
home comes to know a circumscribed repertoire of people and objects slowly and by osmosis, not coming to quick conclusions, but as much as possible
accepting his context without complaint. The traveller can pick and choose,
certainly, but this process also has its responsibilities, both to himself and
other people, since he is very likely to return, possibly several times a year,
to the same city. The friends he makes there will surely expect him either to
work with them again, or at least keep in touch and take an interest in their
lives. Of course such people are more easily avoided than neighbours at
home, and anyway this kind of contact will probably not yield friendships as
mutually serviceable as those between neighbours of long standing. But the
constant process of parting and coming together again may provide a

rhythm which keeps the friendship fresh, not reliably the case between people who bump into each other every day. Variety need not lead to incon-
stancy; and variety is an essential element in the travel compulsion.

I find it almost impossible to think ahead to the next place I am due to
visit, no matter how familiar it is. This is partly a tribute to the concentration of the moment but also a curious reflex of memory. With so many tiny
details to remember my instinct is to restrict myself to those which affect
what I'm doing in the very short term: if packing at home, then choosing
books to read or DVDs to watch on my laptop; if travelling to the airport,
then catching up with the daily papers; when on the aeroplane calculating
exactly how long the flight is and making the best use of that time – a useful
time because telephones and the like are more or less impossible adjuncts.
If any thought is given to the arrival ahead it is likely to be only for the work
itself and any complications which may be attached to it. This kind of
thought will apply to any place – concert halls and churches essentially pose
the same practical problems the world over, though admittedly the willing-
ness of the local organisation to find a solution to them can vary, so the degree of concern may fluctuate. But still, at this stage one is inclined only to
think in general terms.

It is only when I actually set foot in the city of my destination that I instinctively allow my mind to unlock its memories and references. Then the
detail of them can be quite astonishing: how the light falls at different times
of day, telephone numbers previously hidden, the words and phrases used in
long-ago conversations, alongside the more obvious memories of how the
streets lie and where the buildings are. There is a whole rigmarole associated in my mind with arriving. The first meal is the focal point, at which one
puts down vital roots into the local ground, and draws nourishment. One
thrusts them down as far as possible, thrilling to every sensation, savouring
every variation, taking time, slipping from one culture into another, acquiring camouflage. A typical restaurant for this should not be out of the ordinary, but a place where the local genius is on full display, in the serving as
much as in what is served. The Terminus Nord, outside the Gare du Nord
in Paris where the trains from London arrive, is a perfect example. There
one is entertained only by local colour, without any sense of the museum.
The food and the wine are not experimental or themed; the cadenceless
counterpoint which the waiters play out between themselves, underscored

by more subtle layers of seniority than shown by any army in the field, is a Parisian tradition going back centuries. At the conclusion of a meal at the Terminus Nord, London is a distant memory and the restaurant itself has become a surrogate home, welcoming and suddenly familiar.

But even before such an experience – and not every city has so appropriate a restaurant right by the point of entry – at the first sight of the streets the inveterate traveller becomes both knowledgeable and curious, already looking for his 'homes', known or soon to be appropriated. Like an animal marking out its domain, he paces an inner ring of streets, preparatory to more detailed exploration. If the city is well known this takes the form of greeting old acquaintances, with relief that they are still there unchanged, the most loved example of all to me being the corner of West 76th Street and Broadway in New York City, which I have to visit every time I go there, even if we are not staying in the hotel (the Milburn) which introduced me to it in the first place. If it is a first visit the elementary local map provided by the hotel is studied carefully so that the contours of the streets become quickly familiar. Such a traveller as myself will have a need to feel he belongs, however superficially, in every place he visits, and the initial approaches can only be made through a knowledge of its topography. Too often in the routine of professional musicians a venue is scheduled for a stop of one night; and if the travelling to that place takes half the day there will be very little time to embrace one's surroundings. It is possible for us, despite rehearsing, giving a concert and staying the night, to be in a place for no more than fourteen hours, almost all of which will be hours of darkness. A tour which consists only of these one-night visits can be a most unsatisfying event in the calendar: no roots; just music, money and go home. Still, even on an hour or two, the experienced visitor will have picked up enough to be able to say, 'next time I'll know to do this or that'. The unlimited possibility of next time is also an essential part of the compulsion.

Just occasionally one is invited to stay in a place long enough to feel that after a week, say, it would be appropriate to move on. The intention would be to go back in the foreseeable future, of course, but one knows that short of staying months – which is never possible – it is necessary to leave in order to come at the place again from a fresh perspective. This would not be so necessary if one were to be given an apartment of one's own, perhaps, but the restrictions of a hotel room, the positioning of the hotel, the obligation to eat in restaurants, cause one to fall into patterns of behaviour day by day which will not be exactly repeated on a subsequent visit. A favourite restaurant can be instantly replaced by another next time – or remain a place to rediscover at all costs. But each new arrival will subtly alter the view, even in quite a small town. The most elaborate example of this in my experience is Venice, which I have visited countless times in the last twenty years. Without intending it, or even necessarily noticing at the time, the routine by which I make basic choices has gradually evolved not least, typically of Venice, in the combination of streets I may take to get around. These routes, if I can ever find them again just as I had them before, almost never survive intact from one year to the next. Yet I can remember vividly the choices I made on the first two or three visits, and may choose them again if I want to feel young and inexperienced. This is not generally so true of restaurants, incidentally. When one moves on from a restaurant one tends to move on permanently, and be capable of quite cutting disloyalty to rooms where, in a different epoch, one spent many happy hours. Often I hear the old Venice hands suddenly turn against a place, not because of a lowering of standards – the food and wine must be reliable but they are never discussed – but because of change. 'It's not nearly as good as when old Erasmo was there.' Erasmo and his like are always products of Harry's Bar who have semi-retired to run a small place in the remoter parts of the town before fully retiring to the villages in the Veneto where they were born. In addition to the quiet competence which Harry's undoubtedly gives them they are standardly inexhaustible gossips, not to mention experts on artisanal enterprises on the mainland which can yield unusual wines and country produce, alongside a hidden network of old-fashioned craft shops. The fresh-faced cousin or nephew who seems overnight to have replaced Erasmo is viewed with extreme displeasure, and one rarely goes back. In a place as resourceful as Venice one doesn't have to. And so, given the chance, in an instinctive uncalculating way, one deepens one's knowledge and spreads one's roots in the places one loves.

I have learnt to remember towns and cities by their atmosphere. Of course every reasonably-sized metropolis has art galleries, museums, churches and important buildings, but if one goes straight to them, and examines only them, one may come away with very little impression of the city which holds them. The rooms and contents of an art gallery could be literally anywhere – one no more sees a Rembrandt on a wall and assumes one is in Holland than one hears a Mahler symphony and assumes it is being played by the Vienna Philharmonic. (One exception to this immediately springs to mind: the Australian galleries have built up exceptional collections of the best late-nineteenth and early twentieth-century British painting – from Clausen and Wilson Steer through to Paul Nash, Stanley Spencer, Nicholson, Grant and Bell. I assume they don't have the majority holdings of these masters, but for convenience of access – if one is touring the main cities there – it is an unrivalled opportunity. But even in this case the rooms between the cities are interchangeable; and I can't always remember whether a favourite canvas was actually in Adelaide or Liverpool.)

Buildings are more specific, though they too can prove false friends. Does one know the variations in gothic style so well that, once inside a church, it is possible to say without hesitation that one is in Alsace rather than Lorraine? Even to distinguish between the interiors of Peterborough and Amiens Cathedrals requires some specialist knowledge, and to distinguish between Amiens and Rouen yet more. The interiors of many Japanese concert halls are identikit, having been built within a few years of each other. Yet viewed from the outside, with the surrounding streets and shops and accents of the people given their force in the received impression, there should be no confusion. Amiens is not like Rouen, nor Metz like Strasbourg. The outside of the art gallery in Philadelphia is as different from the one in Pasadena as their insides are interchangeable. Step outside the hotel, the airport terminal, the concert hall, the museum, the restaurant, the hospital, even the church, and then one is dealing with the essence. Everything else is supporting cast.

One comes to know those things which depend on local origins for their character but which have been internationalised in the marketplace: wine, ingredients for cooking, clothes, cars (not always the case in the past), hair styles, interior decoration, as much as architectural principles, paintings and music. The Tallis Scholars themselves are a walking internationalism, taking pieces of music from every renaissance culture, putting them together and performing the resulting mix over the globe, in buildings which usually have very little that is genuinely distinctive about them. At the other end of the aesthetic spectrum, consider what the importing chains have done for the availability of different wines. Australian and Chilean growths appear as reliably in London as they do in Chicago; I have found Lebanese, Greek and New Zealand bottles in Madrid, Rome and Tokyo. Even in Paris, where the rest of the world's viticulture was held until recently to be a gigantic irrelevance, there are now preliminary signs of an alternative market. I can buy oranges from somewhere in the world on any day of the year in my local supermarket. I wear clothes from Italy (or is it Japan?). It is said that the best Indian food is served in London, the best Chinese in New York, the best Greek in Melbourne; and Indian, Chinese and Greek food are available in some shape or form in just about every centre of the civilised world. Perhaps for those who are obliged to stay at home the astonishing sophistication of this marketing has quieted an impulse, making life more varied, but it is poor stuff to the serious traveller. By not relying on the resources of any one place for his experiences, the wanderer is likely to reject anything which does not belong to his immediate surroundings.

Surely no one who begins with the streets – the one aspect of a city which is not interchangeable – is going to go into a restaurant and order wine and food from another culture. The idea of pacing the streets of San Francisco and coming to rest in a Japanese restaurant which serves French wine is an anathema to me. The wines which are grown on the doorstep of that city have few rivals anywhere for variety and quality, and to explore them will be the pleasure of many years' research. I do not suggest that this research into Californian produce be undertaken in Cologne, Florence or Lisbon, as is becoming possible these days, because there will be other equally pleasurable researches to be pursued in those places; but the rationale assumes that there will be many visits to the West Coast of the US, or at least to the US, and that in time and with patience the rarest and most splendid bottles will be found. If this principle of action is adopted in every country and is extended to include styles of cooking, actual produce, wildlife, weather patterns and language – the things which cannot be internationalised – the seductive power of constant travel and the attraction of putting down many shallow roots will know no limits.

Such a traveller will in time acquire a great deal of knowledge, a lot of it trivial, about the world. How any memory can cope with so much and such varied information will differ from person to person. As I say, I find I cannot remember anything very precise about the place I'm heading for until I'm actually there. If this is a kind of amnesia, possibly caused by overload, then there are other, more subtle signs of it. I never confuse one pattern of streets with another – even the amorphous nonsense of Los Angeles is sui generis – but the incidental details of street life long ago began to overlap and merge. The most telling of these are the faces of people I talk to, and the sounds which come out of them. The bank of people I have met superficially is now so extended that the features, mannerisms and voices of newcomers can often trigger off exact but unfixable references to other people. My memory is good enough to know that I haven't met this particular person before, and for my mind to be filled instantly with images of someone they resemble, but not good enough to put a name and a face to them quickly. Once this is done, if it ever is, I goggle at the similarities – often visible – for a few brief minutes, and then the torment passes, and I am happy to have put the ghost to rest. The problem is exacerbated by the complete lack of context: colour, sex, dress and venue make no difference. Black men can remind me of white women. It took me twelve tantalised hours recently to work out that the accent of an Italian wife of a friend of mine speaking in English was bewilderingly similar to that of a Greek Cypriot who owns a restaurant near me in Islington. The involuntary racking of the brains which followed her first words to me just about ruined our encounter; and she'd gone before I got to the answer. If I look distracted in conversation it may be because half my mind is processing countless files, like a computer instructed to do something behind another command, and going slow.

Overfilling a memory will cause it to swell in one direction while fusing in another. The end result is likely to be a fair share of comment from those who need to rely on one's grasp of detail. The slightest sign of amnesia can lead to hasty conclusions about one's mental capacities across a broad spectrum, leading to a sharp diminution of authority. For example, because I can almost never remember which day of the week it is – a quite natural problem for an itinerant musician – my family now assume that I don't mean what I say, because I must have forgotten what it was I did say. And if I ever should forget what it was I said, I am sunk without trace for a long time. Indeed trying to re-establish my position has sometimes seemed so difficult that I've been tempted to turn trouble into a virtue and become all mysterious, springing surprises, dangling astonishing feats of long-term memory and generally trying to obfuscate. Another way of putting it would be to say I retreat into my own world, finding the real one too problematic; or insufficiently real; or not real enough enough of the time.

Perhaps, then, I am protecting myself, potentially a relaxing and even genial process for me. However there are side-effects which cause nothing but irritation in myself and at best a kind of bemused (or amused) tolerance in those who share the experiences with me. Reality can retreat to the point where I don't remember whole chunks of certain kinds of day, blanks which can include conversations, places, buildings (especially airports), people and even parts of concerts. If I am tired, or my imagination (rather than my intellect) is absorbed by an image from far away, no doubt often involuntarily conjured up to block immediate things which have become unbearably routine, it is fair to say I am in a dream world, cocooned. The irritation comes later when I realise what I may have missed. For example, I wanted to attend the recent Singer Sergeant exhibition at the Tate Gallery in London. My wife assured me that I had already been, which I vigorously denied until she found the catalogue I had bought at the time, signed and dated. I didn't go again; and I still cannot recall anything about the exhibition, though I can instantly bring to mind the paintings by Sergeant which mean something to me, many of them first seen in circumstances far less striking than an exhibition at the Tate.

If that is an example of fusing inside my head, an example of swelling is my uncertain relationship with language. People often complain of not being able to remember words, sometimes very workaday ones. Such forgetfulness is often held to be a side-effect of getting older (currently often called 'having a senior moment'), and no doubt I have my fair share of that problem, but it is compounded in my case by having picked up bits and pieces of other languages, which sometimes and without warning leap into the limelight. Only to be able to think of a foreign word to fill the middle of a sentence I'm embarked on drives me wild with frustration, especially if I dare not pronounce the word I have thought of for fear of seeming too clever by half. This is the awkward, public side of the matter, though back in my private world it is symptomatic of a pleasure: making comparisons between usages, and so amplifying one's understanding of the nuances of words. I even did a course in Arabic some years ago, partly to this end (and partly because I like taking holidays in the Arab world, the one bloc of countries where I shall never be invited to work, and where as a result holidays are for real). I reckon I may have made some discoveries of my own in the connections department – at least the *Oxford English Dictionary* doesn't mention them. The most obvious is the English word 'lad', which must come from the Arabic for a boy: 'walad'. (The *OED* fumbles with Middle English, concluding the word is of 'obscure origin'.) The most far-fetched connection I have made is between the English dialect word 'wassock', a term of mild abuse, applied one day to me, which sounded as though it had a perfect Arabic formulation. On checking the dictionary I found it does exist in Arabic and means 'filthy, soiled or unclean'. Clearly the crusaders brought back home with them more than just plunder and disease.

The hitch with the days of the week is related to the question of holidays. Concert touring puts the participants in no-man's-land. Very often engagements are on a Saturday evening which, if abroad, destroys any sense of the family weekend (and makes the restrictions of Sundays throughout the Christian world a major trial of one's patience). If there is no weekend then there will be little sense of the week: the grind of Monday mornings and the joyful release of Friday afternoons I only remember from school. A Saturday or a Sunday becomes like any day, and a sense of when one is due a holiday equally has no structure. Since the freelance musician has no salary, holidays are unpaid, which means they are formally taken (by which I mean work is refused because of them) with great circumspection. Besides, freelance musicians have a kind of holiday much of the time: whole days at home unemployed, and many free days in a year on the road, all expenses paid, abroad. No one pretends that these days are an effective replacement for a properly recreational holiday with one's family or chosen friends; but then the cost of two weeks in the sun with those people in one's life one should know better than one does – whose demands can quickly come to seem as unreasonable as they are unfamiliar – may not seem to be as relaxing as the 'work' version of a holiday. Musicians can go for years without a formal break, which may paradoxically be because it is the only way to save their marriages.

And, like any professional doing a job well, one becomes proud of one's professionalism. This sense of achievement can also act on one like a drug, parallel with but separate from the actual business of travelling, for it too can make life at home seem tame. Perhaps at first sight there is not much to this particular thrill: the performer learns to sing, learns to read music, acquires employable stylistic know-how and in time an intimate knowledge of a repertoire. Such a person is obviously well qualified to make a career performing the repertoire in question. However if this person, despite every qualification as a singer, dislikes aeroplanes, is prone to illness, finds the strain of being left to his own devices for countless hours in strange places emotionally too taxing (and needs the companionship of his family), then he has a simple choice: to acquire the necessary shell or stay at home. It can be a brutal decision, because to many people the shell seems to go against nature; nonetheless, with some rare exceptions, the necessary resourcefulness is found, if he wants to join in enough. The finding of it will involve suppressing illnesses, conquering the fears attendant on certain kinds of travel, and above all ignoring or putting to the back of his mind the attachments of home life. A parent of young children may well have to leave them for weeks at a time while travelling to the other side of the world. Admittedly this is not as bad as in the days of empire and slower travel, when a parent might be overseas for almost indefinite amounts of time (my father, who was in the navy in the early 1950s, could be abroad for a year at a stretch; his father, who worked in India in the 1920s and 1930s, was away from England and his children for four years without seeing them); but, unlike in those days, and unlike with modern sports teams, with us there is no provision at all for relatives to tag along. Our tours are just too short, and certainly too underfunded, to make that a possibility. So every touring musician will undergo some degree of deracination in direct proportion to the thickness of their shell. I acquired mine early in life, most of my colleagues suffer more visibly, but we all choose to go anyway.

But this professionalism is not just a matter of putting on a brave face at the airport, sublimating the memory of a child crying their eyes out at the sight of the suitcases lined up in the hall, conquering a visceral dislike of aeroplane turbulence (and sucking down the first palliative gin and tonic), while still singing to the best of one's ability as required on arrival. As I have already described (on p. 34), on the first intercontinental tour the Tallis Scholars undertook – to Australia in 1985 – over half of the ten singers present lost their voices at some stage of the tour, which necessitated extensive rearrangement of the programmes. I remember well the embarrassment of having to announce to a packed concert hall in Melbourne (which means nearly three thousand people) via a PA system, that what we were going to sing bore little relation to what was stated in the printed material they had just bought. This kind of hiccup in a young group trying to establish a reputation is a killer, not least because the changes in effect announce that the music-making is not going according to plan and is likely to be substandard. But a lesson was somehow assimilated, something in our minds activated, and nothing of the kind has ever happened again. Collectively and individually, our bodies have adapted to our wills, which applies not just to those who have been acquiring this knack for 20 years and more, but also to the young singers starting out. When the group was in its infancy, unpaid and amateur singers of every age and type were commonly ill, missing rehearsals just as readily as they were late for them when they were perfectly well. In the early years of paid work we quite regularly endured little mishaps whereby I or my colleagues might miss a flight or go to Heathrow instead of Gatwick. But these things do not happen any more: in punctuality as in health we have become as reliable as machines, for that is what professionalism is.

Such curbing of one's instincts may seem to have been managed by the acquisition of almost magical powers of self-control. Just as natural affection can be buried, so viruses, circulating in air-conditioned buildings and aeroplanes where the air may not be renewed for many hours, can be suppressed and their effects minimised. I have witnessed my colleagues perform astonishing acts of resilience on-stage – singing when they were too ill to speak, standing and delivering when suffering from migraines, influenza or a slipped disc.

No employee on a salary with entitlement to sick-leave would dream of going to work, if he had any common sense, when as ill on the job as we have been. He might also expect to be able to admit to his illness and be openly commiserated with. Not that singers are unsympathetic to each other's troubles – quite the reverse, there is a strong *esprit de corps* – but each of them feels obliged to play down their own physical weaknesses, as men do in an army. Obviously they do not wish to get a reputation for being unreliable, which would surely push them down the pecking-order in groups which travel widely; but, more than that, like the members of any highly-disciplined unit, there is pride in carrying on through thick and thin, honour in not letting your colleagues down when the pressure is on. The results are as I describe them, though what I do not see, except in myself, is the revenge the body can take during holiday periods, standardly in the weeks following

Christmas. Predictably enough, as one relaxes, what has been suppressed rises to the surface; and there is yet another reason why family time for the travelling musician may be painful: family time equals being ill. It is with trepidation that one organises anything – concert or holiday – for the first days of January. Yet no doubt it is as well that there should be at least one period in the year when nature can reassert itself. I have worked with musicians who have fuller diaries than I do, who do not or cannot allow themselves time off. They rarely look healthy; and there will come a point when only the most dramatic of remedies – or disasters – is going to slow them down.

One of the most longed-for powers of this professional body-training is the ability to control jet-lag. Like the common cold, jet-lag afflicts everyone without fail in highly predictable circumstances, yet for all that we live with it and study its effects, there seems to be no cure, *pace* the homeopathic remedies currently on sale. Everybody has their own preferred method of countering it, whether staying awake so that one goes towards meeting the new time-zone; or sleeping so that the body is as refreshed as possible for as much of the time as possible; or drinking so that one's nerves are dulled and one reacts more spontaneously to the needs of the moment; or a combination of these. None is guaranteed to deliver a feeling of wellbeing, even if some semblance of a normal sleep pattern can be maintained, which in itself is asking much. It is a common experience to arrive on the other side of the world, exhausted from travel, sleep eight hours with a sense that one has surmounted the problem, feel increasingly tired and sleep four hours the second night. Meanwhile the work may well have started. My own preference is to spend those hours of the night that I reckon I will not sleep in a bar talking to people, rather than to go to bed early, wake up early and start reading at four o'clock in the morning. I am sure the best answer is to be relaxed, so allowing the evil effects of what one has done to one's body to wash over it as far as possible, without each hurt registering on one's nervous system; but after 24 hours of constant travel, meals meaninglessly distributed amongst them, catnaps taken sitting up, even the most laid-back body is not going to know immediately what to ask for.

It is of course of little comfort that no one knows for certain what the long-term effects of repeated and overlapping doses of jet-lag really are: travelling as fast as we do has not been a possibility for long enough. We are, then, guinea pigs of a rather dubious kind, a status we compound by going to work as soon as physically possible after our arrival. No one has once complained that the first of our concerts after a long journey sounded jet-lagged, yet what it has cost us in physical terms to maintain the standard is unquantifiable. To continue performing when one's mind blanks out and the ground opens at one's feet requires iron concentration. The best argument I have heard in favour of getting straight on with the job, apart from the financial one, is that the concentration needed to give a concert easily overrides the other pains of jet-lag, and in a perverse way this effort offers a kind of respite from more minor irritations. These irritations are of course redoubled once the concert ends, but by then, the adrenalin still pumping, one is in a devil-may-care mood.

One comes to oneself in the hotel room. Nothing is more levelling than a hotel room, because even in the best appointed hotels there is no escaping the fact that this space has been lived in, and possibly died in, by a legion of people one is never going to know. Of course initially the circumstances lend themselves to sleep, and many times I have woken after some time asleep to find myself still clothed. This kind of passionate, irresistible oblivion is a better antidote than alcohol to keeping the demons at bay but there will, inevitably, be a reckoning. When this comes depends on one's metabolism. I have become professional even in the matter of sleeping, able to stay asleep for many hours when it is technically the middle of the day; others I think must suffer dreadfully at 3.30 in the morning. It is as if one has got halfway through the process of being beamed up from the surface of a planet to the Starship Enterprise when the mechanism has got stuck; and the victim is left equally faded in two places, his body tingling with partially-formed particles.

One of the prerequisites for enjoying constant travel is to come to terms with hotels. We have had very little control over the standard of our accommodation, tacitly accepting that espousing renaissance sacred music cannot always lead to five-star accommodation, just as it never leads to business class travel. We put ourselves unquestioningly at the mercy of the resources of the organisation which is staging the concert, of their sense of what is appropriate for an act like ours, of what is available in the area. The results are as varied as may be imagined, though even at best there will always be discomforts and irritations; at worst one is driven back on the 'well, it's only for one night' mentality and keeps quiet. It is essential to call a truce with hotels. In our kind of touring the sheets are always clean, the floor is swept every day and the towels changed, it is not necessary to carry one's own lavatory paper, every room has a telephone. From travelling widely in the Middle East I do not expect even this much; but this is what I get, and I insist to myself on it being enough. To do otherwise is to make sure that those shallow roots one is always hoping to plant stand no chance of surviving at all: every day would become a battle-ground of impotent flaying against people who cannot help you. For receptionists do not vary very much: without exception they want you to keep quiet, and if you don't, all their professional instincts are geared towards returning you to a state of quietude as quickly as possible. Any serious complaint is almost always beyond their remit; they can only pass it on. The most effective of them are either those in English-speaking countries who staff very expensive hotels – I think of the five-star accommodation we customarily experience in Australia – or the wife of the owner in poorer places whose establishment does not qualify for a star in any guidebook, but whose essential good nature will cause her to go to great lengths to ensure that her guests are as easy with their fate as possible. Between these two extremes is a grey hole of infinite depth.

Just occasionally I have walked into my assigned hotel room and felt I could live in it for a week or two in a relaxed way, long enough to put down sufficient roots to give me satisfaction, a surrogate home for however long it takes. The initial good impression could be created by the use of space, the furnishings, the view from the window, anything imaginative in a context which has become predictable to me by endless repetition. Usually a large room or suite of rooms with expensive trappings does the trick, because to the sense of good order which most hotel rooms convey is added the realisation that one is probably never going to be able to afford to recreate such luxury, let alone order, at home. In these rooms I feel cosseted and special, and leave them reluctantly. All the basic needs of life are so magnificently catered for that even the most mundane activity – the putting-on of a dressing-gown or the pouring of a glass of water – seems to acquire a self-conscious magic. Perhaps even this standard of living would pall with familiarity, but I allow myself the hope that it would not. Such a fairyland existence, impossible in these days without servants and difficult in earlier times with them if one was directly responsible for their welfare, represents the height of shallow-root ambition. In fact the hotel room I remember with the greatest affection was notable for being so small that I couldn't open my case properly in it, and my colleagues made a formal complaint to our agent for putting us in such a bad situation. Yet to me this room, in Osaka, Japan, had something which captured my imagination: neatness, calm, self-sufficiency, in one way a daring use of space, an attractive appearance created by shiny surfaces of chrome, plastic and glass. I do not necessarily say that I could have lived in such a room for very long, but the Japanese genius for celebrating smallness, making a virtue of it and giving it beauty, everything needful in place almost like a thing of nature, conveyed itself to me in the design of this room, where I felt safe and refreshed.

The problem with the generality of hotel rooms is that they encourage nervous tics which are the adjuncts of boredom. In having to move on every day or so, the habitual traveller inevitably tries to find some constants. At the most creative end of the scale this may well be a programme of reading and writing; but a restive mind will need more than that. The standard equipment in most hotels provides possibilities which most ordinary houses do not cover, like workout rooms, maybe a swimming pool, an abundance of mirrors in the bathroom. In time any or all of these provisions can result in an inordinate interest in one's physical appearance. Perhaps the precise mix will differ from one person to another – pumping iron to keep my physique in trim is not one of my hang-ups – but the end sterile fascination is the same. I suppose everyone is concerned to observe what effect the passing of time is having on their bodies, but in hotel-bathroom-world it is a daily fixation, which in my case has led to weighing myself wherever I am with embarrassing regularity. In fact in this also I have become 'professional', able to distinguish between different weights at different times of the day, and able to compute the extra weight of different articles of clothing. The utter uselessness of this is shown by the fact that for as long as I can remember in all the conditions this lifestyle has thrown at me, including excessive eating and drinking and the bloatedness which comes from long-distance air travel, my weight has stayed within half a stone (7lbs): all that changes is which end of this scale I find myself at on any given morning, which itself is determined, on an entirely reliable pattern, by the season of the year. Only once has this bathroom life resulted in anything which could remotely be called creative. One morning on a North American tour not long ago I noticed that I was surrounded on three sides by the mirrors which up to that time had only imposed on me on two. I discovered that by standing in a slightly off-centre position and jiggling the door behind me, I could have a view of the back of my head, and of every degree of my profile, such as I had never had before. Overjoyed at seeing in three dimensions what I had only ever seen in one I asked for this angle to be recaptured in my next solo photoshoot. It's a pity I feel like washing every time I catch sight of that photograph.

So in what does the glamour consist? What is that something which outsiders award us and which I, despite everything described here and after many years of it, still strongly feel? Not exactly the concerts themselves, since the actual music-making could take place anywhere, for example in the same hall in London at the end of my street, and the aesthetic satisfaction in the music would be the same. But then we would have sung our thirteen hundred concerts to the same people, or at least to the same stock of people. Plying one's trade, especially a trade like this, in widely differing places is a challenge in communication. To be given the opportunity to communicate with anyone is a privilege; and the effective exercising of it has in my case led to a sense of excitement, of intoxication, which has crowded out a sense of the joys of a more settled life. Part of that excitement rests in introducing audiences to an art form, a beauty, one believes in; another in being given the means through them of growing out of one's native provincialisms. I am alert for this growth, to which at rock bottom I would be strongly resistant if left to my own devices at home, which I have turned into a kind of religion. So it is that perhaps in the end no one, not even those who think my life to be one long responsibility-free holiday, attributes as much glamour to it as I do myself. Perhaps in this, as in much else, I deceive myself. I realise that this is part of the requirement.

1

2

3

4

1. Advertisements at the Grand Theatre, Blackpool 1991   2. Australia, May 2000
3. Local bookshop, Middlebury, Vermont, 1988   4. Riga, Latvia, 1995

Patrick Craig in New York City, 2000

Classic airport scene (before the widespread use of mobiles): somewhere in Canada, 1998

1

2

1. 'Party in Trev's bath': Caroline Trevor's hotel bath became the standard venue for many of our end-of-tour parties. This was the prototype in the Holiday Inn, St Paul, 1989.

2. Matt Beale, Lucy Ballard, Jan Coxwell and Patrick Craig do karaoke in Hong Kong, August 2000

6

SINGERS' ARGOT

Arse (pronounced with exaggerated 'r') A word we relish, partly because of the strange accident of language which has caused American English to drop the 'r' sound, and partly because the initial glottal-stop 'a' and subsequent rolling of the 'r' seems to act as a useful warm-up exercise for singers. The uninitiated may feel at a disadvantage, however, should they come near us before a concert and find this is all we have to say to each other.

'As a matter of fact' A catch-phrase of the New Zealand-born comedian John Clark (alias Fred Dagg). The love affair of some members of the Tallis Scholars with this talented man, who has no reputation that I've been able to detect outside Australasia, has no parallel. It all started on the tour to Australia in 1985, when Nicolas Robertson was listening to the comedy programme, introduced by Frank Muir, on the in-flight entertainment. The sketch in question was 21st Speech, which features a nervous youth on his feet proposing the toast. To give a flavour of Clark's genius, his speech begins with the words, 'On this auspicacious, er, on this auspicionous, er, on this bloody great big occasion ...'. Nicolas immediately spotted what this was worth; and notified all the rest of us by working out how long the tape lasted in total, how long it paused between renditions, and therefore exactly when we could all hear Clark throughout the 12-hour flight in question. Francis Steele still has the timetable Nick handed him that day, made out on a scrap of paper. What with the phrasing and the accent, by the time we arrived a fair few of us, as a matter of fact, were soon imitating him (to the great irritation of the rest of the troupe, who couldn't see the point); and have continued to do so for nearly twenty years. My personal catastrophe is that I spent many hours when on holiday in NZ years later searching for Clark memorabilia, despite receiving a generally hostile reception on the part of the salespeople I questioned, because John had decided to go to live and work in Australia. But I want you to know, John, that in Dunedin I found your first LP, with the 'medley' track you later deleted (I can see why), have seen the film, collected all the discs and thrilled to the Olympic programmes on video. I also want you to know that my wife is called Trev.

At sparrow's fart See 'Oh Christ Hundred'.

Boys, girls A careless way of referring to singers of any age in official documentation or casual conversation. This solecism is usually perpetrated by organisers who believe that singing is a jolly communal activity ideally undertaken by attractive and carefree youths. Any appearance to the contrary – for instance that it might be a life-long commitment for doughty professionals – clearly poses an unwelcome challenge to a simple-minded preconception and must be concealed. How anyone can be so condescending as to refer to fifty-something-year-olds by these words beats me; but whether careless or deliberate, this usage is ultimately a hangover from the days when musicians were held either to be of inferior social status or some kind of elaborate plaything.

Chicken counter To understand this remark one must imagine an airport, a very tall man and a heavy Australian accent. We had arrived at the airport after a bus journey, and indicated our intention to avail ourselves of the facilities immediately. The very tall man, Tony Grybowski, who was our minder at the time, said, 'See you at the chicken counter.' I'm embarrassed to say that this remark triggered off a truly appalling round of squawking, clucking, ruffling of the feathers and strutting about the place. Dear oh dear.
Choir (or, worse, chorus) Professional singers will never accept that they sing in anything referred to as a choir, let alone a chorus. Finding just the right term to describe the Tallis Scholars has been a very sensitive issue, but we find we can live with 'group' or 'ensemble'. 'Chamber choir' (which is what we really are) is too near the bone. On one occasion we were working for someone who really should have known better (Douglas Major at Washington National Cathedral), who, when it was time for us to go on-stage, was seen coming down the stairs into the changing area clapping his hands in a breezy way and calling out, 'Choir, Choir'. This was not a good idea.

Cloggies Dutch singers.

Corpsing The first of these argot terms that I ever met, and probably the one in widest general use. It is not surprising I met it early on, given the amount of it I had to deal with when we were younger; but not only then. It denotes incapacitating laughter amongst the performers when on-stage. It can be triggered off by almost anything – a ridiculous word in the text being sung, a silly noise from one of one's fellow singers, an over-earnest look from the conductor (oh, yes) – and once started is completely anarchic. No matter how serious the public occasion (if it happens in a concert), nor how much time will be wasted in rehearsal, it can be almost impossible to stop not least because the very effort to stop it from the guy out front will seem cripplingly funny in itself. The sensitive conductor dreads corpsing more than any other interruption because it is the one certain time that he has lost all control of his performers. Attempts to master it have led to missing out the phrase which has caused the mirth in the first place; everyone looking at the floor when known danger is on its way; restricting the laughter to silent shaking, which, if it proves as infectious as the out-loud version, can result in the strange vision of a whole row of men holding their copies in front of their faces while giving the impression they have turned into jelly. I once saw a bespectacled singer holding his glasses above his copy to give the impression that he was watching the beat, his puce face hidden by the copy, his body shaking uncontrollably. In cases like these it is never very long before everyone nearby has joined in, though it is generally speaking a male thing, a moment when frustration can hit back at authority. There are many corpsing stories, but my favourite, which did not take place during a Tallis Scholars event, is told of the singer who was singing a long melisma on the final syllable of the phrase 'Ave Rabbi'. At the end of it he deftly added a 't'. The four-part polyphony which surrounded this rapidly degenerated into a series of heaving noises, leading to a vibratoful silence. That piece had to be abandoned. It is a measure of the psychological appeal of what causes corpsing that I am laughing now as I write this, in excess of what it really deserves. Also associated with this term is the idiomatic use of the verb 'to go', as in 'I saw him go' or 'I nearly went'.

Dentes uberaque This extraordinary phrase, which is the Latin for 'teeth and tits', is most likely to be heard about a dressing-room just before we go on-stage, like the German 'toi, toi, toi'. I suppose this is an injunction to address the audience with one's most stimulating features, though it does seem to me to presuppose chorus-girls. The use of Latin here is very fusty and tiresome.

The Distaff side A crotchety term used some years ago by one of the men in the group to refer to the sopranos, who were collectively behaving in a rehearsal in such a way as to annoy him, or to emphasise the difference between his maleness and their femaleness. This particular fellow was not known for his love of women at the best of times.

Dots (as in 'renaissance dots', 'modern dots', 'romantic dots') A simple, no-nonsense indication between singers of what kind of music is expected that day at rehearsal.

'Do we need to rehearse this?' Apparently something I am given to saying in rehearsal when I think we know a piece of music well. What this tends to mean is that most of those present know the music well enough not to rehearse it, but not necessarily everyone. Should a singer find him or herself in this minority position, he or she has a difficult choice. Against the chorus of 'no, we don'ts', which always follows this remark from me, is the possibility of having to sight-read one's part in the concert. Does one speak up or not? Quite recently we found ourselves rehearsing music we all knew backwards except Charles Pott, who thought he knew quite a lot of it and genially assured us he was fine every time I picked up another piece and looked searchingly in his direction. It transpired he was lying. He says he doesn't remember much about the concert which followed.

'Do you know the Victoria Requiem? Good. See you at Heathrow' Our disinclination to rehearse more than the barest minimum is reflected in this anecdote, told by Peter Nardone (countertenor, now organist of Chelmsford Cathedral) after his first appearance for us. He claims that as he took his seat for the London rehearsal I came up to him, asked him this question and without waiting for a reply gave him a copy of the music and an aeroplane ticket. Peter is well known for telling tall stories, always in his heavy Scottish accent, which causes them to be retold (often by Andrew Carwood) in an equally heavy if less authentic Scottish accent. As a result several of the best jokes I know have to be told with a Scottish accent, otherwise they lose part of their public profile. But this Victoria Requiem rumour is nonsense.

Drug-like trance A phrase which has from time to time found its way into comments about our singing, the general idea being that listening to us can induce one. I have wondered which drugs might lie at the back of this metaphor: for example the hallucinatory ones which make you see multi-coloured backgrounds, or the ones that make you giggle. The former would yield an interesting adjunct to the all-round experiencing of polyphony. Perhaps the individual lines would become colour-coded like on those improving television programmes about how fugues were written that we used to watch as kids in the 1960s; or even better they might acquire their own animals, of which the pink elephants in Disney's Fantasia are so memorable a feature when the music gets a bit contrapuntal. The ones that make you giggle are not always needed (cf. 'Corpsing'). But I know what people mean by this. It's just that I never get a chance to sit back as they do and let the music wash over me. I regret this, but the risks of my trying it are too great when conducting, and when it comes to recordings I tend to listen to romantic symphonies for relaxation. Or Tom Lehrer.

Flan-san The common pronunciation of Francis Steele's first name in Japan. However it should be noted that the Japanese only invert 'l's and 'r's on occasion, not standardly. I, for example, am never called Petal. The most difficult phrase of all for them – awkward given the number of times they have asked to hear it and the amount they talk about it – is Allegri's *Miserere*, though Tallis Scholars comes a close second.

The Glamour An ironical term widely used by travelling musicians when the arrangements go wrong. To many people the professional life we lead sounds like one long holiday, and we can only add insult to injury by setting off on another trip days after returning from a previous engagement. We remember this point of view when the flight is delayed, leaving us stranded in overcrowded airports, or our hotel room reeks of cigarette smoke, or we are kept awake by other people's noise, or all the bars have just shut, or we are obliged to put on our concert clothes in public lavatories or in freezing vestries without a mirror. But there are those for whom all these things remain glamorous, and there is no telling them.

Gumby part A non-academic term to describe a cantus firmus part in polyphony. The worst gumbies are those which have very long notes, as in the tenor part of Tallis's *Missa Puer natus*, where the melodic line cannot be enjoyed and the performers are reduced in effect to being drones. Singing very long notes which have no rests between them was once described to me as the equivalent of being crucified: you take shallower and shallower breaths until you suffocate. It is a matter of some satisfaction to most of us that the majority of gumby parts were written for tenors, who, as everyone knows, are the divas of their trade. The other side of that coin is I find it ever harder to keep them – tenors, that is. There are however famous soprano gumbies (Victoria's Requiem) and even bass ones (Sheppard's *Libera nos*).

Gunge Phlegm in the throat, of the kind to which singers are peculiarly prone; or seem to be, given the amount of coughing, spluttering, gurgling and moaning that goes on prior to having to do what they're being paid to do. The need to clear one's throat has become a nervous tic with some of my colleagues, who unintentionally announce their approach with characteristic gunge-related noises. When they do this on recording sessions, for example just before joining a phrase which is already in progress, they become a hazard. I believe the American equivalent of this word is 'grunge'.

Hoovering An unhygienic activity indulged in by singers whose own meal has clearly been in some way insufficient or unsatisfactory, implying the surreptitious removal and consumption of food or drink from one's colleagues' plates and glasses at the end of a group meal. One of the mixed blessings of constant touring is that we find ourselves eating out together more or less routinely (or being branded antisocial). This requirement can have the pleasant effect of convening an instant dinner party with like-minded people without the need to send out invitations (night after night after night, breakfast included); the downside is that nobody is exactly on their best behaviour – why should they be? – which can result in the display of their more relaxed mannerisms. Hoovering is not alone in this category (see 'ID moment'), but it is particularly disconcerting to the organiser since it suggests that the subsistence (q.v.) rate is so low that the poor starving wretch has been driven to do this demeaning thing.

Hostilities An argot rewriting of the word 'hospitalities'. An engagement which involves staying overnight in the houses of the sponsors is not acceptable to professional singers, though the less thoughtful of those sponsors can never understand why. They think to themselves, 'We have this beautiful house; how much more must these sensitive artists want to stay with us than in a dreary hotel.' Which to the singer means not only having to make polite conversation around the breakfast table to the hosts while looking rapturously grateful for the privilege, but also meeting their dog, the grandmother and the contagiously ill child. And any slightly awkward habits the singer may have picked up after a lifetime of actually being in hotels, like smoking or drinking or making long-distance telephone calls all night, usually serve to dim his or her lustre once off the stage, which arguably is best not discovered. The problem essentially is that musicians are all too used to being patronised by people who view them as some sort of clever toy, a fairground source of delight (see also 'Boys, girls'). An extension of this state of mind is the oft-heard remark, 'What a shame you have to rush away tomorrow. Next time you must stay for several days and visit all our friends as well as the local sights, not to mention the village organist who I know is dying to meet you. It would be such fun.'

Hyperventilating John Tavener's music may be popular with the public but it is not popular with many singers. His penchant for writing atmosphere rather than melodic lines, in phrases which often have to be sung within an achingly limited tessitura and are always marked very, very slow and very, very soft (injunctions which in my experience have not once been followed to the letter in performance), can turn a beautiful piece into a nightmare for the performers. The last time we sang a whole programme of his music, which was in New York in May 2000 with Paul McCartney doing the reading, the singers said they began to hyperventilate. This word has now acquired a more general usage as meaning 'inconsiderately written', which I have even heard applied to pieces by Lassus and Isaac.

ID moment, or the 'It's Disgusting moment' Not many years ago one of our colleagues got into the habit of saying 'it's disgusting' every time a dish was brought to the table, no matter who was due to eat it. Unsurprisingly this caused friction. We found that one way of preserving the necessary superficial good feeling about the group at meal-times – which might well be not long before we were to go on-stage – was to say 'ID moment' in the manner of a public warning before anything else could be said. Everyone would join in, and laugh, and it didn't matter so much what followed. I have learnt from years of eating with my colleagues that meal-times can conjure out of our subconscious minds all manner of hang-ups and prejudices, which normally would not be on display. Given the sheer number of occasions when we have to eat together, and the amount of money spent on them, I have always regretted these awkwardnesses. It's a bit like family life. (Further to this see 'Hoovering' and 'I only had a glass of water'.)

'I'm not taking them on the plane' I've got better about this, but I have always found flowers on-stage to be an embarrassment. I never know whether to kiss the girl or woman who hands them over at the end of the concert (it is never a man who performs this task) and I wonder who is really benefiting from this old-fashioned nicety, since in some countries I could mention it is used as an excuse to advertise the agent, who attaches his name on a long streamer to the bouquet. I also find walking around airports carrying flowers in the cool light of the next day something of an invitation to my fellow-travellers to pass comment. Hence the remark. I don't mind taking them home, though.

'I only had a glass of water' The one certain nightmare of eating communally on tour (but see also 'Hoovering' and 'ID moment') is the moment when the bill has to be divided fairly amongst everybody present. Since we are all on the same subsistence rate, spontaneous gestures of generosity are completely unknown at group meals, even between husband and wife. The daily rate makes us all more equal than anything else ever could, and if you look as though you might not pay for that extra tomato you ordered, there will be no escape from massive public humiliation. I know this because I got a reputation for ordering expensive bottles of wine, not passing them round sufficiently, and then sharing out the cost. It wasn't fair of course – I think – but a surprising number of people can claim only to have had beer on these occasions, or water. The problem is trying to agree on exactly what everybody did have, and what repercussions that amount has for the tax and tip. Perhaps the best answer all along – if we really are as bothered about exactitude as everybody makes out – would have been the scientific one of getting out the group pocket calculator, drawing columns for each person involved and working out percentages; but on the one occasion when this was done it was found to be so prosaic that an outcry followed and we immediately reverted to the haggling we were so used to. It has always seemed to me that this retreat from really getting it right exposed a layer of hypocrisy in our dealings with each other, but an unsuspected sensibility had come into play. There are niceties to be observed in group life and one of them appears to be that we would rather argue with each other than have a machine tell us what's what.

'Is there a rit?' Singers used to ask me this, but now they know better. What used to happen was that I would say there wasn't one 'really', and then conduct one. Many copies are marked with the words: 'NO RIT (except when there is)'. Eventually this became codified: we don't rit but we never sing in military time as we approach a final cadence. I find there is never any problem when I want a longer rit in performance, the problem comes when I really don't want one. That is when we can sing out of time.

'It's only for one night' One of the most common of all these argot expressions, in almost daily use. It's the way musicians, alongside many habitual travellers, reconcile themselves to the inevitable. 'It's only for two nights' sounds rather weaker; 'it's only for a week' not even worth trying out, though we badly need a consoling phrase for the longer stays. Musicians routinely tolerate conditions in hotels which are so far below the standard of living they have created for themselves at home that one sometimes wonders why they ever agree to come on the next trip. Perhaps it really is for the music. We still need that phrase.

'Larynx down' A graphic and gentle instruction, peculiar to Andrew Carwood and his Cardinall's Musick, to relax at the end of a big sing. A Fayrfax Mass sung straight through would qualify.

'Let's just start it' Another of my catch-phrases in rehearsal, which usually means what it says since I long ago decided not to mislead people by prefacing a complete run-through with these words: it seemed like a shoddy trick. The upshot is that we can find ourselves singing the beginning of a piece several times and never the rest of it. Mass settings are particularly vulnerable to this oversight: we get to know the Kyrie intimately but not the Agnus, or the middle of the Credo. I have now taken to starting everything in the middle, which can have other drawbacks, but at least the performance will gain in confidence rather than threaten to lose it.

The Lighting One of the more certain time-wasters in the routine of concert-giving, a word which is guaranteed to provoke groans from top to bottom of the group. The most certainly unacceptable side of it is when the promoter has decided that candle-light will provide just the 'churchy' atmosphere on-stage which his understanding of polyphony requires. The amount of time wasted in this case will depend only on how long it takes to

convince him that ultimately the quality of the performance will be improved if the singers get the notes right, rather than looking lovely while
making fistfuls of mistakes because they cannot read their copies. But in fact
the lighting is always an issue, either in concert halls because there is too
much choice, or in churches because there is too little. The order of events
is familiar: the group takes up its position on-stage in the usual semicircle.
Those in less good positions begin to move about, holding their copies in
extreme attitudes as they try to make best use of what light there is. In no
time half the group is saying it cannot possibly continue until there has been
a total rearrangement of what has been provided while the other half pointedly says it is fine and that it needs to get on. The first half has to be
accommodated of course, which means finding the lighting man. Once he
has been located his goodwill is tested to the limit as he is asked to move
heavy constructions about, to the entire satisfaction of nobody. The standard compromise is that all the light should come from behind, because if it
comes from in front it is difficult to look up at the audience without being
blinded. Since this results in a drab or pale appearance of the singers,
because their faces are unlit, I have often wondered whether the looking-up
will not have lost its force. And half the group is still discontented, though
possibly not exactly the same half which started the argument in the first
place. I am reminded that on one of the occasions when the promoter
thought that candle-light would be the very thing, he also thought that the
smell of incense would be. This was in the Grand Theatre, Blackpool, in a
series of events which also featured the Chippendales (see illustration
p.191). Admittedly the venue needed a bit of help, not least because every
church choir in the north-west of England had been dragooned into being
present and the cultural context for all of us was a little uncertain. Picturesque idea as it was, however, incense gets into singers' throats. My ad-
vice to promoters has to remain the same: keep it straight, don't spoof things
up, and the most effective compromise will be reached.

Madrigals A term of abuse, as in 'anyone for some madrigals?' To the professional singer (as to Kingsley Amis's *Lucky Jim*), madrigals and the culture
of jolliness which they imply is an anathema. Some of the most embarrassing moments I have experienced on-stage have resulted from my being
forced into programming secular polyphony and the performers more or

less breaking down with that particular kind of laughter they have which gives no quarter and sees no reason (see also 'corpsing'). Clearly it suits us better to sing Latin we do not understand than to sing the kind of tosh the madrigalists dealt in; at least Latin led to better music, or perhaps one would say overall, music with more integrity. Why did none of those English composers set Shakespeare? (The Italian madrigalists go into the Latin category and so would be exempt, should we ever be asked to sing them.)

NFI stands for Not Fucking Invited, which is what singers say when they are asked by an outsider whether they took part in a concert on such-and-such an occasion, but hadn't been asked. The initials are usually spoken in an unfussed tone of voice and accompanied by a toss of the head. NFI is in very common use, but not so common that a member of the office staff at Hazard Chase didn't have to have it explained to her. However, believing it necessary to spare her blushes, the person who did the explaining told her it stood for Not Flipping Invited. She of the innocent disposition then went round saying, 'Have you heard this amazing Not Flipping Invited they all say?' She was greeted with gentle smiles and knowing looks.

'Noch ein Minibar, bitte' A request put to an unsuspecting hotel receptionist in the middle of the night, the contents of the minibar supplied in the guest's room having been consumed. History no longer relates who said this, though folklore insists it was a brass-player.

Nodule factory A phrase with obvious implications in the singing world. Medically speaking, nodules are blisters on the vocal chords, which can be acquired really quite easily if one is given to singing too much or too forcefully for too long. The first time I heard this phrase was in a story which told of the phone ringing in the song-room of one of our leading cathedrals just before a rehearsal was due to begin. The caller, who turned out to be the organist, was greeted with the words, 'Your friendly local nodule factory – can I help?' The layclerk responsible for this – who kept his job – was some weeks later heard to say that he now had nodules on his nodules. A select band of medical practitioners (I know who you are) are doing a roaring trade on the rampant misuse of voices in the metropolis, the kind of widespread abuse by unscrupulous employers for financial gain which used to be settled by Acts of Parliament.

Oh Christ hundred A term derived from the 24-hour clock (as in 0400) indicating a very early start to a job, sometimes on the concert day itself. When things are really bad we are obliged to leave home for the airport before the underground has started to run (i.e. before 5.30 a.m.) and will have to start singing a concert anything up to 16 hours later, if it's in Spain or Utrecht.

'Oh, I'll have to rethink the whole thing' According to anecdote, a phrase used by sopranos when asked by the conductor to change the smallest detail of their performance, like pronouncing the final consonant of a word more clearly, or breathing less audibly when being recorded. This is just one example of a whole genre of testy exaggeration between conductor and conducted when the chips are down (see also 'Testy co-workers').

Outing Contrary to what might be expected, the use of this word has nothing to do with homosexuality but simply to giving a piece of music an airing in a concert. Thus, 'Tallis's *Gaude gloriosa* hasn't had an outing for months', or 'Let's give the Byrd Four an outing'. Any implication that we might be taking the music, or the listeners, for a ride is unintentional.

Punch and cookies Code for alcohol-free after-concert receptions, especially in churches in the US. These receptions are a very mixed blessing to us. On the face of it punch, cookies, grape juice or fruit cup are the last thing we want after working hard and building up a thirst. The prospect of making polite conversation immediately after a show without proper lubrication is all the more difficult for us in that we tend not to consume much of anything before it. However, given a following wind and the fairly immediate promise of food as well as drink, after-concert receptions can be pleasurable. We really do enjoy meeting the people we have been singing to, and we enjoy going to their houses (to eat and drink if not to stay – see 'Hostilities'). The worst sort of tours are those where we repeatedly sing to people who we never get to speak to. We become too like machines. But as humans our needs are simple and predictable enough.

Retail therapy means with us what it means with anyone else – when morale is low, go shopping. We have uncommon opportunities to do this, of course, travelling widely and having both spending-money and free time thrust at us haphazardly but regularly. The American shopping mall syndrome is part of our communal lives. I have often thought that if our touring to places like

Boston and New York, especially in December, were to be curtailed, the thing we would miss most would be the annual visit to favourite shops, with whose merchandise we have built up an intense relationship over some years. The concerts themselves are much less site-specific to us than shops, despite globalisation. Although I am sometimes dressed from top to toe in clothes made by Banana Republic, these are still not available outside the US. Caroline and I buy jet-lag tablets and lip-salve from a particular shop on Broadway. As for the strange food products I like to bring back from Europe (like horse steaks, tripe, pig's trotters and snouts, boudin noir, pimentão and so on), there will have to be a revolution in the UK before any of these becomes available.

Roving An essential component of our choral technique. The word is applied to a singer who leaves his or her own part and joins another of different range in order to strengthen it, when that part goes uncomfortably high or low for the regular singer. This most often occurs in our repertoire when the alto part goes too low for a falsettist, and a tenor (or even a baritone) has to help out. In a piece such as Parsons's *O bone Jesu*, where the second soprano, alto and tenor parts all begin sections on unusually low notes, there will be multiple roving, with a complete restructuring of the middle voices of the group for a line or two. In Byrd's *Infelix ego*, where all the parts are singing almost all the time and the alto parts are low, one of the tenors will have the complicated task of roving onto both the alto parts, while also joining his fellow tenor wherever possible. His copy will be covered in lines and arrows; and the singer left on the tenor part proper will have a nervous time of it. (In fact when the singers are working really fluently together I have noticed how a quick look or even a slight movement of the body can be enough to indicate that some roving is needed.) Baritones will go to the aid of tenors in this way, and altos occasionally will do the same for second sopranos. The extremes of the group – the first sopranos and second basses – are obviously beyond help. The theory behind roving is to maintain the consistent surface of the sound and can only be realised if the singer joining in can produce a timbre very like those he or she is joining: indeed the whole technique presupposes a fairly smooth transfer of timbre from the top to the bottom of the group, which we have always aimed for. An ensemble sound based on sharp differences of timbre would presumably rejoice in the awkwardness of high and low notes: my view is that much of the time renaissance composers did not write high and low notes for special effects inherent in the text, as later composers did. Their ranges were not our ranges and sometimes the mixing of voices of different natural ranges is the best way round the problem. This is ironic because when we see an old edition of polyphony in which the editor has actually suggested this solution, for example by printing the alto part as if for tenors (c.f. the opening phrase of Parsons's *Ave Maria* in the OUP edition) we go into peals of righteous indignation about the liberties editors of the past took with music we are quick to say they didn't fully understand.

Singing like a drain One of the best-established of all these argot phrases, probably sufficiently so to be known outside the singing world. Its meaning is of course perfectly onomatopoeic, though one wonders if it is the actual noise of liquid going down a drain that is being referred to, or the idea that the throat forms a kind of drain as the sound it is trying to produce becomes rude. For what it's worth, I find the sound of gurgling drains quite attractive in an uncouth sort of way: resonant, direct, powerful even. Come to think of it, one could argue that it makes an ideal model for the lower voices in that kind of spiky medieval polyphony which the Eton Choirbook repertoire came out of.

'The sopranos are young enough to be the basses' daughters' Self-explanatory (first stated, at least in recent times, by the critic Anna Picard, describing the make-up of an ensemble one could mention). Not, in fact, the case in the Tallis Scholars, which leads to some obvious conclusions about my selection policies and general probity.

'So what?' Our Japanese agent, Ogawa-san, has one of the most perfectly restricted grasps of English that still allows it to be serviceable as a means of communication. He is a genius at making himself understood, and understanding us, yet his way of using the language has an infectious quality which will find many of us involuntarily copying him by the end of a tour. It is hard to give a flavour of this. There are the obvious phrases like 'I leccomend' every time he is asked what to eat from a menu. I loved the day he got the hang of how we like to leave hotels at the last possible minute, and that dividing the clock into nothing more precise than 15-minute segments wasn't ideal. The next time we were due to meet he announced we should do so at five past the hour, at which he congratulated himself with the words 'very delicate'. But his most typical remark is 'so what?', uttered without any expression on his face or intonation in his voice, when we tell him something we think will be of interest. Most recent examples have included the day we told him we had notched up 75 concerts in Japan; and when one of our friends was marrying a Japanese woman. Since he is difficult to talk to at the best of times, we find there is not much that can follow this pronouncement.

'Sprem?' Just once in my experience the contract for a concert which was to include Tallis's 40-part motet named the piece as *Sperm in alium*. I decided to make something of this opportunity at the rehearsal but at the last moment came over all coy. Instead of saying it out like it was, I said something like, 'You're not going to believe this, but our hosts have printed an 'r' in *Spem* in the contract.' There was a moment of quiet amusement about the room when one of the sopranos in bewilderment said, '*Sprem?*'

Squawking may stand as a general term for singing out of one's normal range. This word itself is applied to the sound (or lack of it) which countertenors make when they try to produce notes in falsetto which are too low for them. That hollow, burping, bubbling noise in the throat, preceded and succeeded by swallowing and gulps for air, chin tucked in chest, are the more evident signs of the distress which will lead to total silence on the part of the singer and barely-suppressed mirth on the part of everyone within earshot. The imitation of this unfortunate physical limitation is a great sport for bystanders and is about the most irritating thing on earth for the victims, who have on occasion been known to react violently. However, countertenors are not the only singers who have unflattering vocabulary attached to their best efforts. Sopranos singing high have been likened to chipmunks, a reference to those recordings of singers made at 33 r.p.m. and played back (an octave higher) at 45. Even the vowel sounds thin out in perfect verisimilitude. Tye's *Omnes gentes plaudite* is the *sine qua non* chipmunk piece, never needing to be played back at 45 (see 'The Squeaks').

The Squeaks refers to a piece of English renaissance music which has a high treble part, as in 'this one has the squeaks'. There are varying degrees of squeaks, as in medium squeaks or bad squeaks, the bad ones requiring repeated use of top B flat and even C. Christopher Tye is especially associated with bad squeaks, most famously in his *Missa Euge bone* (a.k.a. 'Huge

Bone') which seems to be in a stratosphere more or less by itself. Medium squeaks (for example in White's five-part Lamentations) can be sung by standard first sopranos, the part peaking on A flat, though the point about these treble parts is more one of tessitura than of range.

Staggering This word may have other usages, which may at times refer very properly to the behaviour of musicians, but in the argot it is applied to the business of ensuring that two singers on the same line do not breathe in the same place during a legato phrase. I am often asked what we spend our (very limited) time doing in rehearsal. With new pieces the answer usually is that we sing them once through, in order to have the opportunity (a) to see whether the edition of the music has any mistakes in it, which would cause an audible error in the performance, (b) to work out where the staggering will occur, and (c) to consider some interpretation, more or less in this order. (With pieces we already know we either decide to have a bit more of a go at (c) in the light of experience or move onto the next item.) At the end of such a rehearsal the singers' copies are unlikely to sport many forte or piano markings, but the soprano ones at least will show little pencil flicks above the stave with the initials of their co-worker attached, to indicate where it has been agreed that that person is going to breathe. The co-worker's copy will carry the obverse of this, listing, in different places one hopes, where the other is going to breathe. I don't know how widespread this practice is elsewhere, in the rather elaborate form it has developed in the Tallis Scholars. All I know is that I had nothing to do with it, not being a singer, and that it evolved slowly over the years as a response to one of the most basic requirements in polyphonic singing, a legato sweep of phrase. As a general rule it is only necessary in the top part or parts in the texture, since these are the most audible; the singers on the lower ones can usually get away with snatching breaths and breaking the line. For this reason I am very disinclined to have only one singer on the soprano parts. Of course the more singers on the line the easier the staggering will be; the converse is that if there is only one, a strict legato on a long melisma is going to be impossible, which is why we charge all that money to have two.

Subsistence/ wonga/ washers/ per diem/ séjour/ daily allowance/ spondulicks (etc.) Money is guaranteed to generate argot words in any professional gathering. Ever since we went professional we have made it a condition of working abroad that we receive a daily allowance in the currency of the country we are visiting, paid when we arrive. Whether it will be there or not, as agreed, is a matter of great anxiety for the road manager, as I happen to know: we have heard every excuse under the sun about what has happened to it and why it cannot be paid until after it can be of any use to us. It always seems to me to be a minor miracle when we pile into the coach and eleven discreet envelopes appear from a briefcase. Many groups cannot bear the suspense of all this and decided long ago to pay the daily rate in sterling, or as part of the fee, or just made the fee larger, leaving each member to change currencies as necessary. We soldier on. My favourite subsistence story comes from the early days of trying to make this system work, when we were due to sing in Northern Ireland. Our administrator noticed that the contract made no mention of what we would receive in local currency for subsistence, only a sterling amount, and duly sent it back with peremptory reminders red-inked in. We nearly lost that job. Of the wilder terms for this money (I've never heard of 'wonga' – Patrick Craig assures me it is in use) I find the time-honoured 'washers' wonderfully graphic. Presumably once upon a time the daily rate was dished out in coins so valueless that the best thing you could do with them was try to improve the plumbing in the grade Z hotels which were thought to be sufficient for mere musicians. Things have improved a bit since then.

The Tallis Sisters There have been a number of imaginative misreadings of our name over the years. The Tallis Sisters was the earliest, found in a free listings booklet (in Perth, Australia, in 1992). Another was the Hazard Scholars, perpetrated by the staff of the Globe Theatre in London, who handed out name tags with this inscription, on the occasion of our singing there to the Chinese President. The event itself was a bit of a disaster, causing street demonstrations which the police tried to hush up. Perhaps everyone felt a bit jumpy, though the mention of hazards was attributable to the fact that Hazard Chase are our managers. A third was a genuine misunderstanding by some concert organisers in Latvia, who thought they were promoting a concert by a group called The Tallis Scholars Trust (see illustration p. 191), doubtless because all the correspondence had been on Trust notepaper. And we were met recently at a foreign airport by a driver with a piece of card calling for the 'Tallis Scoohlars'.

Testy co-workers An ill-defined sense amongst my colleagues (usually on tour) that Something is Wrong, leading to a barrage of comment in lowered voices. Until the Something is identified, that is, when the voices get a lot louder.

Three minutes of tele-recording A few simple syllables more capable of sending chills down the spine of anybody trying to fix professional musicians than any other (except perhaps 'Hostilities', q.v.). The request sounds innocuous enough, indeed it might be thought to be offering something desirable, perhaps free publicity on television, usually in some sort of news slot. But no. From long experience one knows that once the cameras are there they are disinclined to leave, and three minutes can become an extendable feast, the cameras increasingly invading the minds of the performers in the most distracting way. One is also mindful of the maxim that once a recording of anything exists it tends to be used, and may, years later, be used for financial gain. The musicians want to be paid for any possible infringement at the point of departure; and everyone else can't believe that they can be so narrow-minded. Since the twain never meet in the heat of the moment, most contracts these days contain heavy-sounding clauses which create a bad smell from the very outset. In theory three minutes of news-filming is allowed, but only tolerated when the cameramen are closely marked by employees of the musicians. I have known performances to stop abruptly sometime into the fifth minute of a gig, when it is obvious the cameras are still there. The whole wretched business is a recipe for a sense of humour failure all round, making one long for a time of innocence.

Waving A word once used by an exasperated tenor in rehearsal when I was trying to cajole him into singing in time. The whole sentence went, 'You do the waving, Petie-pops; we'll do the singing.' The use of 'Petie-pops' to refer to me also stuck, as my children can confirm. 'Carving' is a synonym.

'What do you REALLY do?' The one remark on this planet which is guaranteed to make me see red; yes, even more than 'How do you get your sopranos to sound so like boys?' The questioner is assuming that what he has just heard is the work of a bunch of amateurs having fun, and that it stands to reason we must have 'real' jobs: singing not being held by such people to be a real job. Apart from British ambassadors (reported on p. 163) the people most likely to pop this question are American businessmen, whose experience of life simply cannot encompass the idea that well-educated white middle-class people like themselves would be happy making a living in this way. In fact they probably see it as an affront to everything they hold dear. This disbelief would surely increase if they knew how little we do actually earn.

'What pitch shall we sing this at?' There are a number of danger moments in Tallis Scholars rehearsals, long recognised, when everyone goes on red alert. The posing of this question probably produces the most intense of those moments, because the answer is going to affect everybody's capacity to perform to their best ability. The intensity is heightened by the fact that it tends to be settled by public discussion, which instantly leads to widespread incredulity at one's colleagues' insensitivity to one's own predicament. 'How can they possibly expect me to sing a whole piece at THAT pitch?' It can take a while to hit on the compromise which is going to have to be found sooner or later, including singing the piece through at a crucifying pitch for someone, just so that I can say I don't like the sound and the offended party can say 'I told you so'. We then have to sing it all again, because not having rehearsed a piece at the pitch we intend to perform it at is, strangely, one of those things we never shortcut on. But I dread this question more than most, because it is a decision I have to make in the end. At least two people present are bound to be dissatisfied with my conclusion and are bound to think: why doesn't he respect my voice more than this?

'When you're really into it, you're really out of it' Self-explanatory, if one can get one's head around the syntax. Uttered by a quivering American lady of a certain age after one of our shows in an out-of-town location I forget the name of.

'Where can I get scrod?' A question asked of a cab-driver in Boston by one of our sopranos. Apparently the driver replied that he had never before heard the use of the pluperfect subjunctive in such a context. I sympathise with the cautious reader who may think that the conjunction of cab-drivers in Boston and modern usage of the subjunctive tenses throws doubt on the truth of this story; but then it's effectively impossible to spot the use of the pluperfect subjunctive these days even had you wanted to.

7

NOT AN INTERVIEW

WITH

PETER PHILLIPS

I have given countless interviews, all over the world and in several languages. It transpires that there are a limited number of questions to be asked about performing polyphony, no matter how ingenious or daring the questioner. Maybe the public format of these sessions imposes a certain restraint or politeness, on both of us, which means we never quite reach the heart of the matter. Maybe we don't know each other well enough really to get down to the nitty-gritty. Here is a conflation of some of the more recent of these interviews, with some of the more typical circumlocutions cut out:

Interviewer: Are you rich?

PP: No.

Interviewer: You have a reputation for living well.

PP: I enjoy living. I'm the sort of person who will spend every penny you give him.

Interviewer: If you enjoy living well why did you set out on a career which would guarantee penury?

PP: Well, I didn't quite say penury. We have given a lot of concerts and I have a fee. Also Gimell has sold over a million records, and I am part-owner of it. But it remains a miracle to me that anyone can earn anything at all from putting on concerts of nothing but Latin-texted renaissance polyphonic Catholic sacred music [this is the complete title I always give our repertoire when I want to make it sound its most outlandish]. I have no doubt I would be a lot wealthier if I had decided to do what my mother told me to do in the first place and become a lawyer. Anyway I never set out on a career in music. I just put on a concert 30 years ago with some friends and find myself still doing it. None of the calculation which the logic of hindsight seems to demand came into it.

Interviewer: But surely at some point it turned into a career. You must have given up other forms of employment in order to concentrate on giving concerts and travelling.

PP: The word 'career' suggests a structure which one trains for and works one's way up. There was no structure for me except putting on more concerts and trying to attract attention with them. We did attract attention, but we had the problem, as well as the benefit, of being in England. As I've said elsewhere, our reception here has always been very uncertain, because there are so many other groups trying to do something similar. We attracted the attention of the BBC only to be told to go away and grow up. Gimell got nowhere for years. Meanwhile I planned nothing except one move ahead. I taught at an hourly rate to make ends meet, but had no idea of becoming a professional teacher. It was like living a game of Freecell. I knew what the desired end was – to travel and give concerts full time – and could usually see the next step, but the hundred steps in between those two things were so uncharted that I was in no position to think about them. We built it up piece by piece while technically taking pretty severe risks with our futures – I can see that now.

Interviewer: Would you say you were helped by your timing? The late 1970s and early 1980s saw the advance of early music in every field and in the end, however much you may think you are too grand for it now, you were and arguably still are an early music ensemble, a term you have in fact used freely in the past to describe the Tallis Scholars?

PP: What do you mean by early music?

Interviewer: Er, music written before, say, the classical period, which is susceptible to authentic performance.

PP: Oh dear. As you know very well there have been 'authentic' performances of music written as late as the early twentieth century. And as you also know, there are no voice-boxes surviving from the sixteenth century, nor accurate descriptions of how choirs sounded then, so strict authenticity is simply not an option for us. Go on, ask the inevitable question, the one they all ask ...

Interviewer: Why don't you use boys?

PP: Why do you think? Because it would be a nightmare. Can you imagine going round the world with a bunch of children? Why is everyone so keen for us to use children? Don't say it's because they look pretty and innocent in their cassocks and ruffs on stage.

Interviewer: Because the music was written for them.

PP: Was it? The Sistine Chapel didn't have any children singing polyphony all the time Palestrina was there. Nor did Byrd when he wrote his Gradualia for his recusant friends – unless the kids were singing alongside their mums in those illegal chapels. And how old were the boys in the Chapel Royal choir? There's good reason to believe their voices broke a good bit later than voices break now – perhaps as much as halfway through an average life-span in those days.

Interviewer: You sound a bit defensive, if not over-ingenious. Surely you're not saying that your adult women are more or even just as authentic as boys?

PP: I'm saying we have no idea what choirs sounded like in the sixteenth century, and that we had to start somewhere. Obviously we could mimic a contemporary cathedral choir, using males only. In fact we set ourselves up in the image of a young mixed group – the Clerkes of Oxenford – whose sound I became fascinated by. Incidentally, the next most fascinating sound to my youthful mind was indeed that of King's College, Cambridge under David Willcocks.

Interviewer: Do you mean, then, that you have made no attempt at authenticity at all? I don't think some of your more idealistic followers would like to hear you say that you made the whole thing up as you went along.

PP: I've read the descriptions of what renaissance choirs consisted of in terms of numbers and types of singer; and I've read the accounts of what they sounded like. I have done my homework. But the adjectives they use to try to convey the effect of this singing – words like 'jubilate' – are rather less precise than the words we use today to describe what wine tastes like. They create only the vaguest idea. Given that styles of singing have probably changed dramatically since the sixteenth century, it seems elementary to take the best of today and turn it to the service of the music, rather than try to force people today to ape something we can only guess at.

Interviewer: It would, of course, be a supreme piece of arrogance on your part to assume you know better than the composers themselves how the choir should sound ...

PP: Would it? How do you know they wouldn't be absolutely delighted with the way we sing their music? Perhaps standards have risen since their day. I often dream of Palestrina hearing us sing, and turning his eyes to heaven in ecstasy.

Interviewer: I'll bet you do. But perhaps it would be sort of ... humbler to consider that he might have known what he was doing in the first place, and that your Anglican hands-off approach might not be the whole answer?

PP: Do you realise how lax it was in the Sistine Chapel choir in the later sixteenth century? Half the singers were either absent or too old to do an effective job or not singers at all. Our English choirs work to astonishingly high specifications.

Interviewer: That doesn't disprove the competence of the Sistine Chapel choir to sing a piece by Palestrina, written for them with all their warts, with the active participation of the composer, in a way which would have been in his mind when he wrote it. You are entitled to say that you are doing his music in a modern way – and that that way may be very effective – but not that it automatically must replace every other way, especially not his.

PP: OK, I admit that I find it hard to believe that if you try to respect the nature of the music, as we have tried to do, and then ask for the highest standards from its performers, you can better the results.

Interviewer: How have you respected the nature of the music?

PP: By noticing that it is contrapuntal, which is to say that all the lines are of equal importance in the texture.

Interviewer: Do you suppose Palestrina hadn't noticed this?

PP: Of course he knew what he was writing, but I wonder whether his singers were capable of or interested in singing it with the kind of discipline we think it needs. Did they care whether the contrapuntal web they were collectively creating reached their listeners with the same highly refined and articulated balance we try for – like being able to see all the moving parts of a clock functioning in perfect order – or were they doing it more for themselves and for God, not concerned about what came over to the congregation? I even wonder whether a building like the Sistine Chapel is the best place to sing such music. Reverberant buildings like that are ideal for chant, but arguably not for polyphony, because the echo does what too much vibrato from the singers can do, and muddies the lines. No matter how clearly you sing in those sacred buildings it may be very hard for the listener to hear everything that the music is made of. And polyphony is nothing but a series of highly repetitive chords if you cannot hear the part-writing.

Interviewer: Which buildings would you prefer to sing in, if you reject the Sistine Chapel?

PP: The Sistine Chapel is wonderful for chordally-based pieces, like Allegri's *Miserere*, and chant, which is monophonic. So are many gothic cathedrals. But for something really involved, like an eight-part piece by Gombert, I would ask for a modern concert hall with controlled acoustics, like the Symphony Hall, Birmingham, the new Lucerne Hall, Angel Place in Sydney, or the Taipei Symphony Hall, where everything is as clear as a bell. This is in the same direction of thinking as claiming, as I would, that digital sound on CDs is ideal for polyphony. Both these things of course expose the standard of the singing. In these symphony halls, and on digital recording, there are no hiding places.

Interviewer: What has any of this to do with Palestrina?

PP: In my view, Palestrina inherited a highly cultivated, highly refined compositional style which he loved, but which did not ideally suit the building he found himself working in. That building – the Sistine Chapel – was fashioned for chant and of course was never updated for polyphony. Musical style developed as time went by, religious buildings by and large did not.

Interviewer: By and large?

PP: Well, it has struck me that the very few genuinely renaissance sacred buildings, like the Pazzi Chapel in Florence, do seem quite well suited to the intricacies of polyphony – small, contained, with bloom not boom, to coin a jolly little phrase. But no one thinks to perform renaissance music in them. Renaissance is popularly held to be an adjunct of the gothic period, when in reality it is precisely of its time.

Interviewer: We're getting off the point. So, you are quite happy to take this music out of its original context and put it in completely new clothes for modern consumption: symphony halls, digital recording, evening dress for the performers, a piece written for Lent followed by one for Christmas followed by one for Advent?

PP: Comfortable seating for the audience, heating in the winter, enough lavatories in the building so that the audience doesn't have to disturb us back-stage, proper lighting on-stage, enough money to have all the texts printed, a good income for the promoter and hence for us, in short, a thoroughly professional environment for a thoroughly professional ensemble.

As to liturgical propriety it is completely irrelevant to what we are trying to do.

Interviewer: Doesn't it make any difference to be able to look up during the performance of a deeply religious setting of some beautiful words and see an altar or a devotional object, or even just the walls of a building that has been used for worship for centuries? Surely these things can lead to a performance which has more understanding, more of the right spirit. What is it like looking up and seeing the over-polished surfaces of yet another Japanese auditorium while singing the *Salve Regina*?

PP: My eye glances off the surfaces and moves on to the packed seating. What excites me, and spurs me on to do as well as I can, is the sight of large numbers of people having come to hear us. It is true that cathedrals are large buildings, but they hold surprisingly few people sitting down – usually only a few hundred, and even when packed the lighting is often so bad that we cannot really see them. In the Sydney Opera House we have standardly drawn nearly three thousand people. That is what produces the kind of atmosphere I respond to. You should hear the applause in places like those – and see the faces of the people making it. Very often in churches the audience are so spaced out they cannot build up the weight of noise which exciting applause needs.

Interviewer: A thoroughly secular vision, then, and not a particularly appropriate one, when one comes to think what the words you are singing about actually deal in: humility, solitude, penitence, eschewing wealth, giving to the poor. How does it feel singing about these things when you have three thousand white middle-class Australians cheering you on?

PP: Fantastic. We are not a religious outfit. We are not trying to save souls, at least not in the first instance: we are trying to bring to life great music of the past that we believe in, for modern people. Our ambition is severely limited to singing just this music, and nothing else, in as many places as will pay to have us.

Interviewer: Have you ever sung a Mass in the context for which it was written, i.e. in a church service?

PP: Yes, though not often. The last time, in Holland, was a particularly demoralising experience. The church was cold beyond description – well below the minimum specified by our union – while the priests clearly wanted us to sing something short, because they cut out the whole of the Creed, one of the Agnus Deis, and contracted the Kyrie from three separate invocations into one. And they themselves wouldn't pay, saying they could have a guitarist for nothing: an altruistic secular foundation was paying. Even those priests who admire traditional music tend to think of nothing more elaborate than chant – the best polyphony simply lasts too long for them. Have you ever wondered why the vast majority of Catholic liturgical choirs are so bad?

As a result I've not been able to prove or disprove whether a Mass setting with repeating material, as in a Parody, comes over better when broken up by the spoken parts of the service, as was originally intended, or sung straight through as we do in concert, in movements like a symphony. My instinct, though, is that if you want to understand complex music for what it is worth as music, you need to concentrate on it and not keep interrupting it with talking. I know that the simplest polyphonic Mass settings cannot really sustain that kind of single-minded inspection, and those were probably the ones which served their original purpose the best; but there are other, to me concert-worthy, settings which seem now to be out of place in a church service. Maybe the mood of services then was different and such long tracts of music could be accommodated. Remember that one of the criticisms of contemporary Protestant reformers was that there was too much music in worship.

Interviewer: The secularity of your approach is again noted. So to sum up: not only are you asking us to take on board your wish to be afforded the comforts and securities of big-time artists in the mainstream, you also want somehow to recreate the music in your own secular image. Do the words mean anything to you at all – or is the music just to be a series of abstract sounds, made as pretty as possible?

PP: I am able to find some meaning in the words through what they seem to have meant to the composer, when he had the ability to convey that meaning in his music. So, although personally I find many of the details of the Christian story ridiculous, and the mystification of them in Spanish Catholicism sinister, the compositions of Victoria come over as supremely powerful, because he believed passionately in the texts he chose and was able to turn that belief into passionate music. But it is the music which communicates to me, not necessarily the words. When Victoria writes a beautiful piece about the virgin birth I thrill to the music without feeling anything for the fairy tale. As a result it is no problem for me to find music moving which shows very little apparent interest in the exact meaning of the text which it sets, but which is fine music. I always think of Palestrina in this context. He seems to me at times to come very close to writing the perfect abstract music. Viol consort music can indeed be the perfect abstract music in the polyphonic idiom. So whether the music is by Victoria, Palestrina or William Lawes, what matters to me is the music. I can take or leave the words.

As to your snide remark about pretty noises, I have always tried to make the Tallis Scholars sound attractive. What on earth is reprehensible about that? One of the more standard criticisms of us is that we are narcissistic, that we concentrate on sheer beauty, and that that somehow is suspicious. These critics want something tougher, more questing, they can't relax with it. Perhaps if they understood how difficult it is to produce this easy-seeming sound, and how much easier to make unpleasant noises, they might have more respect for it, but I doubt it. These people want art to reflect the ugliness and violence of the streets they have almost certainly never inhabited, and in that renaissance polyphony can never oblige them. I don't mean to sound weary, but in my experience it is the people who really did grow up in deprived circumstances who can find something crucial to their lives in the beauty of what we do.

Interviewer: The criticism is that this smooth, polished sound is in danger of trivialising, even anaesthetising very powerful concepts. Your hands-off Anglican sonic origins don't help, especially in countries like France and Italy, but even where your sound is admired as sound, there is often an uneasy feeling that something has been lost as a result of it. For instance how do you react to the criticism that you make all this music – two hundred years of it, as you are keen to point out – sound very similar?

PP: A pianist, or even more an organist, will inevitably make everything that he or she plays sound similar because of the limitations of the instrument. The instrument is locked into its sound-world which may perforce be applied to many more hundreds of years of music than we espouse. One of the bonuses of the early music movement, incidentally, was to force a more varied range of sounds on the wide spectrum of music which concert-hall audiences want to hear. We have set our limits in the renaissance. Admittedly that is a very broad remit in its own terms, and I hope that when this music has caught on more securely there will be groups specialising in different areas of it, bringing a wider variety of sounds; but for now we have the run of it, and inevitably we sound similar in everything we do.

I realise that the individual members of the group do not resemble a rank of organ stops, all designed and tuned to perpetuate a particular colour and capable of nothing more. My singers, being very capable and highly trained, left to themselves can produce a truly amazing range of colours. But when they come to sing in an ensemble that prides itself on blend between the voices, they are not being left to themselves. I suppose the responsibility then devolves on me to ask for different colours for different repertoires within the period, but very quickly one learns that that is not practical. What are these different colours? Usually nineteenth-century reworkings. No doubt choirs across Europe didn't all sound the same in the sixteenth century, but we don't know how they did sound. We don't even know for certain how the words were pronounced in the different countries – the researchers keep changing their specifics about this – so what are we supposed to do? Mindful that our first job is to deliver a committed performance of whatever we have chosen to sing, we make it as easy as possible for the performers to communicate to the audience. We don't trip them up with unfamiliar vowel-sounds and voice-production systems, or even with overprecise tuning methods. We make it easy: give them copies which tell them exactly what they have to do, and then ask them to sing as well as they know how. No dressing-up of the music, no hidden agendas. I say to the singers, and through them to the audience: here is music I believe in, we are going to sing just as it is, as well as we can.

Interviewer: Put like that it seems beguilingly simple. But you yourself must have done more than just chose the right singers, give them clean copies and then wave your arms around in front of them. What do you say in rehearsal to get this sound?

PP: I say very little these days. The singers who work with me now only have to take one look at me and 20 years or more of subconscious training comes into play. Of course it was much more difficult when we started, partly because the number of singers prepared to join in with this most uncertain venture was limited and limiting, and partly because the sound was not set in people's minds, by recordings and broadcasts. I don't remember what adjectives I used, but I remember I used to wince a lot, which had a certain eloquence. I couldn't help it, even though it did cause offence. Subconsciously I knew very precisely what sort of sound I wanted; and it must have formed quite quickly, because critics today can find it hard to tell recordings we made 20 years ago from ones we have made recently.

Interviewer: In other contexts that kind of unvarying consistency over many years would be held to be dull and uncreative, the product of a tedious mind. No one would want more than 20 years of the same way of performing Shakespeare, for example. Or the same fashion in clothes. When you are conducting a piece you do often, like Tallis's *Loquebantur*, for example, don't you long for something different, something surprising, if only to keep you on your toes?

PP: No. I love that piece just as it is, and cannot imagine it other than the way we do it. When I get restive with a piece I cease to programme it for a while – Tallis's *Salve intemerata*, Byrd's *Infelix ego* and Palestrina's *Missa Ut re mi* have been examples. There is so much else for us to sing that we are not obliged to find new angles on old favourites, as the directors of Shakespeare's most popular plays are. But that is not to say I think our way is the only way. I would be the first to encourage other groups to do this music in their own ways, because then there would be more of it in the public domain, more to talk about, and each would promote the other. It's just that I personally cannot imagine another way, and I'm not prepared to make one up just because journalists like you have got fidgety and can't think what new to say about us.

Interviewer: What are the most exciting projects that you have in mind for the next year or so?

PP: More of the same.

Interviewer (huffily): You are not being entirely ingenuous when you imply that there are no other groups active in this field. You know the work of the Sixteen, the Cardinall's Musick and the Clerk's Group very well, indeed they might be said to be rivals of the Tallis Scholars and have probably taken work which you might have expected to come to you. And it is a fact that all three of the conductors of those groups – Harry Christophers, Andrew Carwood and Edward Wickham – have sung for you. How well do you get on with them now?

PP: Very cordially.

Interviewer: How do you react to this kind of competition?

PP:

Interviewer: All right, what about the English groups you don't regard as competition? You wrote some less than appreciative things about the BBC Singers in your column in the *Spectator* not long ago, which led to quite a spat in the letters pages with Nick Kenyon. Why bother to do this?

PP: Because when renaissance music is sung in a vocal idiom which is quite unsuited to it, that is, without any proper blend and plenty of scarcely-repressed vibrato, the general public are put off. The cause of popularising polyphony is retarded. When the average concert-goer hears it sung like this he or she will say they know they ought to like it, or some such thing, but find it just isn't for them. On the recent death of Michael Howard, a man who made many recordings of polyphony in the 1950s and 1960s, it was said in one of his obituaries that his work had made the subsequent success of groups like mine possible. I wrote in to say that in all probability the old-fashioned sound he got from his singers has made it harder for us.

Interviewer: How about the non-British groups? You have encouraged ensembles and choirs and conductors all over the world in singing renaissance music, and there are others, like Renaldo Alessandrini, who have specifically ignored your influence and done rather well. To spur you on I would remind you of those musicians, like Alessandrini, who have paid lip-service to the achievements of the Tallis Scholars as a starting point, in order to boast about how far they have subsequently left you behind. No doubt there are yet others – probably French – who didn't think to mention you at all. What does it feel like to be a starting point for others' successes?

PP: The recent advance in stylish performances of polyphony in countries where the standard of singing in church choirs is a byword for incompetence has been very impressive. Suddenly there seem to be groups all over Europe taking on the English at their own game. Suddenly good tuning and good blend seem to be all the rage, with Alessandrini's Concerto Italiano the most prominent example of many. Why? Clearly the impetus has not come from the Catholic Church, but from an entirely secular desire to find a repertoire and give concerts of it. As you say, the English model, as partly disseminated by our recordings, has been influential. It comes as no surprise to me that renaissance music, which is great music, as sung by the English – which is to say by voices trained for the purpose in church choirs which are very good – should be influential. Only people who think in narrow cultural terms would be surprised by this turn of events. To me this broadening of the base of interest in polyphony is desirable and even inevitable. Perhaps now we shall hear the Italians sing Palestrina and the Spanish sing Victoria. Incidentally, the same phenomenon is to be heard in American, Australian and New Zealand music-making, but their link with the Anglo-Saxon/ Anglican world perhaps makes this less remarkable.

Interviewer: How do you choose your singers? I gather you never audition.

PP: I find that aspiring singers all sound wonderfully good in audition. If I relied on audition I would never be able to choose between them, not least because I can't set the audition up in a way which tells me the things I need to know. Like how their voices fit with other voices, and similarly with their personalities. Much more effective is to ask my regular singers who they want to sing with, and let them take some of the responsibility for the final result. There is no surer way of telling how suitable somebody is than in a concert.

Interviewer: Do you still have any of the singers you started out with in 1973?

PP: It would be fantastically unlikely, given that we were undergraduates messing about and having fun. Does it matter?

Interviewer: It would give you a pedigree people could respect. Constant change in the ranks rather undermines your image of craftsmen coming to work year after year, honing their skills in one specialised task for the length of their careers like cabinetmakers or jewellers.

PP: I like that image, and think it accurate. I just wish you people wouldn't be so simple-minded as to expect all the current members of the group to be the ones from the very beginning, as if it proves that I've been running an ad hoc session band all these years when I say only one of them has survived from 1973. Is it not enough that seven of the current ten have sung with me for at least 20 years, and that those who first sang in the mid-1970s have each appeared over a thousand times for us?

Interviewer: OK, but even if one accepts that you met many of the current singers after leaving university in the early 1980s, one can't help noticing how similar their backgrounds are, just the same: usually Oxbridge choral scholars who went on to study at a conservatoire, very white middle-class and middle-of-the-road English, no foreigners. Half of them seem to have known each other at school or university. Just exactly the same types as

30 years ago in fact. Is this deliberate?

PP: Not deliberate, but instinctive. We have never actively excluded those who don't fit the narrow cultural definition you've just described, but such people don't seem to get to the top of the London singing world, or at least our branch of it. And on the longer tours it is an advantage for us to have a stock of common starting points, with which we can all relax. In fact even within your narrow definition there are further subdivisions, one of which is that the group does not encourage flashy or strident characters, no matter how well they may seem to fit on paper, and even vocally.

Interviewer: Exit all toffs and posers, then, even though you might yourself be said to come from a privileged background. Despite this you have managed to hold the thing together all these years. What do you think are the qualities which have kept you on the road for so long? You often point out that the natural life-span of a group is about 25 years and even that length of time presupposes a constant cycle of reinvention. You don't seem to reinvent, and you don't seem to be on the verge of extinction.

PP: My original conception has turned out to be surprisingly robust, centred on nothing more complicated than a sound which can be applied indefinitely to great music. As I've said repeatedly, we make a beautiful sound in order to seduce the listener, to draw him or her in and so in time to consider the meanings which lie beneath the surface of this complex, intellectual music. We do reinvent in the sense that we find new composers and new pieces to sing, knowing that there will be no end to the supply. Ours is a chronically underexplored repertoire, unlike that of those poor bastards who are forever hailing another minor baroque 'masterpiece' because all the major ones have been performed to death.

And then there is me: the sort of person who, for all his love of living, is obsessive about things, about collecting complete runs of journals, or the complete works of X or Y, whether I read them or not. I have kept a journal of the group's activities since 1987, which is now in its 56th volume. I have compiled a database of everything we have ever done, running to nearly 1300 files. Something of this mentality has gone into maintaining the group just as I thought of it 30 years ago, into our one-composer-only discs, into our single-minded exploration of ALL the different repertoires of the renaissance, including the Russian and Mexican and everything in between. Then there is my interest in cricket statistics, especially those of the pre-war

226 WHAT WE REALLY DO

era. Did you know that I'm related by marriage to Gilbert Jessop, the batsman who, against the 1902 Australians, scored the fastest 200 that there has ever been? It was only because of him that I ...

Interviewer: We're out of time.

PP: I thought we might be.

8

AN EXTRACT FROM THE
TALLIS SCHOLARS JOURNAL

TRIP TO LATVIA AND ESTONIA
25 and 26 August 1995
(Volume XLI of the Tallis Scholars Journal, pp. 90–105)

Singers
Deborah Roberts, Sally Dunkley, Jan Coxwell, Sarah Pendlebury,
Caroline Trevor, Michael Lees, Philip Cave, Robert Johnston,
Donald Greig, Francis Steele

Music

Palestrina	*Tu es Petrus* (à 6, complete)
	Alma redemptoris (à 4)
Lassus	*Alma redemptoris* (à 8)
	Timor et tremor
	Tui sunt caeli (à 8)
Allegri	*Miserere*
Taverner	*Dum transisset*
White	*Exaudiat te*
Sheppard	*In manus tuas* I and II
Byrd	*Tribue Domine*
(Encore: Tallis	*Loquebantur variis linguis*)

Venues
25 August Riga Cathedral, Latvia at 1900
26 August Rakvere Church, Estonia at 1900

The opportunity to go to these countries was not to be lightly turned down: indeed Shauni [McGregor, our then administrator] and I put in more than the usual effort to make the concerts happen. The Estonian one got itself organised first, as a result of a suggestion by a Finnish contact putting us in touch with Peeter Vahi and Eesti Kontsert. Once the British Council had agreed to contribute the date was firmed up. On the strength of it, at the first Tallis Scholars Trustees' meeting, held sometime during this summer, I proposed that the Trust should spend its profits on a companion scheme for this event, preferably in St Petersburg. After our Smith Square concert on 8 June I met by chance Kaspars Putnins, who said he came from Latvia. I popped the odd question, and he seemed to think he could find a promoter for us in Riga and set to work. Meanwhile I encouraged Shauni to go hard at the Council, offering Trust involvement; and by the time Kaspars got home he was handed the details of a *fait accompli*. In the end the Trust paid one concert fee, the Council the other and the air fares, leaving the locals to pay hotels, internal travel (in a military bus) and subsistence. I fear these experiences will not be repeated in a hurry.

I realised I knew very little about these not-so-very-small places. Lithuania, Poland, Konigsberg, East Prussia, the amber trade I could do in some measure, but not these quasi-German northern lands, ruled by Danes, Teutons and various others, where old tribes and languages (I think of Liv) have now melded into modern ones. I did once listen to an Estonian-language TV broadcast when I was working in Helsinki, but the Finns at the time were laughing so much at what they held to be a distortion of their language that the words being uttered didn't make much impression on me. But I had deduced from what I heard that day that the Latvians and the Estonians were going to have some difficulty communicating with each other in anything other than Russian, and that was exactly what happened. Estonia is clearly better off than Latvia (and Latvia, I am told, than Lithuania) but still there is so far to go that I'm not sure a generation will be long enough for the levels to come up so that everybody in work will be paid enough in real terms to afford a western lifestyle. Latvia is said to be effectively bankrupt (which begs a few questions about Lithuania), caused in part by trying to restore the capital, Riga, which already looks very good. The obvious signs of the gap between how it is and how it is meant to be include the well-maintained roads with no traffic on them – rush-hour in Tallinn was an object lesson in how to live peacefully in a metropolis, the pollution being provided by other things – and the elaborately westernised (by Finns) hotels and restaurants, the latter sporting lengthy menus, those dishes that were available being without any inspiration in the cooking or even tasty ingredients. However, the communists could not cramp the natural beauty of these peoples: tall and blond.

I have had the impression recently that the singers and I have been up against it on the repertoire front. Ockeghem, Dufay, Woolrich and Browne in the last few weeks have tested us more than usual. But the reappearance of the Lassus 'green book' (a publication by Mapa Mundi of Marian anthems) put us firmly back in the frame of our easy-going 1994 existence. The rehearsal for this trip, which was due to end at 3.30, in fact finished exactly three hours early, surely an all-time record. And this was achieved despite the usual carelessness of singing which can come with pieces we know too well (the first five bars of the Lassus eight-part *Alma* had to be overhauled). It was an easy job, and very welcome as such, most of it great music all the same. Indeed Byrd's *Tribue Domine* is currently sitting in or near my number one favourite item slot at the moment. Apart from its superbly handled sonorities it is one of the most musically intelligent pieces I know. The part-writing unfolds with such compelling logic that should a part go missing for any reason the ear would surely supply at least its points of imitation if not the whole line. The internal strength of this structure is confirmed by the pacing of the phrases: nothing is hurried, all the ideas unfold in perfect spaciousness, the climaxes are completely satisfying. And yet how inadequate are words to express these things.

We flew to Stockholm and thence to Riga. Our room at the Hotel Latvija was on the 21st floor of a Finnish-refurbished concrete lump, which yielded excellent views of the restored city centre and, slightly further away, of the grey unrestored suburbs. I had little option but to sleep at this point and not go exploring, since we had had to get up at 6.00 a m. This would have been earlier if I hadn't been carrying 50 CDs for sale in Estonia and felt able to charge Gimell for a car. After this we were driven through the old centre to the cathedral which had been used until 1988 as an art gallery, after which Gorbachev applied some perestroika and services were again held there. It felt as though the Holy Spirit had been at least on vacation from this building for some years: it is a vast and rather vacuous space of colossal reverberation, dedicated to the Lutheran persuasion. We moved ourselves back and forth on each side of the crossing arch, trying to find somewhere we could hear each other, even if there was no chance the audience was going to hear any of the detail. In such conditions the Allegri is ideal. The common ground around the outside of the building, giving onto the cobbled main square, looked uncared-for, suggesting some lingering lack of municipal pride. However, also in this square were some very new bars, built onto floats topped by cheerfully coloured umbrellas. We repaired to one of these where I met Dick Alford, an old friend from the British Council, who seemed intent on cultivating a Latvian–English feature at the time and left us to it until later.

The concert was reasonably well attended – several hundred paying listeners – though to fill that building would require thousands. Amongst them were Dick and the newly-appointed British Council director Arthur Lawrence and his wife Issie. Kaspars was also there, head and shoulders above everyone else, a solemn and not entirely quiet presence, though appreciative. He looks like a man with a mission, much of which resides in promoting and conducting modern music with the Latvian Radio Choir. I also met and spoke in German to the woman who runs the concert series which we were in. I didn't explain to her that she'd committed the most delightful error in publicising the group as THE TALLIS SCHOLARS TRUST. One of her posters was pinned to the door of the cathedral, and was duly photographed (see illustration p. 191). I subsequently removed another from outside the Conservatory of Music, but lost it in Estonia. By then the printed programmes had already made their own contribution to the language game by introducing the audience to some twilight characters:

> Piters Filipss [Peter Phillips]
> Selija Dankleja [Sally Dunkley]
> Dzeneta Kauksvela [Janet Coxwell]
> Filips Keirs [Philip Cave]
> Maikls Liss [Michael Lees]

A brief reception was held somewhere about the cathedral, hosted by the British Council. Dick was more relaxed than previously, and discussed his new job running the show in Rome. I met Boriss Avramecs, the director of the Riga Early Music Centre (yes, there is one), who may or may not have been responsible for our invitation. Pink-skinned pears were served. After this we embarked – CT (Caroline Trevor), me, Kaspars, a smooth-talking Finn and Deborah – on a restaurant chase. I had been delayed from leaving the reception by doing an interview for a newly-established classical radio station called Radio Amadeus. By the time I had finished – about two minutes after all the rest of my colleagues had disappeared – there was no finding them, so we went to the place they had said they would go to only to find it full. Kaspars then took over and led us to a place he regularly visits after he has finished recording in the church nearby. Going there gave me the opportunity to pace the central streets of Riga at last, whilst carrying a heavy bag. We had a passable meal despite various minor setbacks, like the non-arrival of a course. At this point the Finn became more active and determined to introduce me to Riga Balsam [a local brew of wicked content]. Further foot-slogging and the peeling-off of CT and Deborah led us to one bar which was closed, one which had run out and thence to the hotel bar. This was stocked with Riga Balsam, a lot of very noisy Finns and most of the Tallis Scholars. We were swept out with the fag ends.

The following day we were promised a six-hour bus-drive and that, in the end, was what we got, though it was not as gruesome as the similar epic between Warsaw and Wroclaw in 1993. In particular we stopped at the border and savoured the air, and then did so again shortly afterwards in Parnu to pick up Launi Aav, one of our hosts from Eesti Kontsert. He gleaned, by speaking Russian to the Russian/Latvian driver, that the two anonymous people travelling with us were, respectively, a spare driver and a security official. Since these had travelled into Estonia with us, we assumed they were harmless, but the collection of them added a certain flavour, and not a little body odour, to the business of getting the team from A to B. Crossing the border was a slightly nervous moment, aggravated by the evident lack of experience on the part of all the officials involved. Otherwise the countryside was flat and well-tended, yielding few of the ecological time-bombs which ex-communist countrysides are supposed to be harbouring.

Rakvere is about an hour's journey due east of Tallinn, a pretty town with a ruined castle on a hill, the beautiful church we sang in with its fine organ, and a most memorable main street as though from a late nineteenth-century sepia photograph. It was almost the stuff of dreams. The houses by and large were in sound condition, only two were actually uninhabitable, the-impression being not so much one of dereliction and decay as of the utmost simplicity, which for a principal road in an important city is now impossible in the west. There were shops, but they had no façade or advertisement which told the stranger what he might find inside; there were no more general advertisements or posters of any kind, no signs, no notices, no newly-painted exteriors, no use of synthetic materials, and very little traffic. Thus must so many streets have been before the 1914 war, all over Europe, and I had assumed I would never see them. I loved it, while I understood that such a relic is not entirely healthy for a country in 1995. The hotel we were tipped out at was another communist palace renovated by Finns, replete with light-wood bedrooms, saunas and modern facilities; and a tastefully restored dining-room in which we were incarcerated for 90 minutes while the particularly dreary food was cooked and served at a snail's pace by a waitress who was pure ice. The *coup de grace*, inevitably, was the piped music, cultureless, featureless melodies giving off their reliable impression of international mindlessness, not a good idea for a young country. Peeter Vahi, the director of Eesti Kontsert, made an appearance, as did Arthur Lawrence who had come from Latvia by a different route from ours and got held up at the border.

We went to rehearsal in a cloudburst so ferocious that it seemed highly likely Rakvere high street would be washed away. The church was spared and, according to CT who looked down on the scene from a gallery in the Allegri, presented a most picturesque setting for the concert. It was not large, but had two wooden galleries in tiers much of the way round, which must have doubled the capacity. Eventually it was packed to the rafters, quite literally, and to the back door. Some of the rehearsal was filmed by the state television on a remarkably sophisticated-looking piece of equipment, with exemplary lack of interference. Around the end of this singing two things occurred which fixed this event in my memory: Don found the World Service on his short-wave radio and I met the local priest. As a result of the former we were able to stand in the street of this remote place and follow, at intervals, the progress of the Sixth [cricket] Test against the West Indians. With the series standing at 2 – 2, the outcome was of importance to some of us. Don chalked up on the changing-room blackboard Brian Lara's progress through the rehearsal and then the two halves of the concert. He had reached 170-odd by the end, in astonishingly quick time. The match was eventually drawn. What the Estonians made of the more or less complete score-card on the board, history does not relate.

They probably made as much sense of it as I did of the priest. He was of the mortally shy variety of priest, hardly able to stand up in front of his people and address them, otherwise to be seen rushing around ineffectually about nothing. There was a considerable language problem with this man, who, in order to make his thanks to us understood spoke them in Latin, the first time anyone had used the old international language as a means of communication in my hearing. I missed the first speech he made, at the beginning of the concert, since we were outside the building waiting to go on (and listening to the radio). Peeter Vahi told me at the interval that the man had spoken in Latin, and this put me on my mettle. I knew he intended to speak again at the end, and I determined to answer him. All the way through the second half I worked at my reply, several times losing my place in the music as I struggled with Latin syntax. By the last piece I had it ready: 'Exultemus visitare et cantare in Estonia; et saluemus Estonia liber in futuro et in perpetuo'. I anticipated that the priest would address the assembled company while we stood there, after the encore and applause, which eventually he did. Off he went in Estonian, as it seemed, and that was that. I didn't think I could start speaking in broken Latin if he hadn't, so I didn't. Later I found he could understand German, so I asked him whether he had spoken in Latin on the second occasion and he replied that he certainly had and was mortified to discover that we'd missed it. The problem, of course, was that it had been done in an unrelievedly Estonian accent – and why not? He said with considerable hauteur that as a properly-trained priest he could only speak Latin, Greek and Hebrew (I ducked pointing out, as being too prosaic, that he also seemed to speak Estonian, German and Russian).

After the concert I was beset by a local conductor who wanted to know many, many things, while my colleagues waited for me on the bus, getting more and more impatient. A reception was visited by us all in the hotel, given by the British ambassador, who had been at our Palestrina concert in Santa Maria Maggiore in February 1994: a genial man. After this we boarded the bus and drove in pouring rain to Tallinn, where everyone went to the hotel restaurant for a late dinner.

The following morning we were shown around the city by Mr Lend and his son, which was a memorable experience. Whole streets and squares of buildings of what was once (and soon will be again) the historic centre are derelict, which excited daydreams in those of a romantic disposition. The Lends were interested in meeting us because they want to distribute our records in the Baltic States: the old man is a fine pioneering fellow, the sort who pretends to hail taxis and then tells them they're driving too fast. He is full of ideas and lets nothing get in his way. Communism must have been living death to him; and, indeed, I felt all the people I had met on this trip were learning how to blossom just now.

EPILOGUE

Crossover has become a tired word, almost an insult. Too much money has been made out of dumbing down what originally was something of quality for anyone to have much respect for the processes involved. And once a piece of music or an artist has been thus dumbed, what do we think of them then? What is the future for Vivaldi's 'Four Seasons' amongst melomanes, let alone Vanessa Mae? Can we ever hear them again straight, as they were in their time of innocence?

Part of that innocence was that competent performers were perceived then as making an effort to achieve something difficult. Anyone trying to play a Vivaldi concerto in public has to make some challenging decisions, the first of which is to decide to practise for years. Once they are proficient enough to play the music they must then confront all manner of smaller issues, like whether to follow the latest ideas in authentic performance, or go for a more familiar sound-world. By opting for crossover in whatever form – beat tracks, sexy presentation, acoustically-enhanced effects, overlaying the music with other music – they can be accused of avoiding the difficult decisions, which in serious music-making simply cannot be avoided. And by doing so they may make small fortunes, where the serious tend not to.

But the word in itself has a meaning which is not all bad: it implies that by whatever means, not inherently cheapening ones, a piece of music can be made to appeal to people who would not normally find it interesting. Every artist and every promoter dreams of finding new audiences for something that has an already-established constituency, especially if this audience can be found at the drop of a hat. Many conversations between professional musicians and their managers start with this hope, that by some means or other what they have been doing for years can be made more approachable, it is 'only' a question of presentation. Here lies the opportunity and the danger. The hope is reasonable; the methods resorted to may destroy something fragile.

In this sense I feel we have become a crossover group. We have taken music which was originally intended for one very specific place and purpose, and completely changed the circumstances in which we perform it. In fact when one comes to analyse this, it is such an extreme change in its own terms that I wonder why it is so rarely mentioned – as if it is not quite polite to do so, as if by trying to stage our concerts in churches, which happens often enough, we are somehow anxious not to see what we are really doing and all the concert-hall performances are only tolerable in the context of the church ones. From what was once presented as one element in a complex act of worship, which in its entirety was a highly stylised ritualistic ceremony with significant words, gestures, smells, icons, costumes and music, we have extracted, deracinated and put up in lights by itself for our pleasure and gain. Everything is changed: the words are put into the background; the gestures, smells and icons are banished altogether; the cassock and surplice of the choirman has been replaced, for our men at least, with posh Victorian dinner-wear; the church is often replaced with a concert hall for access to which people must pay. How can this be justified, and how can the music survive the upheaval?

I would argue as follows: in our version the spotlight is now squarely on the music, there are no other distractions. If the music is badly sung, as so often in church services, there is no hiding place in our secular renditions; and I am confident we have shown that the music can stand this degree of scrutiny. We have found that it does not actually need the context of a church service to have meaning, and of course for many of our listeners, whether non-Christian or just non-believers, the church service itself is off-putting. The logical end point to this argument is to present the music in as neutral a place as possible, where people can hear it to best advantage. For this reason I advocate the most modern concert halls with the most up-to-date acoustics and facilities. This may be the sonic equivalent of going to see a Bellini altarpiece in an art gallery, but I do not mind. One can see the painting in the art gallery: it has been hung with the specific intention that the paying public should be able to see it without difficulty, enabling them to admire its technique and consider the relevance of its message to the wider non-Christian world. There one is entitled to enjoy it, luxuriate in it even, and then move on to another painting hanging next to it. I do not object to seeing these paintings on the altars for which they were painted – I do not object to hearing polyphony in church services – but because they are great works of art, products of the human mind, they have the power to transcend the narrownesses of their original commission. The greater the inspiration the stronger the meaning of that artefact to people who live now in quite different circumstances from those of the artist, and yet who need meaning just as much from works of art as people of the past. In their need these modern people can turn to religion if they wish, but most will not, and it is to them that we largely perform, gladly.

I have no regrets about this because I inevitably hear polyphony very differently from the churchmen of the past. At least I suppose I do, though I still wonder whether the more serious priests in Flanders in the late fifteenth century really approved of what they were hearing. It seems so unlikely that a musical style of this complexity and sheer length, requiring such precise conditions for any performance of it to shine, could have seemed like the natural successor to chant in liturgical worship. Chant is like recitative, a monody of infinite flexibility, capable both of presenting stories in a concise but never utilitarian way while being able to wrap the most mystical of texts in appropriate music. There has never been anything to rival it in terms of accompanying worship – every other religious tradition stopped at monophony – yet the Catholic Church allowed part-music to develop until it reached a degree of sophistication which still baffles the minds of the best-informed listeners today, sitting at home in front of speakers with the scores on their laps. Then, as if the journey from chant had not gone far enough already, the authorities eventually sanctioned church music which involved instruments, symphonies, overtures, dance music and coloratura embellishments. Maybe these early renaissance priests, as yet unshaken by the Reformation, were able to take the humanist approach I feel polyphony requires, enjoy the mathematics for what they are worth, and when they couldn't follow them just allowed the smoothness of the idiom to flow over them as they prayed as if it were chant.

But if these priests of my speculations were interested primarily in the communication of the texts which were set in the music, as they were quick to say they were at the Reformation, then I do not understand them. To me the polyphonic idiom had gone too far: the Reformers had a point, the words are obscured and their meaning is not communicated in the surface of the writing. But what to the priest of the mid-sixteenth century had become a drawback is to me, in my 21st-century mindset, the whole point. I do not like storytelling. I detest recitative in its baroque continuo form. I am uneasy with the plots of operas, so predictable, so slow to unfold, so oversized and mawkishly demanding. I even dislike storytelling in its polyphonic forms – madrigals, Lassus's Penitential Psalms and motets which go on and on because the text does, each section an ever thinner attempt by the composer to find arresting music to picture the words. In such writing there is a critical lack of abstraction, of patterns for their own sake.

Whenever I hear polyphony I do not think of original sin, or even of a Bellini madonna, but of patterns: musical shapes converging and dispersing like planets in the cosmos; shifting forms in light. There are many kinds of musical pattern, of which the Vivaldian sequence is only the most obvious and predictable, to me about as interesting as the repetitions of a gyroscope. In polyphony the patterns are infinitely more varied, indefinitely so, as the voices move about inside the texture and react to each other. But the most effective synonyms for my delight in polyphony lie outside music altogether, reinforcing my own sense of crossover. As Kandinsky wrote in his aptly titled *Concerning the Spiritual in Art*, colours and forms must replace material objects and narratives as the content of modernist art, because 'the literary element of story-telling or anecdote must be abandoned as useless'. For some years he borrowed the musical term 'Improvisation' for many of his paintings on the grounds that the total abstraction he was aiming for was the richest, most musical form of artistic expression: 'unconscious expressions of an inner character'. It is no coincidence that the paintings of Kandinsky and his modernist colleagues, especially the drip paintings of Jackson Pollock, send me into the same kind of reverie as an eight-part motet by Byrd. The surface is seductive, the meaning obscure, the desire to grasp something that is too abstract to be grasped only causing me to try again and again, a lifetime of agains, a thrall without end. Music is able 'to draw the hearer, as it were, in chains of gold by the ears to the consideration of holy things', wrote Thomas Morley in his *Plaine and Easie Introduction*: to him 'music' was polyphony, and to me 'holy' has a broad aesthetic sweep. Wouldn't I like my mistress to be more colourful, more chromatic? No. I prefer black and white photographs to colour because in black and white the patterns stand out more satisfyingly: street lights reflected in cobble-stones at night after rain; shadows cast on uneven brick walls by sunlight reflected off water. It is a kind of simple-mindedness.

DISCOGRAPHY

1. English Sacred Music of the Sixteenth Century, eventually released as UACL 10005 and Everst 3421 – (1977; no longer available)
2. Music by Thomas Tomkins (1978? – never released)
3. Missa de la Batalla Escoutez and motets by Francisco Guerrero (1978? – never released)
4. Thomas Tallis Volume One (1979; originally UACL 10006 – no longer available)
5. English Madrigals (1982; originally CFP 4391 and later EMI Eminence AE 34483– no longer available)
6. Werken van Thomas Tallis (1982; KRO klassiek Eurosound 313–33 – no longer available)

GIMELL

Listed in order of recording

7. Allegri: Miserere
Allegri *Miserere*
Mundy *Vox Patris caelestis*
Palestrina *Missa Papae Marcelli*
CDGIM 339

8. Palestrina Masses: Missa Benedicta es
Josquin des Prés *Benedicta es*
Palestrina *Missa Benedicta es*
CDGIM 001

9. Palestrina Masses: Missa Nigra sum
Anonymous Plainchant: *Nigra sum*
De Silva *Nigra sum*
Lhéritier *Nigra sum* (à5)
Palestrina *Missa Nigra sum*
Victoria *Nigra sum*
CDGIM 003

10. Russian Orthodox Music
Anonymous *Izbavlenie posla*; *Budi imya Gospodnie*; *Ot yunosti moieya*; *Blagoviernomu Tsariu*; *Svyatui Bozhe*; *Izhe khieruvimui*; *V Chiermniem Mori*
Bortniansky *Mnogaya lieta*
Rachmaninov *Lord's Prayer*
Stravinsky *Otche nash* (Our Father); *Bogoroditsie Dievo* (Ave Maria)

Tavener *Great Canon of St. Andrew of Crete*
Tsar Ivan the Terrible *Kuimi pokhvalienui mi*
CDGIM 002

11. William Byrd: The Three Masses
Byrd Mass for five voices; Mass for four voices; Mass for three voices; *Ave verum corpus*
CDGIM 345

12. John Taverner: Missa Gloria Tibi Trinitas
Anonymous *Westron wynde*
Taverner 'Western Wind' Mass; Leroy Kyrie; *Missa Gloria Tibi Trinitas*; *Dum transisset Sabbatum*
CDGIM 004

13. John Tavener: Ikon of Light
Tavener *Ikon of Light*; *Funeral Ikos*; *The Lamb*
CDGIM 005

14. Palestrina Masses: Missa Brevis
Palestrina *Missa Brevis*; *Missa Nasce la gioja mia*
Primavera *Nasce la gioja mia*
CDGIM 008

15. Thomas Tallis: Spem in alium
Tallis *Spem in alium*; *Sancte Deus*; *Salvator mundi, salva nos I*; *Salvator mundi, salva nos II*; *Gaude gloriosa*; *Miserere nostri*; *Loquebantur variis linguis*
CDGIM 006

16. Tallis: The Complete English Anthems
Tallis *If ye love me*; *Hear the voice and prayer*; *A new commandment*; *O Lord, give thy Holy Spirit*; *Purge me, O Lord*; *Verily, verily I say unto you*; *Remember not, O Lord God*; Tunes for Archbishop Parker's Psalter; *Out from the deep*; *O Lord, in thee is all my trust*; *Christ rising again*; *Blessed are those that be undefiled*
CDGIM 007

17. Josquin Masses
Anonymous Plainchant: *Pange lingua*
Josquin des Prés *Missa Pange lingua*; *Missa La sol fa re mi*
CDGIM 009

18. Christmas Carols and Motets
Anonymous *Angelus ad virginem*; *Nowell sing we*; *There is no rose*; *Nowell: Dieu vous garde*; *Lullay: I saw* (The Coventry Carol); *Lully, lulla thou little tiny child* (The Coventry Carol)

Byrd *Lullaby*
Josquin des Prés *Ave Maria* à 4
Praetorius *Es ist ein' Ros' entsprungen*; *Joseph lieber, Joseph mein*; *In dulci jubilo*
Praetorius M./Bach J.S. *Wachet auf, ruft uns die Stimme*
Verdelot *Beata es Virgo/Ave Maria* à 7
Victoria *Ave Maria* à 4; *Ave Maria* (double choir)
CDGIM 010

19. William Byrd: The Great Service

Byrd Great Service; *O Lord, make thy servant Elizabeth*; *O God, the proud are risen*; *Sing joyfully unto God*
CDGIM 011

20. Victoria: Requiem

Lobo *Versa est in luctum*
Victoria Requiem; *Versa est in luctum*
CDGIM 012

21. Clemens non Papa: Missa Pastores quidnam vidistis

Clemens Non Papa *Pastores quidnam vidistis*; *Missa Pastores quidnam vidistis*; *Tribulationes civitatum*; *Pater peccavi*; *Ego flos campi*
CDGIM 013

22. William Cornysh: Stabat Mater

Cornysh *Salve regina*; *Ave Maria, mater Dei*; *Gaude virgo mater Christi*; *Magnificat*; *Ah, Robin*; *Adieu, adieu, my heartes lust*; *Adieu, corage*; *Woefully arrayed*; *Stabat Mater*
CDGIM 014

23. Gesualdo: Tenebrae Responsories for Holy Saturday

Gesualdo Tenebrae Responsories for Holy Saturday; *Ave, dulcissima Maria*; *Precibus et meritis*; *Ave, Regina caelorum*; *Maria, Mater gratiae*
CDGIM 015

24. John Sheppard: Media vita

Sheppard *Media vita*; *Christe Redemptor omnium*; *Reges Tharsis*; *Sacris solemnis*; *In manus tuas I*; *In manus tuas II*; *In manus tuas III*; *Verbum caro*
CDGIM 016

25. Sarum Chant

Anonymous Plainchant: *Missa in gallicantu*; *Christe Redemptor omnium*; *Veni, Redemptor gentium*; *Salvator mundi, Domine*; *A solis ortus cardine*
CDGIM 017

26. Orlandus Lassus: Missa Osculetur me
Lassus *Osculetur me*; *Missa Osculetur me*; *Hodie completi sunt*; *Timor et tremor*; *Alma Redemptoris Mater*; *Salve Regina*; *Ave Regina caelorum*; *Regina caeli*
CDGIM 018

27. Josquin: L'homme armé Masses
Anonymous Chanson: *L'homme armé*
Josquin des Prés *Missa L'homme armé super voces musicales*; *Missa L'homme armé sexti toni*
CDGIM 019

28. Palestrina Masses: Assumpta est Maria & Sicut lilium
Anonymous Plainchant: *Assumpta est Maria*
Palestrina *Assumpta est Maria*; *Missa Assumpta est Maria*; *Sicut lilium I*; *Missa Sicut lilium*
CDGIM 020

29. Manuel Cardoso: Requiem
Cardoso Requiem; *Non mortui*; *Sitivit anima mea*; *Mulier quae erat*; *Nos autem gloriari*; *Magnificat secundi toni* (à5)
CDGIM 021

30. Victoria: Tenebrae Responsories
Victoria *Tenebrae Responsories*
CDGIM 022

31. Heinrich Isaac: Missa de Apostolis
Isaac *Missa de Apostolis* (à 6); *Optime pastor*; *Tota pulchra es*; *Regina caeli laetare*; *Resurrexi et adhuc tecum sum*; *Virgo prudentissima* (à 6)
CDGIM 023

32. Thomas Tomkins: The Great Service
Tomkins Great Service; *When David heard*; *Then David mourned*; *Almighty God, the fountain of all wisdom*; *Woe is me*; *Be strong and of a good courage*; *O sing unto the Lord a new song*; *O God, the proud are risen against me*
CDGIM 024

33. Thomas Tallis: Lamentations of Jeremiah
Tallis Lamentations of Jeremiah I; Lamentations of Jeremiah II; *Absterge Domine*; *Derelinquat impius*; *Mihi autem nimis*; *O sacrum convivium*; *In ieiunio et fletu*; *O salutaris hostia*; *In manus tuas*; *O nata lux*; *Salve intemerata*
CDGIM 025

34. Antoine Brumel: Missa Et ecce terrae motus (The Earthquake Mass)
Brumel *Missa Et ecce terrae motus*; *Lamentations*; *Magnificat secundi toni*
CDGIM 026

35. Western Wind Masses
Sheppard 'Western Wind' Mass
Taverner 'Western Wind' Mass
Tye 'Western Wind' Mass
CDGIM 027

36. Duarte Lôbo: Requiem
Lôbo Requiem for six voices; *Missa Vox clamantis*
CDGIM 028

37. Cipriano de Rore: Missa Praeter rerum seriem
Josquin des Prés *Praeter rerum seriem*
Rore *Missa Praeter rerum seriem*; *Infelix ego*; *Parce mihi*; *Ave Regina caelorum*; *Descendi in hortum meum*
CDGIM 029

38. Robert White: Tudor Church Music
White *Magnificat*; *Portio mea*; *Regina caeli*; *Christe qui lux es III*; *Christe qui lux es IV*; *Exaudiat te Dominus*; *Lamentations I and II* (à5)
CDGIM 030

39. Sacred Music by Alonso Lobo
Guerrero *Maria Magdalene*
Lobo *Missa Maria Magdalene*; *O quam suavis est, Domine*; *Quam pulchri sunt*; *Ave Regina caelorum*; *Versa est in luctum*; *Credo quod Redemptor*; *Vivo ego, dicit Dominus*; *Ave Maria*
CDGIM 031

40. Jacob Obrecht: Missa Maria zart
Obrecht *Missa Maria zart*
CDGIM 032

41. Morales: Missa Si bona suscepimus
Verdelot *Si bona suscepimus*
Morales *Missa Si bona suscepimus*
Crecquillon *Andreas Christi famulus*
CDGIM 033

42. The Tallis Christmas Mass
Tallis *Missa Puer natus est nobis*; *Audivi vocem*; Magnificat (à 4); *Ave Dei patris filia*
CDGIM 034

43. Live in Rome
Allegri *Miserere*
Palestrina *Surge, illuminare*; *Missa Papae Marcelli*; *Stabat Mater* (à 8); *Alma Redemptoris Mater*; Magnificat *primi toni* (à 8); *Nunc dimittis* (à 8)
CDGIM 994

44. Johannes Ockeghem
Barbingant or Ockeghem Chanson: *Au travail suis*
Binchois Chanson: *De plus en plus*
Ockeghem *Missa De plus en plus*; *Missa Au travail suis*
CDGIM 035

45. Gombert Magnificats 1 – 4
Anonymous Plainchant: Antiphon for First Vespers, The Feast of All Saints, 1 November; Great Antiphon, 18 December; Antiphon for First Vespers, The Nativity of Our Lord, 25 December; Antiphon for Vespers, Saturday before Palm Sunday; Gombert Magnificat 1, *primi toni*; Magnificat 2, *secundi toni*; Magnificat 3, *tertii et octavi toni*; Magnificat 4, *quarti toni*
CDGIM 037

46 Gombert Magnificats 5 – 8
Anonymous Plainchant: Antiphon for Second Vespers, Corpus Christi; Antiphon for First Vespers, Feasts of the Blessed Virgin Mary; Antiphon for First Vespers, Saint Mary Magdalen, 22 July; Antiphon for First Vespers, Epiphany
Gombert Magnificat 5, *quinti toni*; Magnificat 6, *sexti et primi toni*; Magnificat 7, *septimi toni*; Magnificat 8, *octavi toni*
CDGIM 038

47. Live in Oxford
Byrd *Tribue, Domine*
Josquin des Prés *Gaude virgo; Absalon fili mi*
Mundy *Adolescentulus sum ego; Vox Patris caelestis*
Obrecht *Salve Regina*
Tallis *O sacrum convivium*
Taverner *Gaude plurimum*
CDGIM 998

48. Lamenta
Brumel Lamentations
Ferrabosco the Elder Lamentations I
Palestrina Lamentations for Holy Saturday (à 6), Lesson 3
Tallis Lamentations of Jeremiah I; Lamentations of Jeremiah II
White Lamentations (à5)
CDGIM 996

COMPILATIONS

1. The Essential Tallis Scholars
Allegri *Miserere*
Brumel *Missa Et ecce terrae motus:* Gloria
Byrd Mass for five voices
Clemens non Papa *Pater peccavi*; *Ego flos campi*
Cornysh *Ah, Robin*; *Salve regina*
Isaac *Tota pulchra es*
Josquin des Prés *Praeter rerum seriem*
Lassus *Alma Redemptoris Mater*; *Salve Regina*; *Ave Regina caelorum*
Palestrina *Sicut lilium* I
Rore *Descendi in hortum meum*
Sheppard *Media vita*
Tallis *In manus tuas*; *O nata lux*; *Audivi vocem*
Victoria *Ave Maria* (double choir)
White *Exaudiat te Dominus*
CDGIM 201

2. Christmas with the Tallis Scholars
(2-CD compilation) – available end of 2003

TO BE RELEASED

Music by John Browne (CDGIM 036) – in preparation
Masses by Josquin des Prés (*Missa Ad fugam* and *Missa Sine nomine*) (CDGIM 039) – in preparation
William Byrd (DVD) – in preparation
Live in Rome (DVD) – in preparation

All the other compilation discs have been withdrawn including **Music featured on the South Bank Show**.

LIST OF PERFORMERS 1973–2003

The following is a list of those who have sung with the Tallis Scholars since the group's foundation. Singers' names are given according to the year in which they first appeared; a finishing date is supplied if they last sang more than four years ago. The number of events in which they have appeared is given in brackets after the dates, the total number of events being 1297 (a number which goes up to and includes the concert in Budapest on 3 November 2003). The current regular members are listed at the head of each voice-group.

SOPRANOS

Deborah Roberts	1977–	(1087)	Helen Dixon	1977–8	(7)
Sally Dunkley	1982–	(930)	Ann Gardner	1977–8	(7)
Tessa Bonner	1983–	(870)	Louise Glanville	1977	(19)
Jan Coxwell	1991–	(421)	Angela Hayward	1977–8	(29)
			Veronica Hayward	1977–9	(35)
Catherine Askew	1973–4	(3)	Hilary Phelps	1977	(1)
Kate Brown	1973	(1)	Gillian Russell	1977	(6)
Verity Curry	1973–9	(60)	Jane Armstrong (2)	1978	(1)
Deborah Healey	1973	(1)	Marie Doherty	1978–9	(8)
Isabel Nisbet	1973–4	(2)	Alison Gough	1978–85	(158)
Esther White	1973–8	(6)	Tizzy Lister	1978–85	(6)
Julia White	1973–9	(33)	Cynthia Millar	1978	(1)
Jennifer Youde	1973–80	(12)	Magdalen Pemberton	1978	(1)
Jane Armstrong (1)	1974–89	(72)	Joy Shepherd	1978	(1)
Sarah Cobbold	1974	(1)	Katy Woolf	1978	(1)
Elisabeth Priday	1974–86	(9)	Jane Bovell	1979	(4)
Helen Priday	1974	(1)	Ruth Dean	1979 –	(86)
Alison Stamp	1974–85	(101)	Julia Gooding	1979, 1989	(2)
Julia Williams	1974–80	(73)	Lucinda Houghton	1979–95	(5)
Mary King	1975	(2)	Stephanie Sale	1979–81	(12)
Teresa Armstrong	1976–8	(3)	Mary Seers	1979–85	(8)
Angela Coghlan	1976–7	(3)	Judy Stell	1979–81	(17)
Petronella Dittmer	1976–82	(10)	Rachel Stockley	1980	(1)
Catherine Ennis	1976	(4)	Poppy Holden	1981–9	(12)
Helena Fraser	1976	(1)	Emily van Evera	1981–2	(6)
Judith Liley	1976	(1)	Kate Hacker	1982	(1)
Elizabeth McNamara	1976	(1)	Ann Szreter	1982	(2)
Elizabeth Norman	1976, 1978	(2)	(Caroline Trevor	1982–9)	
Jane Stockley	1976–8	(4)	Frances Jackson	1984–93	(7)
Helen Charnock	1977–8	(3)	Nicola Jenkin	1984–95	(18)

Rachel Platt	1984–95	(58)	Claire Seaton	1993–5	(9)
Teresa Webber	1984,1985	(2)	Helen Parker	1995–	(13)
Caroline Ashton	1985–95	(25)	Carolyn Sampson	1996–2000	(25)
Rachel Bevan	1985,1989	(2)	Lisa Beckley	1999–	(1)
Katharine Verney	1985	(1)	Helen Groves	1999–	(18)
Barbara Borden	1987–90	(17)	Alicia Carroll	2000–	(12)
Olive Simpson	1987–92	(12)	Fiona Clarke	2000–	(6)
Ghislaine Morgan	1988–	(186)	Julie Cooper	2000–	(6)
Susan Winnicott	1988–9	(8)	Clare Dawson	2000–	(1)
Carys Lane	1989–	(65)	Angharad Gruffydd Jones	2000–	(6)
Alison Smart	1989–92	(7)	Kate Hamilton	2000–	(3)
Penny Stow	1989	(1)	Gillian Keith	2000	(1)
Libby Crabtree	1992–	(13)	Cecilia Osmond	2000–	(14)
Susan Hemington-Jones	1992	(2)	Helen Deeming	2002–	(1)
Rebecca Outram	1992–	(32)	Josie Ryan	2002–	(5)
Sarah Pendlebury	1992–9	(29)	Clare Wilkinson	2002–	(1)
Juliet Schiemann	1992–95, 2001–	(5)	Pippa Goss	2003–	(1)

COUNTERTENORS, MEZZO-SOPRANOS AND CONTRALTOS

Caroline Trevor	1982–	(800)

Patrick Craig	1996–	(336)	Christopher Royall	1978, 1985	(8)
			Joseph Sentance	1978	(4)
Jonathan Sharp	1973–4	(3)	Matthew Bright	1979–85	(20)
Ashley Stafford	1973–95	(52)	Richard Baker	1980	(1)
Peter Hayward	1974–7	(31)	David Cordier	1980–4	(43)
Richard Hunt	1974–6	(4)	Nicholas Mitchell	1980–9	(11)
David Parker	1975–7	(19)	Paul Brophy	1981	(5)
Roy Batters	1976–9, 1999–	(55)	Jo Cooke	1981–3	(19)
Michael Cockerham	1976–82	(32)	Wilfrid Swansborough	1981	(1)
Robert Harre-Jones	1976–	(620)	Graeme Curry	1982–9	(9)
Robert Hayward	1976–8	(23)	Margaret Philpot	1982	(1)
Keith Parker	1976	(1)	Alex Donaldson	1983–5	(20)
Andrew Wright	1976–7	(14)	Adrian Hill	1984–	(85)
Robin Barda	1977	(7)	Michael Lees	1984–	(264)
Dara Carroll	1978–9	(19)	Mary Nichols	1984–92	(6)
Michael Chance	1978–84	(78)	Richard Stevens	1984–6	(24)
Julian Clarkson	1978–84	(6)	Timothy Wilson	1984–90	(37)
Christopher Deakin	1978	(2)	Robert Bryan	1985–93	(3)
Jeremy Jackman	1978–82	(15)	John Williams	1985	(4)
Robin Martin Oliver	1978	(10)	Nigel Short	1986–91	(58)
Michael Procter	1978	(1)	Richard Wyn Roberts	1989–	(20)

Duncan Saunderson	1989	(1)	Deborah Miles-Johnson	1993–9	(20)
David Seers	1989	(3)	Peter Nardone	1995–	(16)
Philip Newton	1990–5	(7)	Stephen Taylor	1998–	(21)
William Missin	1991–	(41)	Lucy Ballard	1999–	(37)
Penny Vickers	1991–	(10)	Doug Fullington	2000–	(12)
Stephen Carter	1992–	(11)	Kim Porter	2001–	(12)
David Gould	1992–	(77)	Will Towers	2001–	(5)
Robin Blaze	1993–9	(14)	Stephen Burrowes	2002–	(1)

TENORS

Andrew Carwood	1992–	(121)	Philip Holmes	1982	(1)
Nicholas Todd	1999–	(77)	Neil MacKenzie	1982, 1991	(6)
			Gerald Place	1982, 1985	(2)
Peter Bates	1973	(1)	Nicolas Robertson	1982–	(112)
Philip Cave	1973–6, 1992–2000	(406)	Philip Salmon	1982–4	(9)
Charles Daniels	1973, 1981–93	(247)	Mark Padmore	1983–9	(60)
Antony Sargent	1973	(1)	Simon Davies	1984–95	(48)
(Julian Walker	1973–4)		Angus Smith	1984–	(56)
Alistair White	1973–9	(18)	Richard Edgar Wilson	1984–91	(41)
John Bennett	1974–6	(6)	David Bevan	1985	(1)
(David Saunders	1974)		David Lowe	1985–93	(29)
Harry Christophers	1975–8	(50)	John Mark Ainsley	1985, 1987	(2)
Robin Grayson	1975, 1976	(2)	Simon Berridge	1986–	(86)
Douglas Leigh	1975–85	(21)	Andrew Gant	1987–98	(37)
Neil Lunt	1975–9	(49)	Paul Agnew	1988–94	(96)
John Crowley	1976–85	(67)	Andrew Tusa	1988	(1)
Leigh Nixon	1976–98	(30)	Philip Slane	1989	(1)
Paul Copcutt	1977	(3)	Jeremy Taylor	1989	(3)
Ian Honeyman	1977–8	(5)	Philip Daggett	1990	(14)
Alan Armstrong	1978	(2)	Robert Johnston	1990–	(305)
Graham Bentley	1978	(4)	Tom Phillips	1990–	(51)
David Gregory	1978	(3)	Nicholas Wilson	1990	(1)
Andrew King	1978–82	(58)	Robert Wilson	1990–2	(14)
Rufus Müller	1978–91	(194)	Paul Badley	1991–2	(15)
Richard Day-Lewis	1979	(3)	Steven Harrold	1993–	(265)
Robert Betts	1980–1	(4)	Julian Podger	1994–	(71)
Joseph Cornwell	1980–2	(41)	Toby Watkin	1996–	(62)
John New	1978	(1)	James Gilchrist	1997–9	(9)
Andrew Murgatroyd	1981–4	(14)	Tom Raskin	1998–9	(8)
Harvey Brough	1982–9	(14)	Christopher Watson	1998–	(96)

Matthew Beale	2000–	(39)		Mark Dobell	2002–	(16)
Alex Jupp	2000–	(3)		Julian Stocker	2002–	(18)
Gerard O'Beirne	2000–	(2)		Warren Trevelyan-Jones	2002–	(2)
Nicholas Smith	2000–	(2)		Nick Leitch	2003–	(1)
JanJoost van Elburg	2001–	(7)				

BARITONES AND BASSES

Francis Steele	1976–	(1225)		Richard Barnes	1982	(1)
Donald Greig	1984–	(939)		Gerald Finley	1983–4	(5)
				Peter Harvey	1983–5	(12)
Michael Briggs	1973, 1975	(2)		Jeremy Birchall	1984–	(10)
Stewart Haslett	1973	(1)		Paul Woodmansterne	1984–5	(4)
David Saunders	1973–4, 1981–93	(8)		Simon Littlewood	1985	(1)
Julian Walker	1973–	(197)		Martin Oxenham	1985	(1)
Jeremy White	1973–88	(95)		Stephen Charlesworth	1987–	(95)
Giles Dawson	1974, 1975	(2)		Jonathan Markham	1987–9	(5)
Jeremy Pemberton	1974, 1975	(2)		Adrian Peacock	1988–	(13)
Jonathan Shephard	1974–8	(7)		Patrick Ardagh-Walter	1989	(2)
Andrew Woolmer	1974	(1)		Robert Evans	1989–	(23)
William McKenzie	1975–6	(5)		Christopher Purves	1989–92	(6)
Richard Brett	1976	(2)		Mark Campbell-Griffiths	1992–3	(2)
Paul Cann	1976, 1977	(2)		Charles Gibbs	1992–	(5)
Martin Elliott	1976–9	(8)		Edward Wickham	1992–	(10)
Stephen Jackson	1976–89	(10)		Roddy Williams	1992–4	(5)
Christopher Moorsom	1976–9	(33)		William Clements	1994–	(28)
David Nash	1976	(3)		Robert Macdonald	1994–	(38)
Timothy Rowe	1976	(1)		Jonathan Arnold	1997–	(47)
Andrew Stafford	1976	(1)		Bertie Rice	1997–	(7)
Richard Suart	1976	(1)		Charles Pott	1998–	(26)
Mike Brown	1977	(4)		Matthew Brook	2000–	(1)
Andrew Mayor	1977	(1)		Mike Donaldson	2001–	(1)
Francis Thomas	1977	(3)		David Trendell	2001–	(3)
Alan Leroy	1978–9	(13)		David Woodcock	2001–	(6)
Colin Mason	1978–82	(29)		Jonathan Brown	2002–	(3)
Richard Savage	1978	(1)		Francis Brett	2003–	(1)
Richard Wistreich	1978	(3)		Michael Bundy	2003–	(1)
Howard Arman	1979	(5)		Colin Campbell	2003–	(1)
Peter Hall	1979	(1)		Julian Empett	2003–	(1)
Simon Birchall	1981–	(20)		Julian Perkins	2003–	(1)
John Milne	1981–3	(14)		Edward Price	2003–	(1)
Bruce Russell	1981–7	(4)		Philip Tebb	2003–	(1)

OTHER PERFORMERS

Other individuals or groups who have been involved in Tallis Scholars performances are as follows.

ORGANISTS

Nicholas Carr	1975	(1)	Marcus Huxley	1978	(1)
John Caldwell	1976, 1978	(2)	Robert Betts	1981	(1)
Robert Jones	1976, 1985–9	(4)	Catherine Ennis	1983–4, 2001	(3)
Colin Walsh	1976	(1)	John Scott	1987–90	(3)
Stephen Banfield	1977–8	(5)	Bernard Winsemius	1988	(1)
Iain Burnside	1977	(3)			

OTHER CONDUCTORS

Iain Burnside	1977	(1)	Robert Jones	1985	(2)
Denis Arnold	1984	(1)	Francis Steele 1985, 1991, 1993, 2000	(6)
John Tavener	1984, 1997, 2000	(4)	Andrew Gant	1994	(1)

OTHER CONTRIBUTORS

John du Pré	1976	(2)	Manhatten Brass and		
The Browning Consort of Viols 1977	(1)	Percussion Ensemble	2000	(1)
The Chilingirian String Quartet 1984	(1)	Patricia Rozario	2000	(1)
The Leda Trio	1984	(1)	Stanford Chamber		
London Baroque	1984	(1)	Chorale	2002	(1)
The London Gabrieli			Stanford Early		
Brass Ensemble	1984	(1)	Music Singers	2002	(1)
The Philip Jones			UMS Choral Union,		
Brass Ensemble	1984	(1)	Ann Arbor	2002	(1)
The Folger Consort	1985	(10)	University of Maryland		
His Majesties Sagbutts			Chamber Singers	2002	(1)
and Cornetts	1985, 1992	(2)	Vox Vocal Ensemble,		
Mike Oldfield	1994	(1)	New York,	2002	(2)
The Duke Quartet	2000	(1)	Woodley Ensemble,		
The Flux Quartet	2000	(1)	Washington DC	2002	(3)

NARRATORS IN TAVENER'S IN THE MONTH OF ATHYR

Sting	1998	(1)	Paul McCartney	2000	(1)
Richard Baker	1999	(1)	Vanessa Redgrave	2000	(1)
Nuala Willis	1999	(1)	Susan Sharpe	2000	(1)

INDEX